HOLMAN
Old
Testament
Commentary

HOLMAN
Old
Testament
Commentary

Joshua

GENERAL EDITOR
Max Anders

AUTHOR
Kenneth O. Gangel

NASHVILLE, TENNESSEE

Bible versions used in this book:

Unless otherwise stated all Scripture citation is from the HOLY BIBLE, NEW INTERNA-
TIONAL VERSION®. Copyright © 1973, 1978, 1984 by International Bible Society. Used by
permission of Zondervan Publishing House. All Rights Reserved. The "NIV" and "New International Version" trademarks are registered in the United States Patent and Trademark Office
by International Bible Society. Use of either trademark requires the permission of International
Bible Society.

Scripture passages marked NASB are taken from Scripture taken from the NEW AMERI-
CAN STANDARD BIBLE, © Copyright The Lockman Foundation, 1960, 1962, 1963, 1968,
1971, 1972, 1973, 1975, 1977, 1995. Used by permission.

Scripture passages marked NKJV are taken from the New King James Version. Copyright
© 1979, 1980, 1982, Thomas Nelson, Inc., Publishers.

Verses marked TLB are taken from The Living Bible. Copyright © Tyndale House Publishers, Wheaton, Illinois, 1971. Used by permission.

ISBN 978–0–8054–9464–8

Dewey Decimal Classification: 222.2
Subject Heading: BIBLE. O.T. Joshua

Joshua/Kenneth O. Gangel
        p.   cm. — (Holman Old Testament commentary)
        Includes bibliographical references. (p.).
        ISBN
        1. Bible. O.T. Joshua—Commentaries.   I. Title.   II. Series.

—dc21

4 5 6 06 7 8 9 10   13 12 11 10 09
R

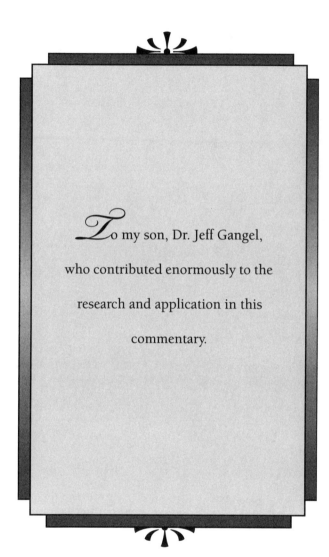

To my son, Dr. Jeff Gangel,

who contributed enormously to the

research and application in this

commentary.

Contents

Contents

Editorial Preface

Today's church hungers for Bible teaching, and Bible teachers hunger for resources to guide them in teaching God's Word. The Holman Old Testament Commentary provides the church with the food to feed the spiritually hungry in an easily digestible format. The result: new spiritual vitality that the church can readily use.

Bible teaching should result in new interest in the Scriptures, expanded Bible knowledge, discovery of specific scriptural principles, relevant applications, and exciting living. The unique format of the Holman Old Testament Commentary includes sections to achieve these results for every Old Testament book.

Opening quotations stimulate thinking and lead to an introductory illustration and discussion that draw individuals and study groups into the Word of God. "In a Nutshell" summarizes the content and teaching of the chapter. Verse-by-verse commentary answers the church's questions rather than raising issues scholars usually admit they cannot adequately solve. Bible principles and specific contemporary applications encourage students to move from Bible to contemporary times. A specific modern illustration then ties application vividly to present life. A brief prayer aids the student to commit his or her daily life to the principles and applications found in the Bible chapter being studied. For those still hungry for more, "Deeper Discoveries" takes the student into a more personal, deeper study of the words, phrases, and themes of God's Word. Finally, a teaching outline provides transitional statements and conclusions along with an outline to assist the teacher in group Bible studies.

It is the editors' prayer that this new resource for local church Bible teaching will enrich the ministry of group, as well as individual, Bible study, and that it will lead God's people truly to be people of the Book, living out what God calls us to be.

Acknowledgments

As the dedication notes, special thanks are due my son, Dr. Jeff Gangel, for diligent research on the project. In addition, I express loving appreciation to my wife, Betty, for assisting with proofreading, and to my manuscript manager, Mrs. Ginny Murray, for impeccable handling of the commentary text. Readers will note my dependence on those who have walked this road before, particularly Campbell, Howard, Redpath, and Schaeffer. It is always a joy to work with editors Max Anders and Steve Bond.

Holman Old Testament Commentary Contributors

Holman New Testament Commentary Contributors

Vol. 1, Matthew
ISBN 978–0-8054-0201-8
Stuart K. Weber

Vol. 2, Mark
ISBN 978–0-8054-0202-5
Rodney L. Cooper

Vol. 3, Luke
ISBN 978–0-8054-0203-2
Trent C. Butler

Vol. 4, John
ISBN 978–0-8054-0204-9
Kenneth O. Gangel

Vol. 5, Acts
ISBN 978–0-8054-0205-6
Kenneth O. Gangel

Vol. 6, Romans
ISBN 978–0-8054-0206-3
Kenneth Boa and William Kruidenier

Vol. 7, 1 & 2 Corinthians
ISBN 978–0-8054-0207-0
Richard L. Pratt Jr.

Vol. 8, Galatians, Ephesians, Philippians, Colossians
ISBN 978–0-8054-0208-7
Max Anders

Vol. 9, 1 & 2 Thessalonians, 1 & 2 Timothy, Titus, Philemon
ISBN 978–0-8054-0209-4
Knute Larson

Vol. 10, Hebrews, James
ISBN 978–0-8054-0211-7
Thomas D. Lea

Vol. 11, 1 & 2 Peter, 1, 2, 3 John, Jude
ISBN 978–0-8054-0210-0
David Walls and Max Anders

Vol. 12, Revelation
ISBN 978–0-8054-0212-4
Kendell H. Easley

Holman Old Testament Commentary

Twenty volumes designed for Bible study and teaching to enrich the local church and God's people.

Series Editor	Max Anders
Managing Editor	Steve Bond
Project Editor	Dean Richardson
Product Development Manager	Ricky D. King
Marketing Manager	Stephanie Huffman
Executive Editor	David Shepherd
Page Composition	TF Designs, Mt. Juliet, TN

Introduction to

Joshua

The angel might well have said to Joseph, "You will call his name Joshua," for the name God chose for his Son on earth is the same as this great captain of ancient Israel. As we shall see in our study, there is also a parallel between this book and Paul's letter to the Ephesians. Here we see historic Israel entering and possessing an earthly inheritance promised to Abraham. In Ephesians we see the church entering and possessing a heavenly inheritance provided in Christ. Major theological themes like rest, godly leadership style, holiness, and obedience appear in both books. Canaan indeed offers a metaphor of something to come but not, as so many songs suggest, heaven. The promised land for believers is walking in godliness and righteousness with the Lord here on earth. As Israel possessed its inheritance in the land, so Christians need to possess their spiritual blessings on earth but with their hearts "in the heavens." For Joshua and for us there is a promised inheritance, a divinely appointed leader, gifts of grace received by faith, and great conflict along the way.

AUTHORSHIP

Some Bible books, like many of the prophets, are named for the author. Joshua is named for the hero or principle character. Nowhere in the book are we told that Joshua wrote it, although most scholars believe he wrote significant parts of it (24:26). Howard claims, "We conclude that portions of the book were written in Joshua's day and that it was substantially complete by the time of David at the latest" (Howard, 30). Howard's work in *The New American Commentary* provides over forty pages of introductory material dealing thoroughly with questions of authorship, date, and other issues.

Some interpreters have suggested that Joshua added intentionally to Moses' work (cp. Josh. 24:26 with Deut. 31:9,24–26), and thousands of words have been written about the Deuteronomic nature of Joshua. Others have suggested that a professional scribe wrote the book as it was dictated by Joshua, or perhaps a group of scribes edited the manuscripts from Joshua's day. In any case, the question of inspiration is hardly influenced by specifically identifying which parts were written by Joshua and which by someone else.

DATE OF WRITING

Great controversy surrounds this question with some critical scholars suggesting a date as late as the 1200s. But evidence for an early date prevails among evangelicals. Obviously such a view (i.e., the 1200s) would preclude any contributions by Joshua who died in 1380 B.C. We also know that the date of the exodus was 1446, so we surmise that most of the book was written by Joshua between 1406 and 1380, and some portions were added by other writers or editors at a later time.

Events in the book cover a time span of less than a decade beginning in 1406, forty years after the exodus. Campbell gets more specific.

> The evidence from Judges 11:26 confirms [1406 as the beginning of the conquest]. Jephthah said the period from the conquest to his time was 300 years (Judg. 11:26). Adding 140 years to cover the period from Jephthah to the fourth year of Solomon gives a total of 480, which agrees with 1 Kings 6:1 (40 years for the wilderness wanderings, plus 300 for the period from the conquest to Jephthah, plus 140 from Jephthah to the fourth year of Solomon equals 480 years). Since the actual conquest lasted seven years, the land was probably occupied about 1399 B.C. The book, apart from minor additions, could have been completed soon after that (Campbell, *BKC*, 326).

PURPOSE AND IMPORTANCE

With the exception of the Syriac version, the Book of Joshua always appears after Deuteronomy in the Old Testament. One would expect this, since this book picks up the story of Israel from the death of Moses to the death of Joshua. But evangelical scholars reject the "hexateuch theory," the idea that Joshua is so similar to the first five books of the Old Testament that they must be viewed as a unit. Actually, the book clearly links much more closely with the historical books than it does with the Pentateuch.

Joshua so closely links with the land promises of Genesis that Isaiah called the Messiah a "second Joshua" who would "restore the land and . . . reassign its desolate inheritances" (Isa. 49:8). We'll make every effort not to overlook the spiritual impact of the book while paying due homage to its historical significance. Page after page depicts the faithfulness of God in fulfilling the promises he had made to Abraham and renewing his promise to those who left Egypt under Moses. The deliverance and promise theme appears in the first part of the book (1:3–4) and is summarized again in 23:14–16.

STRUCTURE

For the most part we will take the book chapter by chapter, combining chapters at a few points but generally following the narrative of the conquest. Certainly there are many ways the book could be outlined, and it may be worthwhile to look at a few of them.

Outline A

    I. Introduction (1:1–9)
   II. Entrance into Canaan (1:10–5:15)
  III. Conquest of the Land (6:1–12:24)
  IV. Division of the Land (13:1–22:34)
   V. Joshua's Farewell (23:1–24:33)

Outline B

    I. The Conquest of the Land (1:1–12:24)
   II. Division of the Land (13:1–21:45)
  III. Farewells (22:1–24:33) (*Nelson Study Bible*, 351–52)

Outline C

    I. The Invasion of Canaan (1:1–5:12)
   II. The Conquest of Canaan (5:13–12:24)
  III. The Division of Canaan 13:1–21:45)
  IV. Conclusion (22:1–24:33) (Campbell, *BKC*, 326–27)

Outline D

    I. Preparations for Inheriting the Land (1:1–5:15)
   II. Inheriting the Land (6:1–12:24)
  III. Apportioning the Land (13:1–21:45)
  IV. Farewells (22:1–24:33) (Miller, 68)

All these outlines look similar and merely form some way of viewing the narrative in blocks rather than a linear flow.

Perhaps this theme of God's faithfulness declared and fulfilled surfaces as a key passage in Joshua 21:43–45: "So the LORD gave Israel all the land he had sworn to give their forefathers, and they took possession of it and settled there. The LORD gave them rest on every side, just as he had sworn to their forefathers. Not one of their enemies withstood them; the LORD handed all their enemies over to them. Not one of all the LORD's good promises to the house of Israel failed; every one was fulfilled."

Joshua 1

Possessing the Promise

I. **INTRODUCTION**
Gilmore's Traps

II. **COMMENTARY**
A verse-by-verse explanation of the chapter.

III. **CONCLUSION**
Ten Minutes a Day

An overview of the principles and applications from the chapter.

IV. **LIFE APPLICATION**
How to Be a Great Follower

Melding the chapter to life.

V. **PRAYER**
Tying the chapter to life with God.

VI. **DEEPER DISCOVERIES**
Historical, geographical, and grammatical enrichment of the commentary.

VII. **TEACHING OUTLINE**
Suggested step-by-step group study of the chapter.

VIII. **ISSUES FOR DISCUSSION**
Zeroing the chapter in on daily life.

"*Leadership is the activity of influencing people to cooperate toward some goal which they come to find desirable.*"

O r d w a y   T e a d

Joshua 1

IN A NUTSHELL

After the death of Moses, the Lord spoke to Joshua and commissioned him to take over the leadership of the Hebrew people. Based on that commission, Joshua commanded the people to get ready to go into the land in three days. He then instructed the warriors of the tribes of Reuben, Gad, and the half tribe of Manasseh to go with the other tribes into the land inside the Jordan River and help them to subdue the promised land. When that military task was done, Joshua told these two and one-half tribes they could return to their apportioned land on the eastern side of the Jordan River.

Possessing the Promise

I. INTRODUCTION

Gilmore's Traps

*I*n his wonderful book *Making a Leadership Change,* Thomas Gilmore identifies some problems leaders face when they assume a new responsibility. He warns that the biggest traps lie in the path of connecting with existing staff:

> Leaders, especially early in their tenure, do not get fully developed options from which they select a path. Rather, a direction begins to emerge from a sequence of choices—about people, issues, resources . . . and from serendipity. . . . Traps arise from misunderstandings and the inability to discuss the situation freely (Gilmore, 136).

Indeed, Joshua faced numerous traps or there would have been no need for God to tell him, "Do not be terrified; do not be discouraged" (1:9). According to Gilmore, the first has to do with *patterns of delegation,* a lesson Joshua had seen in negative form by watching Moses before his confrontation with Jethro recorded in Exodus 18. Yes, Joshua had inherited a staff, and we learn about them in Joshua 1:10 where they are called "the officers of the people." New leaders face a mutual learning experience with existing staff in order to provide a good working relationship within a reasonable amount of time. Since leaders early in their tenure do not want to appear unresponsive, they tend to give out signals suggesting they want involvement in everything. The result is an overloaded desk and staff relinquishing their independence—either eagerly or grudgingly.

The second trap centers on *internal versus external priorities.* Joshua had to keep the people balanced between the physical task of conquering cities and the less obvious but more important task of maintaining spiritual vitality. This is a challenge each of us faces every day as we struggle to enter the spiritual heights of "Canaan."

The third of Gilmore's traps deals with *handling resistance to change.* Picture a pastor who comes to a staff meeting making suggestions and asking for input. The staff responds, and the church leaders get involved. Knowing the practical realities of the church, they often cite difficulties that the pastor's ideas might encounter. He may interpret this feedback as resistance or lack of vision and in the future consult both staff and church leaders on fewer matters. If this happens they may identify less with his ideas and become bystanders, no longer feeling that their leadership is important.

Joshua could not carry out his mission without the supernatural power God promised would be available. But he also could not carry it out if he did not have the support of the tribal leaders, "the officers of the people." Despite the great similarities between Moses and Joshua, we all agree Moses was a tough act to follow. Think again of the new leader who replaced the prophetic icon, Elijah. Despite the striking similarities between their ministries and mannerisms, those two men were quite different. Elijah's miracles were spectacular, national, and highly visible, whereas Elisha dealt more often with "little people" and common things such as water, oil, pottage, loaves, and axe heads.

Elijah was an ascetic, a mountain man who thrived in the wilds by himself; but Elisha seemed to be always in the company of students from the schools of the prophets and apparently exercised some kind of leadership role among them.

The lesson here is simple—but so important. God calls his people to follow others who have served in the same capacity in earlier years. It is tempting to measure ourselves by the record of a predecessor, failing to realize that God does not expect us to be like anyone else. Like Joshua, we must carry out the gifts and commands he has placed on us for our time. We can certainly learn from those who have gone before, but we don't want to fall into any of the traps or in any way restrict God's powerful hand by mimicking the ministry of another one of his servants.

II. COMMENTARY

Possessing the Promise

MAIN IDEA: *Responding to God's call for leadership requires experience, strength, and courage. God had granted Joshua considerable experience before Moses' death. Now he commands Joshua to be strong and courageous.*

A God's Promise to Give (1:1–5)

SUPPORTING IDEA: *The Israelites had to walk by faith to receive God's promises to them. They had to face and overcome obstacles all along the way. These verses tell Joshua and Israel that God will accomplish everything he had promised to Moses.*

1:1. God had set his plan in motion when he called Abram out of Haran and led him to Canaan. In Genesis 12:2 God had said, "I will make you into a great nation and I will bless you." In the very next chapter, when Abram stood on the land, God said, "All the land that you see I will give to you and your offspring forever" (Gen. 13:15). Abraham had been followed by Isaac, Jacob, and Joseph. After four hundred years in Egypt, the family had grown into a great nation—a nation of slaves struggling under the cruel hand of Pharaoh.

God heard their cries for help and moved to fulfill his promise to Abraham. God called Moses who had fled from Egypt and spent forty years as a shepherd in the desert. God told him, "I have come down to rescue [my people] from the hand of the Egyptians and to bring them up out of that land into a good and spacious land, a land flowing with milk and honey" (Exod. 3:8). Moses was hesitant, but God said, "I will be with you" (Exod. 3:12). Through miraculous plagues God freed his people from Pharaoh's grasp and Moses led them through the Red Sea and into the desert where they wandered for forty years until an entire generation died off.

Moses did not enter the land himself because he disobeyed God, but before he died, he had an important request:

"May the LORD, the God of the spirits of all mankind, appoint a man over this community to go out and come in before them, one who will lead them out and bring them in, so the LORD's people will not be like sheep without a shepherd." So the LORD said to Moses, "Take Joshua son of Nun, a man in whom is the spirit, and lay your hand on him. Have him stand before Eleazar the priest and the entire assembly and commission him in their presence. Give him some of your authority so the whole Israelite community will obey him" (Num. 27:16–20).

The first verse of Joshua describes the calling of a new leader. We have already learned in Deuteronomy that Moses is dead, and the narrative continues, almost uninterrupted, from Deuteronomy 34:12. Joshua is reintroduced into the narrative by a direct call of Yahweh himself. We learned in Deuteronomy 34:9 that God had chosen him and prepared him, and now Joshua and the Israelites stood on the western bank of the Jordan River ready to fulfill a promise given to Abraham hundreds of years before.

In addition to Moses and Yahweh, Joshua the son of Nun, the main protagonist of the Book of Joshua, also is introduced in verse 1. He is named about 205 times in the Old Testament, 148 times in this book. After this, his name appears most often in Exodus, Numbers, Deuteronomy, and Judges. Joshua is mentioned twice in the New Testament—in Stephen's speech, where Joshua's leadership in bringing the tabernacle into the land of Canaan is mentioned (Acts 7:45) and in the Book of Hebrews, in the great passage on rest (Heb. 3–4): Joshua's rest is depicted here as incomplete, not fulfilled until Christ's rest (4:8) (Howard, 73).

Later in this book Joshua will also be called "the servant of the LORD" (Josh. 24:29). Here, however, the title is reserved for Moses, a title used of him more in Joshua than in the rest of the Old Testament combined. In addition to the fourteen times it appears in Joshua, this title for Moses also shows up in Deuteronomy 34:5, 2 Kings 18:12, and 2 Chronicles 1:3 and 24:6.

1:2. Let's not forget that Joshua had been one of the spies and had personally seen the enemies Israel would have to defeat and the walls they would have to bring down. There was no question in Joshua's mind where he was headed—**into the land I am about to give to them.** The promise of the land began in Genesis 12:7 and was scattered all over the Pentateuch, but between the place where Joshua stood and the first step in that land flowed the Jordan River. The Jordan begins just below Mount Hermon and flows south into the Sea of Galilee and then the Dead Sea. Joshua and his people were located just north of the Dead Sea and east of Jericho. Like Moses, Joshua viewed a body of water between the nation and the place God wanted them to go.

1:3–5. The Hebrew text here is strikingly like Deuteronomy 11:24–25a, emphasizing again that Joshua fulfilled the beginnings and promises of the Pentateuch. To be sure, the exact land area was not fully occupied until the time of David and Solomon and later again under Uzziah and Jeroboam. There could be no disputing the precise geographical boundaries—the great desert in the south, the Lebanese mountains on the north, the Mediterranean Sea on the west, and to the east **the great river, the Euphrates** (see "Deeper Discoveries").

If the Israelites had listened to Joshua and Caleb and entered the land God intended to give them from the south many years earlier, they would not have been facing the Jordan at this point. The word **give** appears in both verses 2 and 3, emphasizing that Joshua's work was really God's work. Howard tells us the word "is one of the most common in the Old Testament, occurring more than two thousand times. It is one of the fifteen most common words in the Old Testament (excluding particles)" (Howard, 77).

What a promise God gave Joshua! **No one will be able to stand up against you all the days of your life**. And just to reinforce those words, God reminded Joshua of everything his heavenly hand had accomplished through Moses. "The secret of Moses' success had been God's presence with him. It would be the secret of Joshua's success also, and it continues to be the secret of success for the church" (Madvig, 256).

When we stare at the Jordan River in our lives, what do we see? The swirling muddy water of spiritual failures, sins, fears, and habits? Some persistent physical problem? The steady flow of broken relationships? Like Joshua, we need to take our eyes off the river and fix them on the God of the river. But God is not yet finished with his opening speech. In addition to his promises to *give,* he now adds principles for Joshua's *growth.*

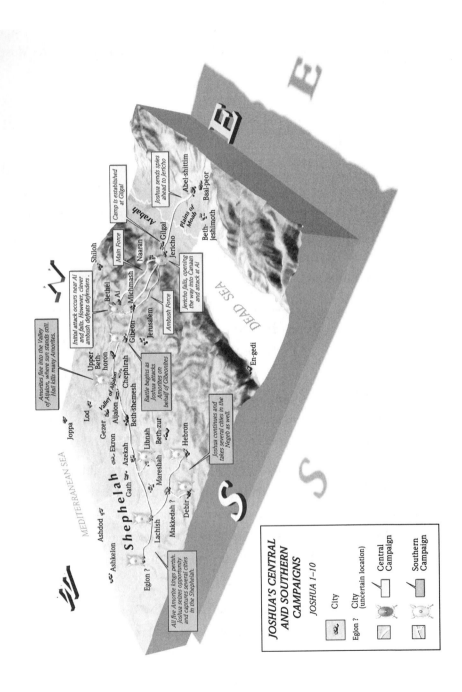

JOSHUA'S CENTRAL AND SOUTHERN CAMPAIGNS

JOSHUA 1–10

City

City (uncertain location)

Eglon ?

Central Campaign

Southern Campaign

Camp is established at Gilgal

Joshua sends spies ahead to Jericho

Initial attack occurs near Ai and fails. However, clever ambush defeats defenders.

Jericho falls, opening the way into Canaan and attack at Ai

Amorites flee into the Valley of Aijalon, where sun stands still. Hail kills many Amorites.

Battle begins as Joshua attacks Amorites on behalf of Gibeonites

Joshua continues and takes several cities in the Negeb as well.

All five Amorite kings perish. Joshua seizes opportunity and captures several cities in the Shephelah.

MEDITERRANEAN SEA

DEAD SEA

Arabah

Plains of Moab

Shephelah

Joppa
Lod
Gezer
Ekron
Ashdod
Ashkelon
Gath
Azekah
Mareshah
Lachish
Makkedah ?
Eglon ?
Debir
Libnah
Beth-zur
Hebron
Beth-shemesh
Aijalon
Chephirah
Gibeon
Jerusalem
Valley of Aijalon
Upper Beth-horon
Bethel
Ai
Michmash
Shiloh
Naaran
Gilgal
Jericho
Beth-jeshimoth
Baal-peor
Abel-shittim
En-gedi

Main Force
Ambush Force

B God's Principles for Growth (1:6–8)

> **SUPPORTING IDEA:** *Joshua had principles for living right in his hands. Moses had received these principles from God and passed them on to Joshua. Now he must think about God's law, do it, and speak it to others. This would bring him success as a leader.*

1:6. Three times in this section of the chapter God repeats his command to **be strong and courageous.** How would Joshua do this? By standing straight and sticking out his chest? No, by leaning on God the same way Moses had done.

- Joshua could be confident because God is competent.
- Joshua could be dependent because God is dependable.
- Joshua could trust because God is trustworthy.

Perhaps the secret lies in the little-known fact that Joshua's name had been changed. Originally called *Hoshea,* which means "salvation," his name was changed by Moses to *Joshua* which means "the Lord is salvation." Joshua was the leader but not the deliverer, the guide but not the giver.

Like Moses, Joshua began his leadership at the age of about eighty. Also like Moses, he could call upon decades of experience to strengthen his faith. For example, when the Amalekites attacked the Israelites in the desert, Joshua led the army into battle while Moses stood on a nearby hill and held up the staff of God. As long as Moses held up his hands the Israelites won. When he grew tired and lowered his hands the Amalekites prevailed. With the help of Aaron and Hur (and a good strong stone to sit on) the staff stayed aloft and the Israelites won.

Did God need that raised rod to guarantee the victory? Of course not. Through that and numerous other incidents he taught Israel that battles are not won in human strength but by divine power. After that battle God had said to Moses, "Write this on a scroll as something to be remembered and make sure that Joshua hears it" (Exod. 17:14).

1:7–8. At the center of Joshua's faith would be the Word of God, **this Book of the Law.** The word **meditate** could be rendered "mutter." As Madvig puts it, "When one continually mutters God's Word to himself, he is constantly thinking about it. Knowledge of God's law is not enough; one must also 'be careful to do' what it commands" (Madvig, 257). Most scholars believe this refers to some portion of the Levitical law already held by the priests. Certainly the Ten Commandments would be a part of it, but the reference would spread far beyond those boundaries. Joshua would receive direct revelation and was in that exact mode while God talked to him, but that didn't change the importance of the written word.

I like the way Francis Schaeffer puts it:

> But though Joshua was going to have this special leading from the Lord, this was not to detract from the central reference point and chief control: the written book. The Word of God written in the book set the limitations. Thus, Joshua was already functioning in the way Bible-believing Christians function. Sometimes God does lead in other ways, but such leading must always be within the circle of his external, propositional commands in Scripture. Even if a person had an Urim and a Thummin as well as a priest to guide him, this would not change his basic authority. The primary leading would come from the written, propositional revelation of God, from the Bible (Schaeffer, 32).

Much has been made of the word **successful** that appears in verses 7 and 8, and also the word **prosperous** to which it attaches at the end of verse 8. It should be obvious to any serious Bible student that financial achievement is not in view here. The so-called "prosperity gospel" cannot be argued from any portion of God's Word and certainly not from these verses in the first chapter of Joshua. Success and prosperity come when a person follows God's will, obeys God's Word, and achieves God's goal, not when the offerings are greater this year than they were last year at this time.

God never forces us to live a victorious Christian life. He teaches and promises and provides principles. But if we fail to cross the river and possess the land, we will remain in a spiritual desert. God is not looking for people with self-confidence but people with God-confidence.

Joshua understood how important the principles of the law are to God. The Lord didn't just airmail the stone tablets to Israel on a windstorm; he met personally with their leader. Exodus 24 tells us that Joshua was the only other person on that mountain with Moses that day. We don't know how close he was to the glory cloud, but it must have been an awesome experience. What looked like consuming fire on top of the mountain engulfed Moses for forty days and nights while he met with God. Joshua was the first to see the glow of God's glory on Moses' face and the first to see the stones etched by the finger of God.

My son Jeff coaches a recreational department boy's basketball team. Half the boys who play have never participated in organized basketball before, so Jeff works hard to build their confidence. He does that by reminding them to remember what they learn and do in practice when they get into a game. If they follow the basic rules and remember the basic skills, they can play well.

In simple terms, this is what God said to Joshua and what he says to us: "Get back to the basics. Remember the rules. Learn the law. Practice the principles."

The problem is that sometimes we become like those little boys. We get out on the basketball court of life where referees blow whistles and people in different colored shirts try to take the ball away, and we lose our confidence and composure. Then we discover that every time we forget God's promises and principles we end up in chaos.

C God's Presence to Guide (1:9–11)

SUPPORTING IDEA: *God's challenge to be strong and coura-geous is not just a suggestion; it is a command. And Joshua had to pass on those orders to the officers and leaders of the people.*

1:9. Surely one of the greatest verses in the Bible, these words echo through the heart of anyone who has ever tried to serve the Lord. God did not tell Joshua that he might be terrified and discouraged some day. The structure of the text leads us to conclude that those words described Joshua's current state of mind. Fear and discouragement go with the territory in any kind of ministry. The only antidote is a constant awareness of the presence of the Lord.

For forty years Joshua had experienced a gigantic visual aid from God to help and accept the reality of the heavenly presence. Exodus 13:21–22 says, "By day the LORD went ahead of them in a pillar of cloud to guide them on their way and by night in a pillar of fire to give them light, so that they could travel by day or night. Neither the pillar of cloud by day nor the pillar of fire by night left its place in front of the people." But it wasn't just people in general or Israel as a nation in focus here, because the three uses of the word **you** in this verse are singular.

All of us can understand the importance of parental presence. We learned it first as children when we thought we had lost Mom or Dad in a crowded room or a giant parking lot. Then as parents we see it again as we watch our children hold firmly to our hands in strange places and want us to go first into dark rooms. Parental presence instills confidence. That's why Jesus taught his disciples about the Father. As the writer of Hebrews put it, "Keep your lives free from the love of money and be content with what you have, because God has said, 'Never will I leave you; never will I forsake you.' So we say with confidence, 'The Lord is my helper; I will not be afraid. What can man do to me?'" (Heb. 13:5–6).

My friend and former boss Chuck Swindoll tells about working with a crusty, rugged guy named Tex when he served as an apprentice at a machine shop. Tex was always washed up and ready to go as soon as the whistle blew for lunch or quitting time. Chuck asked him how he got ready so fast, and he said, "Let me tell you something, sonny. I just stay ready to keep from getting ready." That's what God says to Joshua in this verse—"stay ready."

1:10–11. But Joshua did not stay ready alone. In verse 10 the scene switches from God's instructions to Joshua to Joshua's instructions to the **officers**. We first met these people in Numbers 11, and they reappear in Deuteronomy 1. The word **ordered** shows Joshua's authority and serves as an important concept throughout the Scriptures. Howard tells us:

> The word occurs 496 times in the Hebrew Bible, of which about 60 percent are found in these six books: twenty-seven times in Genesis, fifty-four times in Exodus, thirty-five in Leviticus, forty-eight times in Numbers, eighty-eight times in Deuteronomy, and forty-three times in Joshua (Howard, 90).

The **supplies** mentioned here would have included food and other materials necessary to cross the river and take the land. Once again readiness is important. For the Israelites then and for us now, possessing God's promises means being willing to walk by faith, trusting God to help us over obstacles and difficulties along the way. Perhaps Joshua didn't feel like standing before the people and delivering this message; it was much easier back in the days when he could put the final responsibility on Moses. But in obedience to God and as a result of God's encouragement, he stood up, took the challenge, and gave orders to the people.

Campbell likens this situation to the one Moses faced forty years earlier. "In both cases the obstacle occurred at the beginning of the leaders' ministries. Both were impossible to overcome by natural means. Both demanded implicit trust in and absolute dependence on God's miracle-working power" (Campbell, 329).

D God's Plan for Granting (1:12–18)

SUPPORTING IDEA: *Taking of the land was not just for those who had lived there but for all twelve tribes. It was essential that Reuben, Gad, and the one-half tribe of Manasseh help their brothers conquer the promised land before they settled east of the Jordan River.*

1:12–15. We don't hear much about land grants any more, but in earlier times they were common. The term describes a gift of land usually made by the government and intended for something like a park, a road, or even a college. Agricultural and mining schools (Texas A&M, Florida A&M) came into being because of land grants for a specific purpose.

At this point in the narrative of Joshua, the reader unfamiliar with the Pentateuch is astonished to discover that not all of Israel will be living in Canaan. The tribes of Reuben and Gad and one-half of the tribe of Manasseh have received and accepted their land grant east of the Jordan River. The key here in Joshua's leadership is to keep the two and one-half tribes faithful to the conquest while assuring them that they will be allowed the land they wanted east of the Jordan (Num. 32:20–22). Now it was time for them to leave their families and land and to fight with their brother tribes over in Canaan. **The command that Moses the servant of the LORD gave you** appears in Deuteronomy 3:18–20. They had made their choice, and although questionable it wouldn't determine their future.

As Redpath reminds us:

Look through the terrifying record of the consequences of that choice made by those two and one-half tribes. (Read 1 Chronicles, chapter 5.) You will discover that these tribes who had tasted of God's best and enjoyed God's victory, who had led the army of the people of God into the land of blessing, were the first to be captured by the Assyrians when they invaded Israel. Taken captive, they never returned. They went down to defeat and into bondage, even though at one time they had led the people of God in the way of blessing. Judges 5:16 says this: "For the divisions of Reuben there were great searchings of heart." I should think there were! They chose, they tasted of blessing, they had entered into the land of promise, but they hankered after the world, its pleasure, its indulgence, and its sin, and they were trapped and caught and ensnared in it (Redpath, 44).

Though history may bear out that theme of negative choice, the text before us emphasizes only the military responsibilities of the two and one-half tribes. In fact, as we have noted already, such military language is unusual in Joshua. Throughout the book we see the emphasis on the spiritual dimension and God's control of every situation. Madvig says:

> It is necessary to interpret the phrase "all your fighting men" because Numbers 26:7,18,34 indicates that these tribes had as many as 110,000 men capable of bearing arms. Nevertheless, Joshua 4:13 states that only 40,000 warriors from the two and one-half tribes entered Canaan. Perhaps only the ablest fighting men participated in the conquest while the others cared for the women, children, elderly and domestic animals (Madvig, 258).

Perhaps the two and one-half tribes had made a bad choice, but here they are depicted as passing the test. They would stand with their brothers and enter the land and not return until the conquest was complete.

1:16–18. Let's not miss the importance of the response here. If these tribes had decided not to keep their promise, this new nation could have been fragmented before it got established. If there were ever a reason for rebellion or an excuse for getting cold feet, this would have been it. But they passed the test, and their answer is a model attitude for those who want to serve God.

Whatever you have commanded us we will do. They accepted Joshua as their leader and were willing to obey and do whatever they were asked. **Wherever you send us we will go.** They did not limit the extent of their obedience or tell God where they would serve him.

As we fully obeyed Moses, we will obey you. This may have worried Joshua a bit. They had not always listened to Moses. But it was an important statement of confidence. They had looked up to Moses, and now they would follow Joshua. **May the LORD your God be with you as he was with Moses**. They prayed for Joshua and were willing to trust him as their leader as long as he followed God.

Whoever rebels . . . will be put to death. They were serious enough about this commitment to impose accountability and discipline upon themselves. This punishment actually took place in the case of Achan (see Josh. 7).

How interesting that they reminded Joshua of God's threefold command to **be strong and courageous**. Apparently word had gotten around the camps that the new leader had received specific instructions from on high. Despite Redpath's comments on the bad choice, there is a great lesson here. Sometimes God may ask us to leave our comfort zones east of Jordan to fight alongside other Christians. We like to gravitate to our own causes and march only in our own campaigns. Surely the conquest of Canaan looked to the two and one-half tribes like somebody else's job.

We should notice one more thing. They didn't just tag along into the promised land, grumbling and complaining with every step—they led the army! They were the front line, the first to step into the river. The first to walk up to the wall of Jericho. We need more frontline Christians in the twenty-first century.

> **MAIN IDEA REVIEW:** *Responding to God's call for leadership requires experience, strength, and courage. God had granted Joshua considerable experience before Moses' death. Now he commands Joshua to be strong and courageous.*

III. CONCLUSION

Ten Minutes a Day

Wilma Rudolph was born prematurely and suffered from double pneumonia, scarlet fever, and polio which left her with a crooked leg and a twisted foot. She wore braces for eleven years until she forced herself to learn to walk without them. Then she discovered sports. She went with her older sister to the basketball games but didn't play. Finally she told the coach, "If you will give me ten minutes of your time every day, I will give you a world-class athlete." He did, and she began to run every day. First she beat her best friend and then other girls in her school. By the age of fourteen, she was faster than any other high school girl in the state of Tennessee.

In 1956 she went to the Olympics and won a bronze medal with the 440-meter relay team. That served to motivate her to even greater commitment and sacrifice until running became her life. She would run at six and ten every morning, at three every afternoon, and often from eight to ten at night. For four years she trained and at the 1960 Olympics won gold in the 100-meter, 200-meter, and 400-meter relays. In every race she set a world record.

This chapter reminds us that the Christian life is a daily run, a daily battle. It incorporates all of life. We should wear the armor at all times. We should keep the running shoes on our feet. Earth is not our destination; it's only our temporary dwelling place. We are headed for a different land. Our finish line is in heaven.

PRINCIPLES

- Christian leaders must be convinced that they can trust God enough to enter every situation with confidence.

- God's presence gives Joshua and us the confidence we need to be strong and courageous.

- The way we respond to God's Word and get involved in God's work can communicate strength and courage to those who teach us and lead us.

APPLICATIONS

- In times of fear and danger, trust in God and in his promises, principles, presence, and plan.

- When you make a commitment, stick by it; keep your word even when it's uncomfortable to do so.

- At the center of everything we do is God's Word; our number one task is to be careful to obey it.

IV. LIFE APPLICATION

How to Be a Great Follower

Joshua 1:1 introduces our general as "Moses' aide." We have already noticed how he spent forty years in preparation for assuming this new leadership post. Those of us with experience in church ministry also know that people who are unable to function effectively as followers rarely make good leaders. And recent research in the field of leadership and administration certainly bolsters that notion.

Traditionally we have thought of leadership as gifted people with special traits taking charge of the rest of us in order to make sure things get done. But the recent theme of leadership literature that centers on "the learning organization" is much more in keeping with the biblical pattern, especially the New Testament. It centers on influencing everyone in the organization to achieve at a higher level. Just think how this definition of contemporary leadership fits our man Joshua.

Bornstein and Smith declare:

> We submit that leadership in the future will more closely reflect a process whereby a leader pursues his or her vision by intentionally seeking to influence others in the conditions in which they work, allowing them to perform to their full potential and thus both increasing the probability of realizing the vision and maximizing the organizational and personal development of all parties involved (Bornstein and Smith, 283).

Creative leaders do more than model innovation; they also inspire effective followership throughout the organization. Effective followers are marked by *shared goals,* since people who do not share the goals and vision of ministry cannot exercise creative followership, or, for that matter, creative leadership. Another ingredient is *solid feedback* such as Joshua got from the spies in chapter 2. All leadership is strengthened when leaders and followers communicate.

A third ingredient is *strong credibility.* Trust is a major leadership ingredient. People cannot follow someone they do not trust. But trust works two ways. Leaders generally do not release authority and responsibility to people whose credibility for competence and reliability may be shaky. And everything we say about the credibility and capability of leaders applies to the work and ministry of creative followers, in most cases leaders in the making.

One could argue that Joshua was a great leader because he was a great follower. He had learned the secret of both dimensions of the leadership equation.

V. PRAYER

Father, help us to be like Joshua—strong, courageous, and unafraid—since we know that Joshua's God sustains and blesses us as well. Amen.

VI. DEEPER DISCOVERIES

A. Joshua in the Pentateuch

Joshua is named first in Exodus 17:9 where he is told by Moses to "choose some of our men and go out to fight the Amalekites." Already he was a general and by Exodus 24:13 he stands as a minister under Moses. In Exodus 32:17 he appears with Moses on the mountain and in the very next chapter as a worshiper in the tabernacle.

In Numbers 11:28 he shows some concern about Moses' authority, a potential crisis in his leadership training experience. Schaeffer says of this occasion:

> Joshua had another lesson to learn, and a very serious one: God's glory is to come first. There is a great difference between leadership and self-aggrandizement. There is to be leadership among the people of God, according to the gifts he bestows, but there is not to be glorification of oneself or other men. Joshua asked that Eldad and Medad be forbidden to prophesy because they had not come before Moses and the Tabernacle; but Moses answered magnificently, "Don't envy for my sake." Maybe Moses' response is one of the reasons the Bible says Moses was a meek man. Though Moses

was such a tremendous leader, he would not tolerate Joshua's glorifying him (Schaeffer, 16).

The Book of Numbers tells us that Joshua came from the tribe of Ephraim (Num. 13:8), was one of the spies sent into Canaan (13:16), was a man indwelt with the Spirit of God (27:18–23), was spared from death in the wilderness along with Caleb (26:65), that he wholly followed the Lord (32:12,28), and that he was placed in charge of the division of the land (34:17).

Here is Schaeffer again:

Now, after all these years of preparation Joshua is ready to enter the land: "And Joshua the son of Nun was full of the spirit of wisdom; for Moses had laid his hands upon him: and the children of Israel hearkened unto him, and did as the LORD commanded Moses" (Deut. 34:9). This was not a mechanical readiness. An act of the will was involved. If we do not stress this, we will be giving an inaccurate picture of Joshua's preparation. It is not that you feed preparation into a mill and a leader comes out the other end. It is not that way, any more than that you feed facts into a mill and a Christian comes out the other end. It must be an act of the will in becoming a Christian, and there must be an act of the will for any man, no matter what his preparation, to become a leader in God's work (Schaeffer, 25–26).

B. The Great River (1:4)

Throughout both biblical and secular history **the great river, the Euphrates** plays a dominant role. It nurtured the cradle of ancient Sumerian civilization. Flowing southwest through Mesopotamia, it finally joined the Tigris River to empty into the Persian Gulf. By or near its banks lie the ruins of the ancient cities of Eridu, Ur, Uruk, Larsa, Lagash, Nippur, Nisin, and the great Babylon. Some sixty miles farther up the Euphrates stood Agade, ancient capital of the kingdom of Akkad.

Historian Will Durant wrote of this historic body of water:

No one looking at the site of ancient Babylon today would suspect that these hot and dreary wastes along the Euphrates were once the rich and powerful capital of the civilization that almost created an astronomy, added richly to the progress of medicine, established the science of language, prepared the first great codes of law, taught the Greeks the rudiments of mathematics, physics and philosophy . . . and passed on to the Arabs part of that scientific and architectural lure with which they aroused the dominant soul of medieval Europe. Standing before the silent Tigris and Euphrates one finds it hard to believe that they are the same rivers that watered Sumaria and Akod and nourished the Hanging Garden of Babylon (Durant, 218).

The Euphrates is one of the four rivers which, according to Genesis 2:14, flowed through the garden of Eden and is mentioned again in Genesis 15:18 in God's promise to Abraham. It appears in Deuteronomy, Joshua, 2 Kings, 1 Chronicles, 2 Chronicles, Jeremiah, and again finally in Revelation 9:14 and 16:12 where we read, "The sixth angel poured out his bowl on the great river Euphrates, and its water was dried up to prepare the way for the kings from the East."

No modern political figure or historian would argue that land east of the Jordan River belongs to Israel today. But in the Book of Joshua and throughout the text of Scripture, God's promise stands: "Your territory will extend from the desert to Lebanon, and from the great river, the Euphrates."

C. The Book of the Law (1:8)

We can hardly pass over lightly the great emphasis in verses 7 and 8 on the law and especially on the Book of the Law. This business of walking a straight line according to the law also appears in Deuteronomy 2:27 and other passages in that book. Proverbs 4:27 and Isaiah 30:21 also warn against deviation from God's plan. Of these references Butler says:

The final motif which underlines Joshua 1 is Torah, specifically the Torah commanded by Moses. Torah designated the teaching of the priests (Jer. 18:18; Ezek. 7:26; Hos. 4:6). Particularly important here was the information given members of the community who asked questions of the priests (Butler, 12).

So Joshua worked with the scrolls of Moses written and placed in the ark of the covenant, documents that would judge the kings of Israel and Judah in the future.

The fact that Joshua's generation accepted the Pentateuch as authoritative is more than a mere breath of fresh air in the heavy smog which surrounds present liberal scholarly discussion. To the Israelites, the Canon was not just academic, not merely theological, but practical. Joshua and the people had a continuity of authority as they moved through history. The book was to be their environment, their mentality (Schaeffer, 34).

VII. TEACHING OUTLINE

A. INTRODUCTION

1. Lead Story: Gilmore's Traps
2. Context: Joshua is a bridge book between the pentateuchal writings of Moses and the historical books of the Old Testament. The context is formed by the first words of the first verse, "After the death of Moses."
3. Transition: Deuteronomy ends by saying, "Now Joshua the son of Nun was full of the spirit of wisdom, for Moses had laid his hands on him; so the children of Israel heeded him, and did as the LORD had commanded Moses" (Deut. 34:9 NKJV). This announcement follows immediately the record of Moses' death and sets the stage for the opening of the Book of Joshua.

B. COMMENTARY

1. God's Promise to Give (1:1–5)
2. God's Principles for Growth (1:6–8)

3. God's Presence to Guide (1:9–11)
4. God's Plan for Granting (1:12–18)

C. CONCLUSION: HOW TO BE A GREAT FOLLOWER

VIII. ISSUES FOR DISCUSSION

1. How do you explain the fact that modern Israel possesses so little of the land promised to the patriarchs, Moses, and Joshua?
2. From the information in this chapter, what might we conclude about Joshua's personality and attitude toward leadership?
3. What implications reside in the last paragraph, which describes the reaction of the Gadites, the Reubenites, and one-half of the tribe of Manasseh to Joshua's challenge?

Joshua 2

Strangers in the Attic

Quote

"*F*aith is more than thinking something is true. Faith is thinking something is true to the extent that we act on it."

W . T . P u r k i s e r

GEOGRAPHICAL PROFILE: SHITTIM

- Hebrew word for Acacia Grove
- Israelite encampment east of the Jordan River (Num. 25:1)
- Located some distance east of the river, possibly near Mount Nebo

Joshua 2

IN A NUTSHELL

*T*his chapter contains a fascinating story of military intelligence and intrigue. It includes a walled enemy fortress, two brave Israelite spies, one surprising prostitute, a house of ill repute, a search and cover-up, a manhunt, an intelligence gathering, a back window getaway, and a three-day hideout. What a story!

Strangers in the Attic

I. INTRODUCTION

Turning Points

In an article in *USA Today,* William Strauss and Neil Howe offered an extensive essay reflecting upon the terrorist attacks of September 11, 2001. They argue that history, while not repeating particulars, does flow in rhythms that relate to the cycle of generations. The 1990s, they say, bore significant similarity to the 1920s, and 2001 looked much like 1930 in which "an old order was giving place to the new, a reflecting and aching disillusionment of the hard-boiled era, its oily scandals, its spiritual paralysis, the harshness of its gaiety." They argue that turnings come in cycles of four, roughly eighty to one hundred years, with the first turning representing a high; the second turning bringing an awakening; the third turning producing an unraveling, and the fourth turning, a crisis. They conclude, "For a long time, Americans have been waiting for history to happen. It's happening. Let's hope we, and our leaders, handle it well" (October 2001, 15a).

Whether Strauss and Howe can demonstrate substance for their theory poses another question. What seems clear, however, is that Israel was facing a major turning, this one just two generations (forty years) after the last one, the great exodus from Egypt. This huge turning point would finally place Abraham's land in the hands of his people, but not without a great deal of trauma and terror assuaged only by courage and faith. The lessons of Joshua 2 remind us to obey God, perhaps especially when great change enters our lives, and to recognize that he is in control and the process and the outcome of turning points rest in his hands.

II. COMMENTARY

Strangers in the Attic

> **MAIN IDEA:** *This chapter centers not on the spies or Joshua himself but on Rahab the prostitute. She demonstrates for us the wisdom and value of choosing faith and acting upon that choice. Her reward was enormous.*

A Undercover Assignment (2:1–7)

> **SUPPORTING IDEA:** *Somehow tuned to the plan of God rather than the paganism all around her, Rahab chose to follow the God of the Hebrews in faith and therefore models for us spiritual courage inspired by faith.*

2:1. Jericho lay some fourteen miles west of the Jordan River. It was a walled fortress city that served as a bridgehead for all advances west, south, and north into the land of Canaan. Joshua sent out the spies not to decide if they should attack the city but to gain information to help them know how and when to attack.

The use of the spies was not a lack of faith but rather a demonstration that true faith is active faith. Like Joshua, we must use common sense and caution as we march through our Christian lives.

But why go to Rahab's house? Schaeffer says:

> They went where they could easily "get lost," where they could find shelter with some degree of freedom. There is no place like a harlot's house for people coming and going. There is no indication whatever that they went there for any immoral purpose; this simply does not exist in the story (Schaeffer, 71).

It seems superfluous to say that the spies were sent **secretly**, since all spy missions are supposedly secret. Likely we are to understand here that even the Israelites did not know the spies had been sent. Joshua would well remember the disaster of an earlier spy mission (Num. 13–14). The original mission sent them to **look over the land** with special focus on Jericho. Events there brought to a quick close any exploration of additional portions of the land. Indeed, the military assignment quickly turned into a dangerous game of hide-and-seek.

2:2–3. So much for undercover work. The presence of the spies was detected immediately. The king of Jericho, suspecting that a local prostitute might be involved in undercover treachery, sent a message to Rahab to turn them over to the authorities. According to Madvig, "In antiquity too, as in modern times, prostitutes frequently were involved in intelligence activities. The king expected Rahab to do her patriotic duty and turn the spies in" (Madvig, 260).

2:4–7. But the story takes a surprising turn. At her own initiative, apparently based on belief about the God of Israel, Rahab lied to the king's men and sent them on a wild goose chase. In "Deeper Discoveries" we will explore the question of the morality of Rahab's lie, a central issue in this chapter. Here let's just remember to distinguish between what the Bible reports and what it recommends, what it records and what it requires. Rahab's lie is never condoned and certainly God could have saved the spies another way. But we should hardly expect spiritual behavior from a heathen harlot, especially one involved in espionage during a time when war was imminent. With the king's men heading east toward the river and the spies still hidden in Rahab's house, **the gate was shut**.

B Undercover Intelligence (2:8–13)

> **SUPPORTING IDEA:** *God's selection of Rahab for this mission parallels Joshua's selection of the spies. She was a usable instrument because she demonstrated a readiness to know the purpose, power, and person of God.*

2:8–13. Rahab and her fellow citizens of Jericho had heard stories about the Red Sea and the defeat of Sihon and Og. Apparently those miraculous works of God made greater impression on her than they had on some of the Israelites. She concluded God had given the land to Israel and, along with her neighbors, she desperately feared this invading nation.

But this prostitute also came to a personal conviction about the nature of God when she said, **The LORD your God is God in heaven above and on the earth below**. This is an amazing statement of faith from a woman who had never tasted manna, had never seen the glory cloud, and had never read the law. Howard reminds us that "Rahab's words become even more significant when we realize that the last part of her affirmation—the phrase 'in the heavens above and the earth below'—is found only three times prior to this, all in contexts that affirm God's exclusive claims to sovereignty" (Howard, 103). Those texts are Exodus 20:4, Deuteronomy 4:39, and Deuteronomy 5:8.

Some interpreters have criticized the spies for forming this treaty of amnesty with a prostitute and a Canaanite and have argued that such behavior violated the principle of separation. But Rahab's testimony makes her a *de facto* Israelite in that she chose to join sides with the God of Israel and the success of his people. One could claim that she became the first "proselyte of the gate," the system used by foreigners to affiliate with Israel and enjoy a relationship with Yahweh in Old Testament times.

Based on her knowledge of God's judgment and her belief in his sovereignty, she asked the spies for mercy. She begged for the lives of her family members and some sign of assurance that they would all be saved. Her motivation seemed far beyond just saving her own skin. She reflected a deep spiritual understanding of the heavenly nature involved in the fall of Canaan and wanted also to protect the lives of her family.

🅲 Undercover Agreement (2:14–21)

SUPPORTING IDEA: *These verses center on the covenant between Rahab and the spies. There were certain conditions to be kept. When fulfilled, they would lead to deliverance for Rahab's entire family.*

2:14. **Our lives for your lives.** That was the deal. The spies never wavered in their confidence that God would give them the land. But there were conditions that Rahab must fulfill in exchange for which she would be treated **kindly and faithfully.** The word *kindness* appears in verse 12 in Rahab's request and is promised again in verse 14. This significant Old Testament term (*hesed*) appears some 250 times in the Old Testament. It refers to a steadfast and genuine love based on some kind of promise or covenant. She made a *hesed* agreement with them by saving their lives, and they in turn made a *hesed* agreement with her to spare the lives of her family.

2:15–16. Rahab's house was set into the city wall. She pulled off a simple rope trick right through a window and sent the spies to some limestone clefts and caves about one-half mile west of Jericho. A scarlet cord would be a symbol for the "scarlet woman" and her family. Matching the color of

Jesus' blood, this cord would serve as an early reminder of how salvation takes place.

2:17–21. Several conditions marked this covenant: Rahab must help them escape, put the scarlet cord in the window, keep their secret, and stay in the house. When she tied the cord in the window, it was an act of faith and a sealing of the deal. Hamlin observes:

> Rahab was a paradigm of hope, showing that the old idols, the old corrupt ways of the past, could be given up. What Rahab did just before the fall of Jericho, Israel could do before (or after) the fall of Jerusalem. The contrast between Rahab at the bottom of the social scale and the kings and nobles of Jericho at the top illustrates well what Jesus said: "Harlots go into the kingdom of God before you" (Matt. 21:31) (Hamlin, 18).

We should note that the long conversation recorded in verses 16–21 did not take place after the men were on the ground with Rahab still up in the window, shouting back and forth. The text at the beginning of verse 16 is quite precise: "Now she had said to them." All these agreements had been made before they rappelled down the wall.

We should also note that the rope used to let the spies down and the scarlet cord symbolizing the location of Rahab's house were two different items indicated by two different Hebrew words. With regard to the color of the cord mentioned earlier, Howard says:

> This is a typological approach to understanding Scripture, and it is one that the Scriptures themselves employ and endorse. For example Paul argues that Adam "was a 'type' of Christ in Rom. 5:12–21; nv. 14, he states explicitly that Adam "was a pattern ['type'] of the one to come." Peter argues that the waters from which Noah was saved were a "type" of the water baptism that saves Christians "by the resurrection of Jesus Christ" (1 Pet. 3:20–21) (Howard, 115).

We don't want to push the typology too far and argue that the cord is definitely a type of the blood of Christ and Rahab represents the church, since no such association appears in the New Testament. Nevertheless, there is certainly a symbolic connection related to the salvation of undeserving people through grace and faith.

D Undercover Report (2:22–24)

> **SUPPORTING IDEA:** *God kept his word. As a result Rahab's name shows up in the first chapter of the first book of the New Testament.*

2:22–24. When the spies left, they went into the hills and stayed there until the pursuers had completed their search and returned to Jericho. The Hebrew is somewhat tricky here. Old Testament scholars note that all that is required in the reckoning of three days is that some part of each day be counted. The point is that the entire adventure from the sending out of the spies to their return may have taken three days.

The confidence of the report of these spies was very different from the majority of the spies who had returned thirty-eight years before. Their hair-raising adventure produced confidence and courage. They quoted Rahab herself (v. 9) when they told Joshua, **All the people are melting in fear because of us**.

What can we learn from this amazing story? It seems that God had two purposes in mind for this spy mission, and both have to do with faith. Joshua may have thought he was sending spies for military purposes; God used their mission to reward Rahab's faith and reassure the Israelites. We find faith in the "stalks of flax" (v. 6), since the spies were surely surprised to find an ally in Rahab the harlot, a heathen woman involved in an immoral profession living in a condemned city. God approached her much the way Jesus approached the woman at the well in John 4. He always looks for faith in the midst of unbelief and moves in astounding ways to reward that faith.

Rahab risked her life to hide the spies, and because of this act, the writer of Hebrews singles her out as a hero of faith (Heb. 11:31). But she had to continue demonstrating faith by letting the spies go and fulfilling other covenant conditions. James says that Rahab, like Abraham, was justified by faith (Jas. 2:25), a living active faith despite her limited knowledge of God.

Campbell observes:

> While the two young spies and their remarkable exploits are not to be minimized, Rahab's supporting role leaves lasting and even

deeper impressions. Whenever she is spoken of in the Bible, she is referred to as a harlot. This is not to humiliate her or to demean her memory, but to cast in bold relief the grace of God that saved her. Regardless of the kind of life a person has lived, there is forgiveness for sin and eternal life available in Jesus Christ (Campbell, 24).

In God's unique sense of humor, not only was Rahab's house the only part of the Jericho wall that didn't collapse and her family the only one in the city to survive, but God gave her a Jewish husband named Salmon. They had a son named Boaz who had a great grandson named David who became Israel's king. So Rahab shows up in Matthew's genealogy of the Savior (Matt. 1:5)—from heathen harlot to messianic matron. God's grace is amazing!

And we are Rahab. We are not of the original family or nation of God. We live in a corrupt and degenerate world. We are sinful harlots, unfaithful to God. But God moves in a strange and powerful way to bring his salvation to us. And like Rahab we turn our backs on the world around us, hang the scarlet cord of redemption in our windows, and claim Christ's blood sacrifice for our sins—then we wait for Christ to come and get us. Let's recognize too that the other residents of Jericho could have done what Rahab did. According to her report, all of them had heard about Israel's God and trembled in fear. Any others who called on the name of Lord would also have been saved. But they chose to remain in fear while Rahab turned her fear into faith, giving up everything to trust God. Today, as in Rahab's day, the only salvation lies in the scarlet cord of faith.

MAIN IDEA REVIEW: *This chapter centers not on the spies or Joshua himself but on Rahab the prostitute. She demonstrates for us the wisdom and value of choosing faith and acting upon that choice. Her reward was enormous.*

III. CONCLUSION

Athanasius of Alexandria

For seventy-eight years the great Christian leader Athanasius, who was born in Egypt about A.D. 295, served as virtually the sole defender of what we call orthodox Christianity. Over and over he defended the deity of Christ, recognizing that the hope of salvation depended on that crucial doctrine. Athanasius was opposed on every side. Emperors denounced him, and five different times he was exiled from his bishopric. At times even the church turned against him, and for decades it seemed to be Athanasius against the world. Yet his steadfast faith helped preserve the church of Jesus Christ. Today he is recognized as one of the leading church fathers of the early years of the Christian movement.

Like the spies and Rahab and Athanasius, we can extract encouragement from our enemies. When Joshua sent the spies to Jericho to find out more about the enemy, he discovered that the enemy cringed in the fear of God. Perhaps he expected this if he remembered back to the song of Moses and Miriam in Exodus 15:15–16a: "The chiefs of Edom will be terrified, the leaders of Moab will be seized with trembling, the people of Canaan will melt away; terror and dread will fall upon them." So the fear of the enemy brought encouragement to Joshua, the spies, and all of Israel. It wasn't a report about a weak point in the wall or a failure of the armies of Jericho. There was no hope that the enemy would sign a friendly peace agreement. They simply feared the power of Israel's God.

We should see the parallel here for us. Paul wrote: "Our struggle is not against flesh and blood, but . . . against the powers of this dark world and against the spiritual forces of evil in the heavenly realms" (Eph. 6:12). But our enemy also knows that he is defeated already. Satan was thrown out of heaven (Ezek. 28), and his defeat was pronounced as early as the third chapter of Genesis. Christ's death sealed Satan's fate (John 12:31; Heb. 2:14). One day he will be cast into the lake of fire for eternity (Rev. 20). Satan knows he is doomed, so he has become a desperate but defeated enemy.

And that truth is our spy report—God's message to us that the battle is his and the victory is sure. The enemy is melting and the land is ours.

Each year on Valentine's Day most of us receive cards from loved ones. We believe those people love us. We really don't need the cards to prove it, but it is still a wonderful encouragement to receive those messages of support. The cards build our confidence in those relationships. In this story Joshua and the Israelites received a love note, an encouragement card from God. The card contained his message of assurance and victory; he sent it to build their confidence and faith.

PRINCIPLES

- All Christians need to live out their faith like Rahab did.
- Christians need to find support and encouragement in the victories God sends their way.
- The enemy of our souls will seize every opportunity to disturb the spiritual equilibrium that the Holy Spirit wants to bring into our lives.

APPLICATIONS

- Hang your hope of eternal life on the scarlet cord of faith in Jesus.
- Consider the specific ways the Lord has dealt with you in grace and kindness as he did with Rahab.
- Know that when God sends you into a difficult place, he will provide protection as he did for the spies.

IV. LIFE APPLICATION

Christmas Crossing

By Christmas of 1776 the cause of American liberty seemed lost. General George Washington's troops were in retreat after a devastating defeat in New York. They ended up in New Jersey barely one step ahead of the red coats. They reached Trenton on December 2, gathered every bullet they could find, and took six thousand Colonial troops across the Delaware River into Pennsylvania. On December 19 Thomas Paine's essay was published, and Washington's weary and nearly naked soldiers read the challenge:

These are the times that try men's souls. The summer soldier and the sunshine patriot will, in this crisis, shrink from the service of their country; but he that stands by it now, deserves the love and thanks of man and woman. Let it be told to the future world, that in the depth of winter, when nothing but hope and virtue could survive, that the city and country, alarmed at one common danger, came forth to meet and to repulse it!

Washington was inspired to plan the now-famous crossing of the Delaware River. Nine miles north of Trenton he took about twenty-four hundred men to attack the Hessian garrison. He sent word to Col. Joseph Reed: "Christmas day, at night, is the time fixed upon for our attempts on Trenton. For heaven's sake keep this to yourself, as the discovery of it may prove fatal to us."

The crossing began at 6:00 p.m. as the shallow boats under the command of Col. John Glover made their way across the ice-choked river, and it continued for the next nine hours. Then with rags on their feet, marching against freezing wind and hail for nine miles, the patriot army headed southward, leaving bloody footprints in the snow. The Americans attacked the Hessians shortly after dawn in a complete surprise. Nine hundred of the one thousand Hessian soldiers were taken prisoner. It was a rout. Continental General Henry Knox, chief of the artillery, wrote to his wife that "the fury, fright, and confusion of the enemy was [not] unlike that which will be when the last trump shall sound."

That victory proved the psychological turning point of the American Revolution. The morale of the troops soared, and the cause of freedom and victory was secured.

To be sure, Joshua 2 does not talk about the coming battle, just the preparations for it. But already we sense that God's hand so completely guided the attack on Jericho that victory is sure. Like Washington, Joshua will lead his troops to conquest with hardly a shot being fired.

V. PRAYER

Father, give us the faith and courage of both Rahab and the spies. May we undertake dangerous missions for our Lord with confidence that he will make them successful and victorious. Amen.

VI. DEEPER DISCOVERIES

A. Rahab (2:1)

Rahab, for all her negative beginnings, rises like a star throughout the pages of biblical history. In the honor roll of faith in Hebrews 11, she and not the spies makes an appearance: "By faith the prostitute Rahab, because she welcomed the spies, was not killed with those who were disobedient" (Heb. 11:31). James tells us, "Was not even Rahab the prostitute considered righteous for what she did when she gave lodging to the spies and sent them off in a different direction?" (Jas. 2:25). Of this latter text Thomas Lee writes:

> This section turns to the example of good works from the life of Rahab. Abraham was a man of prominent position and exemplary character. Rahab came from the background of degradation and insignificance. James insisted that these contrasting personalities showed deeds which demonstrated their righteousness (Lee, 289).

Rahab's acts of faith place her with four other women in Jesus' genealogy in Matthew 1: Tamar, Ruth, Bathsheba, and Mary. Mary was of course a Jew, but all the others were foreigners who became part of Israel. Howard notes, "This reflects the inclusiveness intended in the Abrahamic Covenant, whereby God stated he would bring blessing to the nations—to those who were not descendants of Abraham, like Rahab—through Abraham and his descendants" (Howard, 105). Perhaps the reason James mentions Rahab is that she is a classic example of someone who demonstrates her faith by her works. The spies could have smuggled her and her family out with them, but that would have taken considerably lesser faith than staying in the house throughout the battle and surviving by God's grace.

Schaeffer says of this fascinating prostitute:

> This woman Rahab stood alone in faith against the *total* culture which surrounded her—something none of us today in the western world has ever yet had to do. For a period of time she stood for the unseen against the seen, standing in acute danger until Jericho fell. If the king had ever found out what she had done, he would have become her chief enemy and would have executed her. . . . This is exactly how the Christian lives, and Rahab is a tremendous example for us. But you and I have stepped from the kingdom of darkness into the kingdom of God's dear Son, we're still surrounded by a culture controlled by God's great enemy, Satan. We must live in it from the moment we accept Christ as our Savior until judgment falls. We are also encompassed by one who was once our king but who is now

our enemy. It is just plain stupid of a Christian not to expect spiritual warfare while he lives in enemy territory (Schaeffer, 79–80).

B. Lying

As the 2001 football season ran down, a popular head coach at one university was appointed the new head coach at a prestigious school. But the coach lied on his resume, claiming a master's degree that he did not have. The job offer was revoked and the coach was left for a time out in the cold, another victim of lying.

From a number of sources the *St. Petersburg Times* gathered some observations about what a reporter entitled "Lying in America."

- 32 percent of Americans believe "the way things are today, lying is sometimes necessary."
- 36.2 percent of teenagers say they would lie to get a good job.
- 25 percent of public relations professionals say they lie on the job.
- 60 percent of Americans say it's OK to lie to "protect another person's feelings."
- 42 percent of workers who make $50,000 say they sometimes fake sick days.
- 22.7 percent of workers who make less than $22,000 say they sometimes fake sick days.
- 71 percent of high school students have cheated on an exam in the past twelve months.
- 74 percent of college students admit to "serious test cheating" (1–20–02, 19a).

But all Christians know the Bible condemns lying. It is the very nature of God himself that he cannot lie (Num. 23:19). Some would say Rahab's lie was acceptable because she chose the greatest good. As the argument goes, a person is often faced to choose between two sins, and one should take the lesser. In this case that would mean that Rahab chose to lie to the officials in Jericho rather than surrender the lives of the two spies.

Perhaps. But it is also possible that Rahab's lie was a sin and God forgave it along with all of her other sins because of her faith and his grace. *The Nelson Study Bible* makes a good observation here:

> We must be careful to make a distinction between Rahab's faith and the way Rahab expressed it. The Bible praises Rahab because of her faith in God, not because of her lying. That is, her actions would have been more noble had she protected the spies in some other fashion; as it is, she did the best she could. The Bible calls Rahab a prostitute, but we are not meant to take that as an endorsement for immorality. Rahab, like the rest of us, had a mixed character, but she believed in God and strove to honor Him and His people. That is what draws her praise (355).

VII. TEACHING OUTLINE

A. INTRODUCTION

1. Lead Story: Turning Points
2. Context: Since Joshua is a book of history, one chapter leads into the next. From Joshua's call in chapter 1, we move to the story of the spies and Rahab in chapter 2, which prepares us for the crossing of the Jordan River in chapter 3.
3. Transition: The transition at the beginning of both chapters 2 and 3 is achieved by our historian with the use of a different word to launch his narrative. Things are progressing in exactly the order that God intended for the conquest of Canaan.

B. COMMENTARY

1. Undercover Assignment (2:1–7)
2. Undercover Intelligence (2:8–13)
3. Undercover Agreement (2:14–21)
4. Undercover Report (2:22–24)

C. CONCLUSION: CHRISTMAS CROSSING

VIII. ISSUES FOR DISCUSSION

1. Consider again the issue of Rahab's lie. Does the explanation offered in "Deeper Discoveries" seem satisfactory, or do you wish to consider other options?

2. What is the central lesson we learn from the behavior of the spies?

3. How do you account for the difference in this spy report compared with the report brought thirty-eight years earlier by eight of the ten spies?

Joshua 3

On Jordan's Stormy Banks

I. INTRODUCTION
Looking Beyond the Jordan

II. COMMENTARY
A verse-by-verse explanation of the chapter.

III. CONCLUSION
Delayed Excitement

An overview of the principles and applications from the chapter.

IV. LIFE APPLICATION
Close to Home

Melding the chapter to life.

V. PRAYER
Tying the chapter to life with God.

VI. DEEPER DISCOVERIES
Historical, geographical, and grammatical enrichment of the commentary.

VII. TEACHING OUTLINE
Suggested step-by-step group study of the chapter.

VIII. ISSUES FOR DISCUSSION
Zeroing the chapter in on daily life.

Quote

"*P*rogress also involves risk. You can't steal second and keep your foot on first."

Frederick Wilcox

GEOGRAPHICAL PROFILE: ADAM AND ZARETHAN

- Cities located fifteen to twenty miles up river from the crossing
- Adam stood just south of where the Jabbok River meets the Jordan
- Adam is usually identified with Tell ed-Damiyeh

GEOGRAPHICAL PROFILE: JORDAN RIVER

- Flows from the slopes of Mount Hermon south into the Sea of Galilee and down to the Dead Sea
- Mentioned frequently in the Old Testament, including references to Elijah, Elisha, and Naaman
- In the New Testament Jesus was baptized in the Jordan

GEOGRAPHICAL PROFILE: SALT SEA

- More commonly called the Dead Sea where the Jordan River ends 1,285 feet below sea level
- A lifeless body of water full of bromide and sulfur and completely undrinkable
- Fifty miles in length and eleven miles in width at the widest point
- Also called Arabah

This popular story of the nation of Israel crossing the Jordan River comes to life as God directs Joshua to prepare the people spiritually and physically to enter the promised land.

Joshua 3

On Jordan's Stormy Banks

I. INTRODUCTION

Looking Beyond the Jordan

Compared to the Tigris and Euphrates, those mighty rivers of the Mesopotamian valley, the Jordan is a humble body of water that repeatedly pops up for mention and even star billing in the dramatic history of Israel. Often in poems and hymns, the Jordan takes on the image of a barrier between life and death, between earth and heaven, between a struggling, death-infested physical existence and the glories of eternity.

Such was the image used by Samuel Stennett in a song with a rousing melody still sung today. Stennett was an influential preacher among the Protestant dissenters in London during the eighteenth century. He pastored a Baptist church on Little Wild Street all his adult life and wrote the poem some time before he died in 1795 though it was not published in its present form until 100 years later. The tune with which it is usually associated is called "Promised Land," a traditional American melody popular during the early part of the nineteenth century. The tune's lilting styles and Stennett's encouraging words should not blind us to the fact that he missed the metaphor when deciding that Canaan somehow represented heaven.

> On Jordan's stormy banks I stand,
> And cast a wishful eye
> To Canaan's fair and happy land,
> Where my possessions lie.
>
> All o'er those wide extended plains
> Shines one eternal day;
> Where God the Son forever reigns
> And scatters night away.
>
> No chilling winds nor pois'nous breath
> Can reach that healthful shore;
> Sickness and sorrow, pain and death
> Are felt and feared no more.

When shall I reach that happy place,
And be forever blest?
When shall I see my Father's face,
And in His bosom rest?

I am bound for the promised land,
I am bound for the promised land;
O who will come and go with me?
I am bound for the promised land.

Promised land, yes. Heaven, definitely not. The warfare, suffering, struggles, and death awaiting Israel on the western side of the Jordan River hardly represent our hope of heaven. This is one of those places where Christians need to get a grip on the Bible rather than imaginative poetry and to grasp the significance of the promised land that symbolizes our righteous walk with God after salvation, our willingness to move forward with him in spiritual life and our ability to handle, with his help, the battles of spiritual warfare described in Ephesians 6.

Redpath puts it succinctly:

I would suggest that the clue to the interpretation of this Old Testament book is found in the Epistle to the Ephesians and Epistle to the Hebrews. For example, in the third and fourth chapters of Hebrews we find that the land of Canaan is a picture of the spiritual rest and victory which may be enjoyed here on earth by every believer, a rest of faith in the Lord Jesus Christ. Again, the Ephesian letter speaks of life "in the heavenly places"—not in heaven, but in the experience of oneness with our Risen Lord in His victory here and now, the place of the fullness of God's blessing. I believe that we shall understand the real significance of the Book of Joshua only if we recognize that what it is in the Old Testament the Epistle to the Ephesians is in the New. This suggestion, of course, has to be substantiated from the Word of God itself (Redpath, 18–19).

II. COMMENTARY

On Jordan's Stormy Banks

MAIN IDEA: *The task of ridding the promised land of pagan peoples requires careful preparation and dedication on the part of Israel. These are qualities God not only required but provided for them.*

A Preparation for the Crossing (3:1–8)

SUPPORTING IDEA: *The ark becomes the centerpiece of the crossing of the Jordan River, and God's plan unfolds one step at a time. At this time God elevated the credibility and status of Joshua in preparation for the task ahead.*

3:1–4. In northeast Georgia where I live six months of the year, crossing the Tallulah River down in the deep gorge requires only dexterity in jumping from rock to rock during most of the year. But when one enters the visitor's center and sees the video of that river when the dam is open and the river flows deep and fast, he discovers immediately that it cannot be crossed by rock-jumping at that time. A kayak will make it in a zigzag fashion, and Karl Walenda once crossed it on a high wire, but wading large groups of people through is impossible. This is the problem the nation of Israel faced in Joshua 3.

The morning after Joshua received a favorable report from the two spies, he told the Israelites to move to the banks of the Jordan River and make camp in anticipation of crossing over. We learn in verse 15 that the river was at flood stage, a one-mile-wide, raging torrent moving about ten miles per hour, probably filled with tangled brush and floating debris. A bridge or a solid ferryboat would have been nice, but neither was available. Once again it was miracle time.

This preparation required some time, so the Israelites camped by the river for **three days**. During this time they had an opportunity to see what they were up against as the melting snows of Mount Hermon filled the river channel and probably caused the Jordan River to overflow its banks.

Furthermore, the symbol of spiritual leadership now switches from the cloud to **the ark of the covenant**, both of those symbols representing Yahweh himself. Madvig describes this unique representation of God's presence:

The ark was a portable shrine built as a rectangular box, twenty-seven inches wide by twenty-seven inches high by forty-five inches long. It was overlaid with gold. The cover of the ark had a golden cherub on each end facing toward the middle. It was between these two cherubs that God met with Israel (Exod. 25:10–22) (Madvig, 265).

All the priests were Levites, although not all Levites were priests; hence the designation in verse 3. No trumpets yet, no Moses at the front waving a magic rod—just the spiritual leaders leading the way forward.

The **distance of about a thousand yards** strikes us as interesting and gives an even more graphic picture of what this march may have looked like. Perhaps they stood back so they could see the ark from all directions and all points of the march. The distance would have been more than half a mile. Butler suggested:

> Such great distance does not derive from the need to follow the ark to find one's way. Again we have signs of theological reflection. The concept of keeping a distance from divine holiness has entered the passage. Our text thus gives two emphases to the ark. It shows God's people God's way into the Promised Land, but it also represents a holy presence from which the people must keep their distance (Butler, 46).

3:5–6. God did not reveal his plan immediately. Joshua told the people to consecrate themselves—not to inflate rafts, sharpen swords, or build a bridge. Their preparation for entering the promised land was spiritual, not physical or military. We will deal with the meaning of the word **consecrate** in "Deeper Discoveries." Here we focus only on the general preparation it provides. A church dedication service is a kind of consecration for the congregation, a spiritual preparation. The same with a baby dedication that targets the commitment of the parents rather than the baby, just as a building dedication is more about the commitment of the church than about the structure.

Christians consecrate themselves to God's Word, to God's will, and to God's leadership. This is not at all unlike what was happening here in the history of Israel. Joshua and Caleb could still remember the Red Sea crossing. Some of the other Israelites who were children at the time would also have remembered, and the entire nation would have heard the stories. But this time it was a bit different. Joshua didn't raise his staff and stretch out his hand over the water but instead talked directly to the priests, the spiritual leaders: **Take up the ark of the covenant and pass on ahead of the people.**

This drama symbolizes the personal presence of God moving before the people. The ark contained the words of God on stone tablets, God's promises to Israel covered by the mercy seat to remind them of God's love and grace. It also represented God's sovereignty and leadership over the people, a leadership that would carry them through the next forty years of conquest in Canaan. The ark is mentioned no fewer than ten times in this chapter, and it dominates the scene before us.

3:7–8. Joshua tells us that our lives and battles are all a part of God's work and God's leadership. If God does not go before us, we cannot cross "Jordan" to receive his blessing. We wait for his timing and his way. But the ark didn't jump into the Jordan River by itself or sail across in a basket like Moses in the Nile. Remember, at the crossing of the Red Sea, the whole nation saw the path before taking a step. Here the waters didn't move until the priests got their toes wet. Imagine being one of those priests. What if Joshua had received the wrong message? With the weight of a gold-covered ark on their shoulders, they could have sunk like rocks. There is a great spiritual lesson here.

The leaders of Israel and the leaders of the church today must be first to demonstrate faith in God. If pastors, elders, and deacons are unwilling to walk into the waters of spiritual warfare, the congregation will never cross.

Redpath observes:

> The passage of Jordan means facing the impossibility, following the dying, rising, ascending Jesus into the place of all power. Get a clear view of Him who can deal with the impossibility of your life before you have reached it. For in the name of the Lord Jesus I declare this truth, that, however subtle, however strong it may be, there is no attack of Satan on the child of God but first has struck the heart of the Lord. He overcame it at the Cross, and He bids us, His children, to get a clear view of Him, to face again the impossibility

that we have faced so often, then look up into His face and say, "Now, Lord Jesus, I believe that, although I cannot, you can." In that moment the roar of Jordan will be silent, its violence be checked, and we will go through on dry land (Redpath, 56–57).

This was also Joshua's "big day." Certainly he had been acknowledged as Israel's leader several times before this moment, but now God said, **Today I will begin to exalt you in the eyes of all Israel.** As Campbell puts it:

> It was time to establish the credential of Joshua as God's representative to guide Israel. What better way to accomplish this than for Joshua to direct their passage through a miraculously parted river? After the crossing it was recorded, "On that day the Lord exalted Joshua in the sight of all Israel; so that they revered him, just as they had revered Moses all the days of his life" (Campbell, 29).

B Purpose of the Crossing (3:9–13)

SUPPORTING IDEA: *God required Israel to be relieved of worldly influence and completely dependent upon him before they were ready to cross the Jordan River and enter the land. The warfare they were about to face was much more spiritual than military.*

3:9–11. The task of ridding Canaan of the seven wicked nations loomed large. The people, as always, needed some sign that God would be with them. Joshua promised a sign, but the exact nature of it is not revealed until verse 13 where Joshua says "its waters flowing downstream will be cut off and stand up in a heap." The seven nations of Canaan worshiped dead gods, but the people crossing the Jordan worshiped **the living God.** Howard observes, "This exact wording—'this is how you will know . . .'—is found only one other time in the Old Testament, in Num. 16:28, where God was authenticating Moses' position as his chosen leader. . . . Here, he is doing the same for Joshua" (Howard, 125).

Perhaps we need a word about the listing of seven nations which appears twenty-three times in the Old Testament, including five times in Joshua (3:10; 9:1; 11:3; 12:8; 24:11). A total of twelve peoples are actually named in the various lists, but this core of seven is the "short list." But weren't all these people Canaanites? Why would "Canaanites" be used as a separate ethnic identification? Howard helps us here as well:

> The term "Canaanites" sometimes is an all-inclusive term denoting any people living in Canaan regardless of their ethnic identity (e.g., Gen. 12:6; 36:2–3; Exod. 13:11; Ezek. 16:3). Often, however, the Canaanites are distinguished from others who lived in Canaan as they are here. . . . In this case they are probably the peoples living by the sea and near the Jordan River (see 5:1, which mentions Canaanites along the coast, and Num. 13:29, which mentions them by the sea and near the Jordan) (Howard, 126).

3:12–13. This selection of **twelve men from the tribes of Israel, one from each tribe** anticipates chapter 4 and their task of carrying stones. These were not priests and certainly not necessarily tribal leaders but just representatives of the tribes. We anticipate in a historic narrative like this that the storyteller will repeat himself several times to make significant points, and we see that at various places in chapters 3 and 4.

ⓒ Process of the Crossing (3:14–17)

SUPPORTING IDEA: *These few verses contain one of the greatest miracles of the Bible as two million people walk across a river on dry ground.*

3:14–16. This passage begins and ends with the priests and in the middle describes the power and flow of the river. Most evangelical churches are blessed to have people of faith on the elder or deacon leadership teams. These spiritual leaders work and pray about issues related to ministry before it takes place. Many times they have to step into the river of faith in order to keep the church moving forward. All the while they believe that God will meet the needs of their churches, even when they don't know exactly how this will happen. This is called leadership. Hence the phraseology in verse 14, **went ahead of them.**

In the ancient calendar it was the time of Nisan, approximately March or April, the first month of the Israelite year (4:19). Spring floods were in full strength. But as soon as the feet of the priests **touched the water's edge, the water from upstream stopped flowing.** Some fifteen to twenty miles north of their crossing point near Adam and Zarethan a wall of water built up, providing a dry riverbed for that distance. Many have challenged whether this was a miracle at all or some natural phenomenon.

Campbell addresses this challenge:

> They point out that on December 8, 1267 an earthquake caused the high banks of the Jordan to collapse near Tell ed-Damiyeh, damming the river for about 10 hours. On July 11, 1927 another earthquake near the same location blocked the river for 21 hours. Of course these stoppages did not occur during flood season. Admittedly God could have employed natural causes such as an earthquake and a landslide and the timing would still have made it a miraculous intervention. But does the biblical text allow for such an interpretation of this event?
>
> Considering all the factors involved it seems best to view this occurrence as a special act of God brought about in a way unknown to men. Many supernatural elements were brought together: (1) The event came to pass as predicted (3:13,15). (2) The timing was exact (v. 15). (3) The event took place when the river was at flood stage (v. 15). (4) The wall of water was held in place for many hours, possibly an entire day (v. 16). (5) The soft, wet river bottom became dry at once (v. 17). (6) The water returned immediately as soon as the people had crossed over and the priests came up out of the river (4:18) (Campbell, *BKC*, 335).

3:17. In one verse this miraculous deed is announced, but the ark did not lead the people all the way across. The priests stopped in the middle, holding it high while two million people **passed by until the whole nation had completed the crossing on dry ground.**

MAIN IDEA REVIEW: *The task of ridding the promised land of pagan peoples required careful preparation and dedication on the part of Israel. These are qualities God not only required but provided for them.*

III. CONCLUSION

Delayed Excitement

At the risk of promoting the incorrect metaphor of Canaan as heaven, I venture a corny old joke about an eighty-five-year-old couple, married for almost sixty years, who were killed in a car crash. They had been in good health right up until their death mainly due to the wife's interest in health food and exercising. When they reached the pearly gates, Saint Peter took them to their mansion decked out with a beautiful kitchen, master bath suite, and a jacuzzi. After walking through the rooms, the old man asked Peter, "How much is all this going to cost?"

"This is heaven," responded Peter. "It's all free."

They went out beyond the backyard to survey a championship-style golf course where they would have golfing privileges every day. Every week the course miraculously changed pattern until it represented fifty-two of the greatest golf courses on earth throughout the year. Instantly suspicious, the old man asked, "What are the green fees?"

Again the same answer: "This is heaven; you play for free."

The tour next visited the clubhouse with its lavish buffet lunch featuring the cuisine of the world, and again the man asked the price and received the same answer. In unbelieving exasperation the man asked, "Will my prescription medication be free as well?"

Peter, amazed at the man's ignorance of his surroundings, nevertheless replied patiently, "This is heaven. You don't need to worry about cholesterol or heart problems; you eat as much as you like of whatever you like and you never get sick. This is heaven!"

Upon hearing that, the old man went into a fit, throwing down his hat and stomping on it while screaming wildly. After Saint Peter and his wife got him calmed down, they asked him what could possibly be wrong with what he had seen and heard. The old man looked at his wife and said, "This is all your fault! If it weren't for your blasted bran muffins, I could have been here ten years ago!"

Silliness, to be sure. But exactly the point of the Jordan crossing in our chapter. If it were not for sin, complaining, murmuring, and doubt, the Israelites could have crossed over the Jordan River thirty-eight years earlier. Spies had been sent, the land surveyed, and the possibility of entrance considered, but lack of faith kept them out. Now finally they put their feet into the water and followed the priests into the promised land. All this excitement reminds me of an old chorus we used to sing some decades ago.

> Got any rivers you think are uncrossable?
>
> Got any mountains you cannot tunnel through?
>
> God specializes in things thought impossible;
>
> He can do what no other friend can do.
>
> (Copyright Singspiration. Written by Oscar Eliason © 1945 renewed 1973.)

From time to time I like to offer little outlines that can be used by teachers or pastors in treating these great portions of Scripture. Check out the following four points as a possibility for this chapter.

1. The Consecration of the People
2. The Humility of the Leader
3. The Encouragement from the Lord
4. The Obedience of the Priests

PRINCIPLES

- When God says move, he means it.
- God acts decisively when we believe and obey completely.
- Miracles are no problem for God; he can dam up any stream of trouble and give us ample room to walk through.

APPLICATIONS

- When it's time for a church to move forward, good leaders step in the river first.
- Be careful and prayerful in the presence of an awesome God.
- Christian leaders should not promote themselves—that's God's work in his timing.

IV. LIFE APPLICATION

Close to Home

How many religious people are lost in sight of home? How many people attend church with regularity, join congregations, participate in denominational activities, and yet have never been born again? How many thousands of people may be wandering in the desert all around the promised land, some unsaved, others believers who have never entered into the spiritual rest of Canaan? I've often thought that Judas represents the classic example of how close a person can get to Jesus Christ and still be lost. He was a public worshiper, an esteemed follower, and even a church treasurer—but he was lost.

In the later books of the Pentateuch and the early chapters of Joshua, we see a nation still lost in sight of home. They are not "unsaved" in the sense that we would use that word to describe nonbelievers today, but they were the people of God unwilling up to this point to exercise sufficient faith to cross into the promised land and face the spiritual battles God had in store for them.

We talk a lot about people who relocate after retirement and move to the Sun Belt. The demographics support a significant migration over recent decades to states like Florida, Texas, Arizona, and California. But in fact more than two-thirds of U.S. natives live in the same state in which they were born. And the states (along with the percentages) are surprising. For example, 82.4 percent of people born in New York still live there; 81.7 percent in Pennsylvania; 80.3 percent in Louisiana; 78.9 percent in Michigan; 76.6 percent in Ohio; and 76.5 in Iowa. These are Census Bureau records, and they probably surprise everyone except residents of those six states who would call them "home."

Furthermore, that most studied of generations, the baby boomers, are already showing a pattern of retirement. They are drawn to "yogurt cities"— a new term describing places with active culture, meaning access to books, music, and art. They spurn the retirement communities of Florida and Arizona and head for places like San Diego, Seattle, and Austin.

The only final lesson here, of course, is to be where God wants you and when God wants you there. It's refreshing after the struggles of the

Pentateuch to picture in our mind's eye this massive congregation of people moving across the Jordan River to march into the land that God promised Abraham.

Let me emphasize again the significance of this crossing. For believers in the twenty-first century, crossing Jordan is not a television program but a movement from a lower level of Christian living to a higher level of Christian living. It describes our entrance to the spiritual warfare of Ephesians, a rejection of a life lived by the flesh and human effort, and the beginning of a life centered in faith and obedience.

One of the keys to understanding these historic chapters is the reference to the promise of rest in Hebrews 4. Here is the text of the early verses of chapter 4:

> Therefore, since the promise of entering his rest still stands, let us be careful that none of you be found to have fallen short of it. For we also have had the gospel preached to us, just as they did; but the message they heard was of no value to them, because those who heard did not combine it with faith (Heb. 4:1–2).

The whole Canaan narrative seems to portray a double meaning, highlighted here in Hebrews where we find a temporary rest of deep spiritual living and dependence upon the Lord on earth and then a final rest. *The Nelson Study Bible* comments:

> By merely entering the Promised Land, the Israelites had not entered God's rest, for David (years after Joshua had led the Israelites into the land) had warned his generation to not harden their hearts so that they could enter God's rest. . . . This word [*rest* in Hebrews 4:3, 5, 10; 3:11, 18] means 'Sabbath rest' and is found only here in the New Testament. Jews commonly taught that the Sabbath foreshadowed the world to come, and they spoke of "a day which shall be all Sabbath" (2,082).

V. PRAYER

Father, give us the courage and the faith displayed by your ancient people as they stood on the banks of the Jordan River. May our modern church leaders be like priests who step into the water of challenge to lead us into deep Christian living, willing to face the battles of spiritual warfare and to depend on an eternal God for the victory. Amen.

VI. DEEPER DISCOVERIES

A. Ark of the Covenant (3:3)

According to Deuteronomy 10, the priests were responsible for carrying the ark but had to do so with poles, never touching it (Exod. 25:12–13; 37:3–5; Num. 4:4–15). The ark stood for the presence of God and the character of God. The ancient Jews were prohibited any kind of icons for worship, but the ark was a physical representation of the character and covenant of the Lord. It was not just a religious symbol that preceded the people into that riverbed. Rather, it was the living promise of a living God who would take them across, into the land, and give them the land. In verse 13 this symbolic box is called "the ark of the LORD—the Lord of all the earth" indicating that it was not some religious symbol of a certain ancient sect.

Hamlin offers a helpful paragraph of description:

The simplest description is "the ark" (3:15; 4:10), which could mean simply a sacred box containing some objects. When the terms "ark of the Lord" (4:11) and "the ark of the Lord your God" (4:5) are used, the references point to the ark as the portable throne of the invisible God. God was described as "seated on the cherubim" (Pss. 80:1; 99:1). The cherubim were represented as winged lions with human faces and were placed on either side of the ark (Exod. 25:18–19), in the royal style of ancient west Asia. The ark of Yahweh, carried as the people journeyed, symbolized their belief that Yahweh went with them, guiding them to places of rest (Num. 10:33). The ark was thus a symbol of the mysterious and awesome presence of God in their midst as they crossed over into the new land. It was this presence, symbolized by the ark, that made this people unique (Hamlin, 24).

So the whole picture offers up a cosmic dimension to what seems like a somewhat trivial bit of Israel's history—crossing the Jordan. It indicates that this event was as great as the exodus, the giving of the Law, the manna in the wilderness, and other ways that God evidenced himself to be with his people. What about the presence of the ark today and its possible significance for the future?

Here's Schaeffer again:

> We do not know what happened to the ark. It is conceivable that it was destroyed when Jerusalem was laid waste by Babylon, or it may have been brought back from Babylon and been in the temple when Titus demolished it in A.D. 70. Perhaps the ark did not come to an end. It is not far fetched to think it exists somewhere and will one day reappear. Whatever happened to it, we must understand that what it represented did not end. The covenant and the oath of God (which reached all the way back to Genesis 3:15) has come up to today through different forms. From the times of Noah and Abraham, sweeping on through the Old Testament into the New, the promises of God will continue right up to the end of this era and beyond it into eternity (Schaeffer, 89).

B. Consecrate Yourselves (3:5)

Throughout the Book of Joshua we see that spiritual preparation and spiritual warfare far outweigh the importance of military preparation and physical warfare. Another possibility here would be the word *sanctify*, meaning "to set apart," although *The Living Bible* prefers a longer version, "to perform the purification ceremony for themselves." The concept of sanctification is found only six times in the Book of Joshua (3:5; 5:15; 6:19; 7:13 twice; 20:7), and each time it fits in with a general Old Testament theme of holiness and separation. This would have included a variety of ritual washings and preparation to face the contamination that lay on the other side of the Jordan.

For forty years Israel had remained in something of a monastic existence with only occasional brushes with outside influence. But now they would enter the "hornet's nest" itself. An understanding of who they were as the separate people of God was absolutely essential to the battle. The word here is *kadash,* and Gridlestone says:

> Perhaps the English word *sacred* represents the idea more nearly than holy, which is the general rendering in the A.V. The terms sanctification and holiness are now used so frequently to represent moral and spiritual qualities, that they hardly convey to the reader the idea of *position* or *relationship* as existing between God and some person or thing consecrated to Him; yet this appears to be the real meaning of the word (Gridlestone, 175).

This is one of the most important words in the Hebrew Scriptures, not only theologically but practically, and we see both dimensions in the Jordan experience.

C. Amazing Things (3:5)

Amazing things indeed. The damming up of the Jordan at flood time! God will display his presence, his power, and his promise within the next few days. But then that was hardly anything new for Joshua and Caleb. For most of the people, however, the great stories of the past would soon become the realities of the present, and God would move a body of water to get his people where he wanted them to go. Howard says that the Hebrew word behind the phrase *amazing things*

> . . . is the closest word in the Old Testament for what we today call "miracles." These wonders were such impressive acts that they astonished people and called forth their praise of God. . . . They included God's miraculous acts among the Egyptians [and] they were so abnormal as to be unexplainable to people experiencing them except as mighty acts of God (Howard, 123).

VII. TEACHING OUTLINE

A. INTRODUCTION

1. Lead Story: Looking Beyond the Jordan
2. Context: Joshua 3 continues the crossing narrative that began in 1:11 and continues into chapter 4.
3. Transition: Joshua 3 and 4 are tied together by the last verse of chapter 3 and the first verse of chapter 4, both of which contain a reference to finishing the crossing. Joshua 3:17 uses the word *completed* and 4:1 uses *finished*, but the transition is clear as the story continues.

B. COMMENTARY

1. Preparation for the Crossing (3:1–8)
2. Purpose of the Crossing (3:9–13)
3. Process of the Crossing (3:14–17)

C. CONCLUSION: CLOSE TO HOME

VIII. ISSUES FOR DISCUSSION

1. Since we don't practice ritual washings today, what would the command "consecrate yourselves" mean for Christians in our time?
2. In what ways do modern church leaders "step in the river" to lead a congregation into deeper spiritual life and the struggles of spiritual warfare?
3. Since we don't have an ark of the covenant as a symbol of God's presence and power, what sustains and guides us in the twenty-first century?

Joshua 4

Rocks of Remembrance

I. INTRODUCTION
Trick Play

II. COMMENTARY
A verse-by-verse explanation of the chapter.

III. CONCLUSION
"Rock of Ages"

An overview of the principles and applications from the chapter.

IV. LIFE APPLICATION
Special Selection

Melding the chapter to life.

V. PRAYER

Tying the chapter to life with God.

VI. DEEPER DISCOVERIES

Historical, geographical, and grammatical enrichment of the commentary.

VII. TEACHING OUTLINE

Suggested step-by-step group study of the chapter.

VIII. ISSUES FOR DISCUSSION

Zeroing the chapter in on daily life.

"*That* man who deposits experiences carefully in his memory will draw rich returns from his life. A flashback from such a past will be rewarding, not remorseful."

Anonymous

GEOGRAPHICAL PROFILE: GILGAL

- Lay about two miles northeast of Jericho
- Means to "roll away" or perhaps "circle"
- Probably equally important as a national base with Shiloh and Shechem
- The city where Saul was made king

GEOGRAPHICAL PROFILE: JERICHO

- Canaanite city located six miles west of the Jordan River and about ten miles northwest of the northern end of the Red Sea
- Located near a large fresh-water spring
- 825 feet below sea level

The actual experience of crossing the Jordan River was not enough. God wanted to make sure the future generations would hear the story of his deliverance of an entire nation and the keeping of his promise about the land.

Joshua 4

Rocks of Remembrance

I. INTRODUCTION

Trick Play

*N*inety percent of prescription drugs today have been developed in the last seventy years and many since 1990. Every physician must maintain a continuing education program, or he cannot keep up with the changes in the pharmaceutical field. Creativity in ministry has become essential for churches, since no congregation wants a dirt-road church in an interstate world. Some things never change, like God himself and the message of Scripture. Overall, when measured by the Great Commission, the mission never changes. But methods change all the time and so do locations—as 20 percent of Americans move across state lines every year.

I heard a pastor tell about a high school basketball team in his midwestern town that was one point behind with two seconds left on the clock. It was their turn to inbound the ball. Three players ran to the free throw line, kneeled down, and began barking. The other team was so frustrated that they rushed toward the barking players, leaving one player free to grab the ball for a layup.

That may be the ultimate gadget play, but it emphasizes again how new ideas and change are important in the progress of the Christian life. That's where Israel was at this point—facing a major national and geographic change. Nevertheless, the very fact of the change established the necessity for a remembrance exemplified in our passage by the memorial stones. Perhaps the key phrase of the chapter comes at us in question form: "What do these stones mean?" Change for the sake of change itself usually has no value. Change related to accomplishing the mission reflects positive willingness to adapt to shifting surroundings in order to achieve the will of God in our lives.

Faith requires that we look forward, but it also requires that we look back. Someone has said, "The greatest enemy of faith may be forgetfulness." If we forget how God has worked and provided in the past, we may fail to trust him for the future. God told Joshua to arrange for a visible memorial that could be an object lesson. He knows we have memory lapses and faith failures, so he often acts to remind us when we need the change, or how we have been changed.

II. COMMENTARY

Rocks of Remembrance

MAIN IDEA: *The crossing of the Jordan River taught Israel that overcoming by God's power and remembering God's work in their lives would require reviewing past victories. This would also encourage them for future battles—quite a necessity at this point in their history.*

Twelve Men, Twelve Stones (4:1–9)

SUPPORTING IDEA: *The pile of stones in the Jordan River helped Israel remember that spiritual monuments in themselves are not as important as the realities they signify.*

4:1–3. Once the Israelites crossed the Jordan and the river resumed its flow, they might have thought it was all a dream. No one had video footage or photographs, but they did have stones from the middle of the Jordan— one for each tribe. Gilgal would become a memorial park, a visual testimony to future generation of Israelites and to the other nations of the world. Why a pile of rocks? So that fifteen years later, when an Israelite father might bring his children to Gilgal Memorial Park, they would say, "Hey, Dad. What's with the pile of rocks?" Dad could then tell them about God's faithfulness and miraculous power in damming up the Jordan so Israel could enter the promised land.

In the context of Joshua 3 and 4, the words of 3:12 connect chapter 3 with the early verses of chapter 4. The timing seems a bit confusing here, the men possibly having been selected earlier or perhaps 3:12 only anticipates the selection. Certainly Joshua's status has changed between the chapters, and the exaltation mentioned in 3:7 has taken place by the fulfillment of the crossing. Now we understand the actual duties of these twelve important men—to take stones from the middle of the Jordan River where the priests were still standing firmly and carry them to the first campsite in Canaan.

The words **put them down** could literally be rendered "cause them to rest," picking up again a major theme of this book.

Commentators debate whether the men crossed all the way over and went back for the stones or picked them up on the way, but that seems to miss the point. The stones themselves and what they would become are the spotlight of these verses. Furthermore, Madvig reminds us that "the phrase 'the Lord said to Joshua' emphasizes the fact that everything was done in obedience to God's commands" (Madvig, 269).

4:4–7. Raising stones as a monument and memorial is a common behavior in the Old Testament. We see it clear back in Genesis 28 and 31; we see it here in Joshua 7 and 24; and it appears again in 1 Samuel 7:12. We probably cannot overemphasize the focus of the stones as a memorial to prompt questions from children about spiritual values and the work of God. Indeed, this point of setting up markers deliberately intended to provoke questions about spiritual matters in the minds and hearts of children is a central theme of biblical education in the Old Testament and a technique still used today. We'll deal with it just a bit more in "Deeper Discoveries."

4:8–9. When one reads the NIV marginal note at verse 9, there seems to be an indication that we have two piles of stones and not one. The obvious one is on the bank at Gilgal, but the other would be in the river itself. Campbell suggests that

> Joshua joined these men on their strange mission and while they were wrenching up great stones from the bed of the river, he set another pile of 12 stones in the river bed itself to mark the precise spot where the priest stood with the ark of the covenant. This was apparently done on Joshua's own initiative and expressed his desire to have a personal reminder of God's faithfulness at the very beginning of the conquest of Canaan (Campbell, *BKC*, 336).

This view seems less attested in the text however than the more normal reading of one pile of stones. Howard interprets the passage like this:

> When we read about the twelve men taking up twelve stones from the river bed to take up on the banks of the river, it becomes clear they were taking up the twelve stones that Joshua had set down previously. Their purpose initially was to mark the importance of the

spot where the priests stood with the ark. However, when the crossing was complete, these stones were set up on the river bank as a perpetual memorial (Howard, 136).

The phrase **and they are there to this day** clinches the significance of the memorial to emphasize the greatness and goodness of the God who made this crossing possible.

B Priests Left High and Dry (4:10–18)

> **SUPPORTING IDEA:** *The two and one-half tribes that settled east of the Jordan River provide a great lesson for Bible readers: they make good on their promise.*

4:10–13. While the priests stood patiently in the middle, this procession of over two million people was led by the two and one-half Transjordanian tribes, following Joshua, of course. This harks back to Numbers 32 where Moses commanded Joshua and Eleazar the priest to make sure the Transjordanian tribes made the crossing well armed with everyone else. We might note that this whole operation was completed quickly and efficiently because of the obedience of the people. When God tells you what to do, do it with dispatch.

The people had stood on the eastern bank and watched the priests enter the water and stand in the middle of the river. Now they stood on the western bank and watched the priests walk out of the dry riverbed, a signal that the crossing was complete. The unity of the nation had been preserved and forty thousand fighting men **armed for battle** were ready to head into Jericho and take up the conquest. We use the symbolic expression "he burned his bridges behind him." There are no bridges here, but when that river came roaring down from the north—once again a mighty flood—the people knew they had no route of return and must turn their faces toward Jericho.

Hamlin observes, "The important message of the twelve stones is that every transition, every new task, requires a renewal of the whole, undivided people of God" (Hamlin, 27).

4:14. The exaltation promised in 3:7 is now affirmed in 4:14. Joshua had faithfully conveyed God's word to the people, and God had made everything happen just as Joshua had said. The word **revered** appears as the word *fear* in verse 24. But Joshua was not God. Reverence and honor to a human leader is in line with God's word, but the holy fear and reverence—the awe in worship of God—belong to him alone. Howard says:

> Joshua is now, in effect, the "new Moses." After the great cross-ing of the Red Sea, "the people feared the LORD and put their trust in him and in Moses his servant" (Exod. 14:31b). Here, now, Joshua found himself in a remarkably similar position after a remarkably similar miracle. He was growing into Moses' job as Israel's leader (Howard, 139).

We should notice, however, that the reverence accorded Joshua (like that given Moses) did not extol military victories but spiritual leadership. Up to this point, and throughout most of this book, Joshua is not so much the military strategist as he is the servant of the Lord echoing God's word to the people. All of this emphasizes again that Joshua is not nearly so much a book of military victory and land acquisition as it is spiritual victory and acquiescence to the plan of God.

4:15–18. Now the language changes. We have been focused on crossing the Jordan River, but now we read that the priests were **to come up out of the Jordan**. They had entered the land, and the focus rests no more upon a wandering people but upon a nation that has achieved the goals their God set for them. We also have new phraseology about the ark—**the ark of the Testimony**. The words *testimony* and *covenant* are used interchangeably in Scripture. The Old Testament could be called the old covenant, and likewise the New Testament could be called the new covenant. The focus of *testimony* always centers on God's promises and covenants with Israel. The ark, as we have noted, was a living and mobile reminder of God's presence and prom-ises.

Just as the river had parted when the priests first placed their feet in from the eastern shore, so now the torrent of flood season began again as their feet left the waters at the western shore.

Schaeffer observes:

> As we see what happened in Joshua's day, we can take heart in the midst of our struggles. The God who kept His oath and promise to the children of Israel at the traumatic moment of their walking over the Jordan and entering the land will keep His word to the very

end. As Bunyan's Pilgrim crossed another river, the river Death, the oath and promises of God gave him absolute assurance. Not only in the river Death but in the whole of life, we can count on God to keep His living promises (Schaeffer, 89).

Ⓒ Memorial Moment (4:19–24)

SUPPORTING IDEA: *The Gilgal stones were a physical remembrance like a picture or an object. And the Israelites knew that reminders of God's power, however important, must never be worshiped in themselves.*

4:19–20. So Gilgal became the first encampment in the promised land. Just six miles away, the residents of Jericho could see two million people hustling about putting up their tents and had doubtless already been watching the movement after the spy episode of chapter 2. Mention of **the tenth day** reminds us of Exodus 12:3, another link with Moses. Madvig speculates, "Joshua may have placed the stones in a heap, as in 7:26, or he may have placed them in a circle. Gilgal sounds like the Hebrew word for circle" (Madvig, 271). The day coincides with the selection of the Passover lamb and, in Howard's words:

> . . . foreshadowed the keeping of the Passover in 5:10 on the fourteenth day of the month in accordance with the Passover calendar (when the lamb was actually killed) (Exod. 12:6, 18). And the fact that this happened at Passover helps to connect the crossing of the Jordan even more closely with the events of the exodus and the crossing of the Red Sea, which is made explicit in v. 23 (Howard, 141).

Gilgal would go on to become a place of historic significance as well as the first encampment. In chapter 5 circumcision and Passover are celebrated there; Samuel will make it one of his cities of judgment (1 Sam. 7:16); Saul will be anointed king in Gilgal (1 Sam. 11:14–15); and the apostasy of the city will be condemned by Hosea (9:15; 12:11) and Amos (4:4; 5:5).

4:21–23. At the church we attend in Florida, the congregation frequently pauses in a morning worship service to observe what is called "a memorial moment." Usually these offer opportunity for reflection upon the death of one or more church members, and a quiet stillness descends on the sanctuary during that time. Israel had many memorial moments, and this was one of the great ones. And as a word in the bulletin and flowers on the platform offer visual reminders of what has happened, here Joshua's stones provided a memorial for the future. They had a very distinct purpose, or purposes.

When children asked about these stones, they were to be told that **Israel crossed the Jordan on dry ground** and that **the LORD your God dried up the Jordan**. Not only what had happened, but why it had happened. Not just "Why are these stones here?" but also "What do these stones mean?" Those children may never have gone back to the Red Sea to view the site of the crossing of that body of water, but now the land which belonged to Israel provided opportunity actually to make a journey to this famous national monument and reflect upon what God had done. These twelve stones became like the Lincoln Memorial or the Washington Monument for future generations of Israelites.

4:24. The purpose of the stones was to show God's power in the crossing, but the purpose of the crossing was to show God's power. Again here we have two purposes, one related to other nations (**that all the peoples of the earth might know that the hand of the LORD is powerful**) and one related distinctly to Israel (**that you might always fear the LORD your God**). Everyone was to know God's power and respond in worship and reverence. God provided for his people so that others (like Rahab) would trust in him too.

Our ministry accomplishments are like our Gilgal, our monument. Memorials of human achievement are quite popular, and many can be found in our nation's capital. The Gilgal stones memorialized God's power and provision. Churches are somewhat like mobile homes. There is nothing sacred or special about them any more than there was anything special about the twelve stones. But the buildings provide a constant reminder of the power and provision of God. They symbolize God's work for his people and through his people.

> **MAIN IDEA REVIEW:** *The crossing of the Jordan River taught Israel that overcoming by God's power and remembering God's work in their lives would require reviewing past victories. This would also encourage them for future battles—quite a necessity at this point in their history.*

III. CONCLUSION

"Rock of Ages"

In 1776 the newly formed United States declared its independence; in England, Augustus Montague Toplady was writing hymns. The familiar "Rock of Ages" actually first appeared a year earlier in the *Gospel Magazine* that Toplady published. Only the first stanza appeared in 1775, and the entire hymn in March 1776 under the laborious heading, "A Living and Dying Prayer for the Holiest Believer in the World." Toplady died three months shy of his thirty-eighth birthday. In 1866 as the steamer *London* sank in the Bay of Biscayne, the last human sounds heard from the helpless passengers were the words of "Rock of Ages."

The Old Testament proclaims that Yahweh is the rock of Israel in passages such as Isaiah 26:4: "Trust in the LORD forever, for the LORD, the LORD, is the Rock eternal" and Psalm 18:2: "The LORD is my rock, my fortress and my deliverer; my God is my rock, in whom I take refuge."

This metaphor is not often used of Jesus, but in 1 Peter 2:7 we learn that "the stone the builders rejected has become the capstone." Toplady may have taken a bit of poetic license in the metaphor, but we cannot fault him for the theology of his hymn.

> Not the labors of my hands
> Can fulfill Thy law's demands;
> Could my zeal no respite know,
> Could my tears forever flow,
> All for sin could not atone;
> Thou must save and Thou alone.

The rocks of remembrance in our passage remind us that God is our foundation, whether the Father or the Son, whether the rock of the Old Testament or the stone of the New. We rest all our hope and faith on our blessed Rock of Ages.

PRINCIPLES

- Biblical leaders lead; they never drive.

- God's care and blessing in our lives are the key to victory and the banner over our families and churches.
- Memory provides an important tool in spiritual formation.

APPLICATIONS

- Look for the spiritual lessons in historical experiences.
- We should expect miracles in our lives, however small or great, and always see God's hand behind them.
- Throughout this book we dare not overlook the truth that spiritual victories are more important than physical victories.

IV. LIFE APPLICATION

Special Selection

One Sunday a pastor told his congregation that the church needed extra money, and he asked the people prayerfully to consider putting a little something more in the offering plate. To enhance his stewardship efforts he indicated that the person who gave the most would be able to pick out three hymns.

After the offering plates were passed, the pastor glanced down and noticed that someone had placed a thousand dollar bill in the offering. He was so excited that he immediately shared his joy with the congregation and said he would personally like to thank the person who placed the money in the plate, stopping the service right then to take care of the three hymns.

A quiet, saintly lady all the way in the back raised her hand. The pastor asked her to the front, and she slowly made her way to the platform. He told her how wonderful he thought it was that she gave so much and in gratitude asked her to pick out three hymns. Her eyes brightened as she turned from the pastor to look out over the congregation, pointed to the three most handsome men in the building, and said, "I'll take him and him and him."

A silly anecdote at best, but it helps us notice the important selections of this passage: (1) the careful geographical selection of where the nation would enter the river and where they would exit, (2) the selection of the twelve men to carry the twelve stones, and (3) the selection of the stones themselves. This entire crossing was carefully orchestrated to fulfill God's plan. And the churches in which we worship serve as physical reminders or memorials of what God has done for us and what he wants from us.

Being in Gilgal meant that Israel had reached the place God had for them—and we worship in places God has given us. Places where spiritual victories are won; places where biblical teaching goes forth; places where eternal decisions are made.

When our children ask us about our church buildings, may we be quick to tell them about God's faithful provision. And may those buildings be places in which other people come to know God's power and love. When the Israelites camped at Gilgal that night, the river flowed behind them and the land of Canaan stood before. Now there was no turning back. God has given us our congregations and our buildings to use for his glory. There is no turning back. We must dedicate ourselves to God's ministry to do God's work and to trust his promises that he will help us conquer the land and win spiritual victories for his glory. Standing above all that we do is the heartfelt awareness that God has selected us in a special way and enabled us to hear his plan, to respond, and to serve him as part of that response.

V. PRAYER

Father, may we be careful to remember your grace and blessing when we think of the way you care for your people as you have throughout all the ages of history. When we see any kind of monument or memorial, let us remember that we must reverence God and teach our children about the meaning of what he has done. Amen.

VI. DEEPER DISCOVERIES

A. Stones (4:3)

As we have already seen in our "Conclusion," stones and rocks are very important in the Bible. As early as Genesis 29, Jacob pushed a stone off a well so Rachel's sheep could drink. The stone sealed the well and helped keep the water clean. When Rachel died, Jacob set up a stone pillar over her grave, actually the first time the Bible mentions a monument erected over a burial site (Gen. 35). By the time we get to the historical books, Solomon is bringing in quarried stones for the building of his magnificent temple. This kind of thing happened again during the time of Josiah when he made repairs to the temple. The work of stonemasons was vital (2 Chr. 34:11,31).

But those temple stones were in a sense "manufactured" as are the stones we use in buildings and bridges today. Joshua and his people were working with the common stones that still litter the landscape of the Middle East. As now, in ancient days they became the building materials for houses, city walls, and fortifications. Throughout Genesis and the Pentateuch we have seen them raised as altars (e.g., Deut. 27:5). Nor is this the first time we have seen stones piled up as a memorial. In Genesis 28:22, Jacob said, "This stone that I have set up as a pillar will be God's house, and of all that you give me I will give you a tenth," an act which he repeated at Mizpah in his encounter with Laban (Gen. 31:45–50).

In line with our earlier observations, the *Nelson Study Bible* suggests:

> Because a stone was commonly used as a foundation for a structure, God Himself was called the "Stone of Israel" (Gen. 49:24). But Isaiah also described the Lord as a "stone of stumbling" for those Israelites who rejected Him (Is. 8:14). These same images were applied to Jesus Christ in the New Testament (Is. 28:16; 1 Pet. 2:4–8) (359).

B. When Your Children Ask (4:6,21)

Perhaps no more needs to be said about the pedagogical significance of the rocks of remembrance. On the other hand, the theme is so dominant in Joshua 4 that we probably cannot overemphasize its importance. The reminders here in this chapter hark back to Deuteronomy 6, one of the key passages in the Bible on the religious instruction of children at home.

In the famous Shema passage we read:

> Hear, O Israel: The LORD our God, the LORD is one. Love the LORD your God with all your heart and with all your soul and with all your strength. These commandments that I give you today are to be upon your hearts. Impress them on your children. Talk about them when you sit at home and when you walk along the road, when

you lie down and when you get up. Tie them as symbols on your hands and bind them on your foreheads. Write them on the doorframes of your houses and on your gates (Deut. 6:4–9).

Then after further admonition of obedience and worship, Moses said, "In the future, when your son asks you, 'What is the meaning of the stipulations, decrees and laws the LORD our God has command you?' tell him: 'We were slaves of Pharaoh in Egypt, but the LORD brought us out of Egypt with a mighty hand'" (Deut. 6:20–21).

We know that in later years the Pharisees took the words of Deuteronomy literally and tied little copies of the law on their wrists and foreheads—a distorted view of the passage. Surely what the paragraph means is that children in godly homes should constantly be reminded by a variety of symbols and celebrations that the work of God and the Word of God are revered in that house. Families create and sustain traditions to make this possible.

It is always a danger to remember the monument and forget its meaning. People climbing the stairs of the Washington Monument focus more on its height and view than they do on the person and era of the country in whose honor it was erected. The imposing size of the Lincoln Memorial brings to mind more readily the steps and the gigantic figure of that sitting president rather than the struggle for freedom and national unity connected with his leadership.

Only in recent years at sites like "The Wall," the National Vietnam Veterns Memorial in Washington, D.C., the Oklahoma City National Memorial, and the Twin Towers disaster site do we see a greater willingness to remember the people involved and the meaning rather than the monument itself. Yet these latter examples demonstrate people remembering within their own generation. The rocks of remembrance were set up to indicate meaning to future generations.

Obviously the key is not in the symbol itself but in the willingness of parents and teachers to point out the meaning of monuments and memorials like Joshua's twelve stones.

VII. TEACHING OUTLINE

A. INTRODUCTION

1. Lead Story: Trick Play

2. Context: Joshua 3 takes place on the eastern bank of the Jordan River and Joshua 4 on the western bank. The crossing has been completed and the people have come out of the river. This marks a huge change in their status.

3. Transition: The river also represents the transition from the desert to the promised land and leads them into chapter 5 where there is yet another duty before the conquest can proceed—circumcision—which must follow the crossing but precede the campaign.

B. COMMENTARY

1. Twelve Men, Twelve Stones (4:1–9)

2. Priests Left High and Dry (4:10–18)

3. Memorial Moment (4:19–24)

C. CONCLUSION: SPECIAL SELECTION

VIII. ISSUES FOR DISCUSSION

1. Do you think the text offers a stronger argument for two piles of stones or for one?

2. In what specific ways can we use monuments and memorials to provoke our children to ask, "What do these stones mean?"

3. What kinds of things can we use in families and churches as "memorial stones" upon which to build our own and our children's understanding of God?

Joshua 5

Holy Ground

I. INTRODUCTION
A Tailor-Made People

II. COMMENTARY
A verse-by-verse explanation of the chapter.

III. CONCLUSION
Friendly Frisbee

An overview of the principles and applications from the chapter.

IV. LIFE APPLICATION
"To God Be the Glory"

Melding the chapter to life.

V. PRAYER
Tying the chapter to life with God.

VI. DEEPER DISCOVERIES
Historical, geographical, and grammatical enrichment of the commentary.

VII. TEACHING OUTLINE
Suggested step-by-step group study of the chapter.

VIII. ISSUES FOR DISCUSSION
Zeroing the chapter in on daily life.

"We should be less concerned about making churches full of people and more concerned about making people full of God."

C .   K i r k   H a d a w a y
a n d   D a v i d   A .   R o o z e n

Joshua 5

IN A NUTSHELL

Physically and geographically, the Israelites were ready for war. They had crossed the Jordan River and set up camp just a short distance from Jericho. The conquest of the land seemed imminent. But their hearts were not ready until circumcision was reinstituted and their diet was changed.

Holy Ground

I. INTRODUCTION

A Tailor-Made People

*B*ack in the early twentieth century, time and motion studies were conducted in every major business by stopwatch-toting consultants measuring distances between feet and pedals, and everything else that might cut seconds off a project at the factory. The Carnegie Foundation for the Advancement of Teaching decided that approach might work in universities as well, so it turned to Frederick Taylor, the father of modern scientific management, who passed the project on to his protégé, Morris Cooke. Selecting the physics departments of eight universities, and determined to ferret out inefficiency, Cooke discovered that classrooms sat empty for days at a time, professors routinely showed up a few minutes late for class, and entire campuses would grind to a halt in time for a big football game.

Furthermore, these universities operated at a loss, and Cooke and Taylor could only understand profit as a measure of efficiency and motivation. So Cooke designed "the student hour" by dividing a class's total cost by the number of hours it met and the number of students enrolled. Obviously in the chemistry department or the library, the idea was a disaster.

All seemed to fail except that another idea of Cooke's actually caught on. Cooke discovered that professors were routinely setting university policy, recruiting students, and ordering supplies. He pronounced, "The industrial world has freed itself from the slavery of the idea that to get a thing well done you must do it yourself." So in order to free professors' time for teaching and research, he invented a new class of university employee—the administrator. Some of my friends would consider that a less-than-gracious gift, but no institution of higher learning today operates without that "Taylor-made" lineup of officers.

On the western bank of the Jordan River, God wanted to tailor-make his people. That would require the renewal of circumcision and observance of the Passover. This would be the final stage of God's preparation of his chosen people for the holy war that awaited them. The inhabitants of Canaan were terror stricken, so Joshua could afford to let his warriors remain immobilized a few days by circumcision, a prerequisite to the Passover feast (Exod. 12:44,48).

II. COMMENTARY

Holy Ground

MAIN IDEA: *It seemed like a perfect time to attack. The enemy was afraid and perhaps even assumed it had months to prepare while Israel waited for the flood waters to recede. Now suddenly the armies of Israel were across the Jordan River and on their doorstep. Conventional military wisdom would say, "Attack now!" But God delayed them because they were not yet ready. Why? Because spiritual preparation is more important than military advantage. In this chapter God takes his people through three major events—the circumcision of the Israelite men, the celebration of the Passover, and the submission of Joshua.*

A Ancient Rite (5:1–3)

SUPPORTING IDEA: *In God's design physical acts like circumcision reinforce and strengthen the covenant with the nation of Israel. Their spiritual meaning and purpose are more important than the acts themselves.*

5:1. This same formula **now when . . . heard** begins chapters 9–11. Our narrator wants us to see that the nations had no will to fight and stood virtually helpless before the armies of Joshua. Some suggest that the word **we** in verse 1 indicates an eyewitness report by Joshua, and they may have a point, although this alone hardly establishes authorship. Let's also notice that just because the nations feared Israel doesn't mean that they repented and accepted the God of Israel as Rahab had done. This verse confirms Rahab's judgment of her countrymen and their fear of Israel and Israel's God. We learn that this will not be Joshua's battle. All the victories in Canaan will come as a result of God's power, not the military tactics of the Israelite army. Here the **Amorite kings** and **Canaanite kings** apparently serve as representations for the seven people groups we have already discussed in chapter 3.

5:2–3. This story is hardly embellished; in two short verses the text describes the circumcision of all Israelite males at **Gibeath Haaraloth**, the name which means "hill of foreskins." Circumcision, the physical sign of the

Abrahamic covenant, goes back to Genesis 17 where God said to Abraham, "You are to undergo circumcision, and it will be a sign of the covenant between me and you. For the generations to come every male among you who is eight days old must be circumcised" (Gen. 17:11). This was a visible sign of commitment to God. It proclaimed a national distinctive: "We are different and we belong to you." It also reminded the nation of God's promise to Abraham to make them a great people and give them the land. How important then to have the sign in place when preparing to enter this promised land.

The use of **flint knives** for this ritual seems to have been demanded (Exod. 4:25). *The Nelson Study Bible* describes the instrument:

> Flint is a rock found in abundance in biblical lands, and its use is known from almost all periods of ancient history; many flint knives have been found in excavations. Flint was gradually replaced by metals, such as cooper, bronze, and iron. Only in two places in the Old Testament is the Hebrew word *flint* found, here and in Ex. 4:26, both in connection with circumcision (360).

The Israelites had forsaken the covenant symbol while in the desert for forty years, although the passage does not tell us why. We do not know whether it was direct disobedience, oversight, or whether the rite was impractical while they were on the move through the wilderness. Nevertheless, none of the Israelite men born in the desert had been circumcised, and this was necessary now.

So God asked Joshua to do the unthinkable, to incapacitate his entire army while camped in the shadows of enemy walls. It took great faith to sit there unable to fight. But in order to demonstrate their covenant commitment to God, the Israelites had to become completely vulnerable. Circumcision was just one more way in which they completely trusted God to protect them.

So it is with us. Our commitment to God often requires vulnerability on our part. When we say to God, "I belong to you," we are also saying, "Do with me as you please." This has nothing to do with spiritual warfare but everything to do with preparation, since it is a heart issue. Even for the Israelites the outward sign indicated an inward condition. Moses said to them in Deuteronomy 10:16: "Circumcise your hearts, therefore, and do not be stiff-necked any longer." In God's plan, having their hearts right was more important than having their swords sharpened.

Every spring I watch the NCAA tournament. Imagine a player getting all ready to play—shoes, shorts, shirt, headband, and tattoos in place. He warms up and never misses a shot in practice but does not listen to or do what the coach says. That player is not ready to play, and if that attitude persists, he will sit on the bench.

If our hearts have not been circumcised, if we do not have a wholehearted commitment to God's cause and the Christian life, we are not ready for spiritual warfare. For these Israelite warriors willingness to submit to the flint knife and be marked as belonging to God's covenant required the same total commitment.

Let's be careful to recognize that the outward act is insufficient. We know that other nations such as Egypt, Edom, Ammon, and Moab practiced circumcision but were uncircumcised in their hearts (Jer. 9:25–26). As with baptism, the heart attitude—not the outward ritual—makes the difference.

Schaeffer says it well:

> There is a flow between the circumcision of the Old Testament and the baptism of the New. The New Testament speaks of baptism as the Christian's circumcision. . . . Abraham was not saved by circumcision; he was already saved. And the New Testament argues, especially in various Pauline sections, that a person does not have to be either circumcised or baptized to be saved. You can be saved without the sign. The Book of Romans argues that neither the Jews nor the Gentiles needed the sign of circumcision for their redemption. First Corinthians also argues it. Galatians, strongest of all, argues against any legality that would add an external sign such as circumcision or baptism to the way of salvation. Salvation is all by grace, all on the finished work of Jesus Christ. You can add nothing to it—nothing at all (Schaeffer, 98–99).

B Accountable People (5:4–9)

SUPPORTING IDEA: *As generations pass, spiritual heritage is forgotten and must be renewed if corporate spiritual life is to remain strong. That is exactly what God is doing with his people in these verses.*

5:4–7. Many interpreters have speculated on why circumcision of Israelite males did not continue during the desert wanderings. We have already noted it may have been inconvenient, impractical, or perhaps just pure neglect. Possibly God may have prohibited the practice because the nation stood under his judgment. They had rebelled against God repeatedly, had practiced idolatry, and had refused to enter the land (Num. 14). Maybe they were forbidden to place on their children the sign of the covenant which, in spirit and reality, they had broken.

Howard points out:

> While the elements of this covenant would not be broken by God and they remain in effect throughout all generation, each generation of Israelites—indeed, each individual Israelite—had to make its own decision whether to obey the covenant. That is the point of circumcision as the sign of the covenant (Gen. 17:9–14): an individual's failure to circumcise was tantamount to breaking the covenant, and whoever did not do this was cut off from the rest of Israel (17:14). . . . God's promises to Abraham's descendants would be fulfilled to the nation as a whole, but not every last individual would automatically participate; faith and obedience were required. Joshua 5:7 shows this by stating that God raised up another generation to replace the one he had consigned to perish in the wilderness (Howard, 150–51).

So circumcision as a sign has no role in the church today; God has given us baptism instead. Nevertheless, both Old Testament circumcision and New Testament baptism demonstrate our personal relationship with God, in the New Testament sense with the crucified and risen Christ. Both symbolize our belonging to God and our commitment to live for him.

5:8–9. Gilgal, lying just southeast of Jericho, was the place of this great event. The word sounds like the Hebrew word for *roll*. The phrase **the**

reproach of Egypt does not refer to the taunts heaped upon Israel by the Egyptians or to the misery that the Israelites endured as slaves in Egypt. Rather, it refers to the suspension of the Abrahamic covenant agreement of which circumcision was the sign.

The word for **reproach** (*herpa*) refers to shame or disgrace. Even though the people had been delivered from Egypt geographically, they had wandered around with the stench of Egypt upon them throughout all these forty years. The Abrahamic covenant and the Mosaic covenant lay idle while awaiting this revival at Gilgal. Recognizing national apostasy, Moses had exhorted the Israelites to repent before the Lord, implying the figure of circumcision (Deut. 10:16). Now by faith they had crossed into the promised land and showed their willingness to accept God's covenant terms again by submitting to circumcision, so the shame of their idolatry and lust for Egypt was finally rolled away. The old name meaning "circle" now took on new significance connected with the word *roll*.

◖ Alternate Diet (5:10–12)

SUPPORTING IDEA: *Israel was not ready to fight any enemy until the nation had been assured of its position before God and his provision for them. This would give them the courage to fight. The reinstitution of the Passover was important preparation for the task before them.*

5:10. Here we find only the third recorded Passover since the second (Num. 9:5) had been the first anniversary of the institution of the event. On the first month and fourteenth day they circumcised Israel, then celebrated the Passover in the land of promise, putting behind them the years of rejection and wandering. As Madvig puts it, "Many years later another 'Joshua' ate the Passover with his disciples and constituted them as the new people of God under the new covenant (Matt. 26:26–28)" (Madvig, 275).

Passover celebrated the deliverance of Israel from the angel of death during the final plague in Egypt. The Israelites put the blood of the Passover lamb on their doorposts, and they were saved. Israel had celebrated the Passover the next year at Mount Sinai, but we have no indication that they celebrated Passover for the next thirty-nine years in the desert; here we see the reinstitution of this celebration.

The celebration of Passover was important because the Israelites needed a reminder of God's commitment to them. Their dramatic and miraculous deliverance from Egypt provided a powerful demonstration of God's love for the nation and his intention to settle them in the promised land. Since most of the Israelites present were not even born at the time of the exodus, this memorial celebration became crucial.

5:11. Passover always carries with it the feast, so the text tells us **they ate some of the produce of the land: unleavened bread and roasted grain.** Just in case they needed another demonstration of God's care and provision for them, they began to eat food from Canaan, no longer dependent on the miracle manna provided in the wilderness. The God who had saved them from Pharaoh and provided for them in the desert would certainly give them victory and food in Canaan. Campbell notes:

> Since they gave evidence of wanting to be fully obedient to the Law of God it is probable that they first brought the wave-offering of a sheaf of grain, prescribed in Leviticus 23:10–14. . . . Roasted ears of grain are still considered a delicacy in the Middle East and are eaten as a substitute for bread (Campbell, *BKC,* 338).

5:12. The day after the feast the manna ended. Let's remember that the manna had not stopped when the people complained about it (Num. 11:6) nor even at the various points of unbelief in the wilderness. God continued to provide for his people throughout that forty-year journey and only stopped the manna now that they had ample food provisions in the promised land.

Sometimes the Christian life involves jumping into difficult circumstances, conflict, and warfare. We need to remember that God has committed to walk beside us and to go with us in all our moments of difficulty. Jesus' blood covers us, and his manna feeds us until we're able to eat the fruit of the land of normalcy once again. Barley would have been available during harvest then in progress at the Jericho oasis. We can only imagine the people's delight to think that they had now come to a place where they could eat again in a normal way.

Ⅾ Angelic Commander (5:13–15)

> **SUPPORTING IDEA:** *Before Joshua or Israel could attack, they had to remember the real commander. They had to bow down before him in submission and worship because he always leads his people into battle. He never brings up the rear.*

5:13–14. What a fascinating scene! Surely by this point Joshua thought he had done everything possible to get ready for the conquest of Canaan. But he still didn't have a battle plan from God. He had worked through his fears, crossed the Jordan River, consecrated the people, celebrated the Passover, eaten from the land, and now he was ready to take up the sword and charge ahead into battle. But God had one more hurdle for Joshua to clear before he could fight, even before he dared hear about God's battle plan.

Joshua was confronted by someone he recognized as a soldier (the drawn sword gave it away). Joshua didn't recognize him, so he asked the logical question: **Are you for us or for our enemies?** This was no mere vision but an actual appearance, possibly of the preincarnate Son of God himself—what we have called a Christophany. Redpath observes:

> Surely this was the same One before whom a leper fell and worshiped in thanksgiving for having been cleansed. Surely this was none other than the Saviour at whose feet Peter fell in a fishing boat and acknowledged Him to be his Lord. He is the One of whom John tells us in the Revelation that He is "King of kings and Lord of lords." Here is none other than Jesus Christ, our Lord and Saviour, who has come at that moment to meet Joshua (Redpath, 94).

Joshua was hardly prepared for the answer he received. He faced the **commander of the army of the LORD**, so he fell to his face in worship. The commander acknowledged and accepted his worship. The text does not say directly that Joshua perceived the presence of a supernatural being. But given his deeply spiritual and long experience with God, that would not be an unfounded conclusion. Though the NIV capitalizes LORD, the word *adonai* could be used to address human beings.

The commander put everything in perspective. This was not Joshua's war; it was God's war. God assumed sovereign control of this operation from the beginning. The commander would not help but take over, and Joshua would become his servant. We will soon read the account of the conquest (Josh. 6–11) and discover that all the military strategy was divinely directed. God sent them against the center of the land, first capturing Jericho and Ai, thereby securing the passes to the central ridge and driving a wedge between the northern and southern sections of Canaan. They then moved south to conquer the Amorite coalition and finally wipe out the northern confederacy.

But why did the commander answer **Neither**? Why didn't he say, "Joshua, I'm here to represent God. You have nothing to fear." I belabor the point when I say that God did not come to fight *for* Joshua and Israel but rather to take charge of the campaign. We talk often about God being on our side, but in fact we must always serve on God's side—and that's where Joshua found himself in this situation.

When people invite you to their house for dinner, you do not dictate the menu. You don't ask them to cook this or that. You eat what they serve or you don't eat at all. You come to eat the meal, but it is not really your meal. In the same way Israel approached God's promised land table as his guest. He would serve them, but he would also choose the menu and call the shots.

5:15. The reminder that God had taken command prepared Joshua for the battle plan that God would give him. That plan would require great trust and obedience in the true commander. But instead of a battle plan, Joshua heard, **Take off your sandals, for the place where you are standing is holy.** One final act of consecration and commitment before the conquest. Joshua needed to worship before warring. To bow before battling. To submit before serving. No, this location was not some holy shrine that Joshua had accidentally stumbled upon. Any place one meets God becomes holy ground, as Jacob discovered at Bethel (Gen. 28) and Moses at the burning bush (Exod. 3).

But Gilgal would not always remain a holy place. During the days of Amos and Hosea, the Gilgal shrine became a point of apostasy where people took false oaths (Hos. 4:15) and empty sacrifices were offered by insincere worshipers (Amos 4:4). Eventually God abandoned it, even though people thought they genuinely sought him there (Amos 5:5). Ultimately Amos prophesied that Gilgal, where the first Passover on the land of Canaan had been held, would be the first place to go into exile (Amos 5:5).

We read yet one more historical reflection in Micah 6:5, but other than that we find no later mention of Gilgal in the Old Testament. Hamlin is right to observe, "The history of the Gilgal sanctuary would lead us to believe that the emphasis of the Teacher was not on that particular place, but rather on what happened there: Israel's military leader bowed down before the covenant LORD and accepted the divine guidance" (Hamlin, 42).

> **MAIN IDEA REVIEW:** *It seemed like a perfect time to attack. The enemy was afraid and perhaps even assumed it had months to prepare while Israel waited for the flood waters to recede. Now suddenly the armies of Israel were across the Jordan River and on their doorstep. Conventional military wisdom would say, "Attack now!" But God delayed them because they were not yet ready. Why? Because spiritual preparation is more important than military advantage. In this chapter God takes his people through three major events—the circumcision of the Israelite men, the celebration of the Passover, and the submission of Joshua.*

III. CONCLUSION

Friendly Frisbee

One day last summer we had a family game night at church. A number of us went out to the soccer field to play ultimate Frisbee. It was one of those events where people come and go, so my son Jeff, our pastor, switched teams a number of times to try to keep it even. After a few rounds he wasn't sure who his team members were any more. It really didn't matter because as people entered and left they played only for the fun, not for the competition. When you are not committed to a cause, it's hard to feel passionate about winning.

But war is very different from a friendly game of Frisbee. When German planes bombarded England during World War II, a keen sense of national loyalty and resolve arose from the ashes. Commitment to the allied cause ran deep in the hearts of the British people. One Englishman wrote in a letter, "As one man the whole nation handed over all its resources to the government. We have invested the cabinet with the right to conscript any of us for any task, to take our goods, our money and our all. Never have rich men set such little store by their wealth; never have we been so ready to lay down life itself, if only our cause may triumph" (Campbell, *Leader Under Fire*, p. 39).

That's what Joshua and the Israelites needed before they headed into Jericho. No selfishness, no sin, no spiritual shoddiness. As unusual as it might seem, this was still war and there could be no holding back of consecrated people and resources. I like the way Madvig summarizes Joshua 5:

> The events of this chapter are further evidenced that the conquest was to be accomplished by God's power, not man's. From a human point of view, it would have been wise to fulfill the rituals of circumcision and the Passover on the other side of the Jordan where the Israelites were not exposed to their enemies. Celebrating them in the promised land, however, symbolized that the covenant relationship between God and Israel was a pre-requisite for possessing the land. With this encounter the preparation for the conquest was completed (Madvig, 276).

The last four words of this chapter are powerful: "And Joshua did so." All the way along, wherever he found himself and whatever God asked of him, Joshua did it. Circumcise the troops—yes, sir. Celebrate the Passover—yes, sir. Take off your sandals and worship—yes, sir. Hardly the typical position for a great military commander but precisely where God wanted Joshua—and where he wants us.

PRINCIPLES

- God can change the hearts of our strongest enemies to fear him and us.
- Sometimes God wants us to take off our shoes and worship before we hurry to a task—to slow down and acknowledge his sovereign leadership in our lives.
- God wants us to be vulnerable before him and to anticipate that whatever difficulties or battles we face are really his and he will win the day when we allow him to have complete control.

APPLICATIONS

- List some of the enemies or obstacles you face. Before you engage them, bring each one before the one who met Joshua at Gilgal.

- One by one, turn those obstacles you face over to God's control.

- Next time you come before the Lord in prayer, worship, or Bible study, stop and remember that you stand on holy ground.

IV. LIFE APPLICATION

"To God Be the Glory"

Fanny Jane Crosby was blinded for life at the age of six. She began writing songs two years later and went on to become a concert singer, organist, and harpist. She married Alexander Van Alstyne (also a blind musician), and they both taught at the New York City School for the Blind. Fanny began to write hymns when she was forty-four years old. During the next half century she produced over eight thousand hymn texts. Interestingly, "To God Be the Glory" was first introduced in Great Britain by Sankey and Moody and first published there as well in 1875. Its popularity, however, most likely springs from its use in the Billy Graham Crusade at Harringay in 1954.

The first two verses of Psalm 29 call angels to worship the name of the Lord. They responded and so should we, joining and proclaiming, "Great things he hath done!" Here's the text: "Ascribe to the LORD, O mighty ones, ascribe to the LORD glory and strength. Ascribe to the LORD the glory due his name; worship the LORD in the splendor of his holiness."

> O perfect redemption, the purchase of blood!
>
> To every believer the promise of God;
>
> The vilest offender who truly believes,
>
> That moment from Jesus a pardon receives.

The earth cannot hear the Lord's voice unless it is communicated through his people. Our praise reaches upward and outward to glorify his name and exalt his greatness. Now the land of Canaan would see the greatness of Almighty God. Joshua had learned from the commander of the Lord's armies that whatever victories might lie ahead, he must be willing and ready to say, "To God be the glory."

V. PRAYER

Give me the love that leads the way,
The faith that nothing can dismay,
The hope no disappointments tire,
The passion that will burn like fire,
Let me not sink to be a clod:
Make me Thy fuel, O flame of God.

—Amy Carmichael

VI. DEEPER DISCOVERIES

A. Circumcision (5:2)

Many commentators suggest that circumcision as introduced in Genesis was a new concept to humanity and that when it appeared later in other Semitic peoples it must reflect that great revelatory chapter in Genesis. But wider research does not seem to support that view. Egyptians almost certainly practiced circumcision before that point in history, as did most Semitic tribes in the area of Canaan as well. So God took a common social custom and transformed it into a spiritual rite.

But that should not determine our emphasis. The fact that God chose this particular symbol to bring honor to himself places greater importance on it than the historic fact that other nomadic tribes may also have practiced it. Circumcision was established as the sign of the covenant. Yes, Israel departed from it in the desert, so Joshua reinstituted the practice on the western bank of the Jordan River before the battle of Jericho. By the time of Joshua, every Israelite understood that circumcision was more than an outward sign—it represented an inward commitment.

The relationship of circumcision to baptism has already been mentioned. But here is another strong paragraph on the meaning of baptism from the pen of a reputable theologian:

Theologically, baptism may be defined as an act of association or identification with someone, some group, some message, or some event. Baptism into the Greek mystery religions associated the initiates with that religion. Jewish proselyte baptism associated the proselyte with Judaism. John the Baptist's baptism associated his followers with his message of righteousness (he had no group for them to join). (Incidentally, John was apparently the first person ever to baptize other people—usually baptisms were self-administered.) . . . To be baptized into Moses involved identification with his leadership in bringing the Israelites out of Egypt (1 Cor. 10:2). To be baptized for the dead means to be identified with the Christian group and take the place of a believer who had died (15:29). Christian baptism means identification with the message of the gospel, the person of the Savior, and the group of believers. Some of the baptisms listed do not involve water. Also observe how impoverished we would be without a proper understanding of the meaning and ramifications of baptism (Ryrie, 422).

B. Army of the Lord (5:14)

Two possible interpretations come to mind as we look at this phrase. Did this divine messenger command angelic armies that would provide unseen victory from the skies while Joshua's troops carried out the work on earth? Or was the army of Israel actually going to become the army of the Lord and be supervised visibly by Joshua but in reality by God's commander? The phrase **the army of the Lord** is found only in this passage, although the plural appears in Exodus 12:41 where it refers to the ranks of Israelites as they left Egypt.

The word *saba* generally used for *army* also commonly refers to angelic hosts. More than 250 times in the Old Testament God is known as the Lord of hosts—or as *The Message* put it, "God of the angel armies." Howard favors this latter view:

In this passage, the likelihood is that it was Yahweh's heavenly army, placed to fight on Israel's behalf. There is no indication that the man Joshua met was taking personal command of Israel's army, displacing Joshua, and the language of v. 15 (concerning holy ground) strongly suggests that this is a divine being representing God and his host. Even the syntax of v. 14 highlights the commander: a literal translation of his response is 'No. For I, I am the commander of the army of the LORD.' The focus on himself points to a divine being with a divine mission (Howard, 158).

Since we have already hinted that this may be another Christophany—a literal representation of Jesus on earth in a preincarnate form—the view that "army of the Lord" refers to angelic forces takes on even greater possibility.

VII. TEACHING OUTLINE

A. INTRODUCTION

1. Lead Story: A Tailor-Made People
2. Context: Between the setting up of the crossing memorial and the actual battle for Jericho, three more steps of preparation were necessary.
3. Transition: Chapter 4 begins with *when* and chapter 6 begins with *now*, but chapter 5 begins with *now when*. We find no great geographical transition as we did from chapter 3 to 4 but rather a pause for spiritual preparation in order to face the battle ahead.

B. COMMENTARY

1. Ancient Rite (5:1–3)
2. Accountable People (5:4–9)
3. Alternate Diet (5:10–12)
4. Angelic Commander (5:13–15)

C. CONCLUSION: "TO GOD BE THE GLORY"

VIII. ISSUES FOR DISCUSSION

1. In addition to baptism, what are some other modern parallels to circumcision?
2. Is circumcision a practice that Christians should follow today?
3. What is the correlation between the Old Testament Passover and our modern celebration of Easter?

Joshua 6

On the Jericho Road

I. **INTRODUCTION**
Mission Possible

II. **COMMENTARY**
A verse-by-verse explanation of the chapter.

III. **CONCLUSION**
"Battle Hymn of the Republic"

An overview of the principles and applications from the chapter.

IV. **LIFE APPLICATION**
Perfect Melody

Melding the chapter to life.

V. **PRAYER**
Tying the chapter to life with God.

VI. **DEEPER DISCOVERIES**
Historical, geographical, and grammatical enrichment of the commentary.

VII. **TEACHING OUTLINE**
Suggested step-by-step group study of the chapter.

VIII. **ISSUES FOR DISCUSSION**
Zeroing the chapter in on daily life.

"*If* you pray in a time of victory,

you will never have to plead in a time of defeat."

Alan Redpath

Joshua 6

IN A NUTSHELL

The battle for Jericho was really a spiritual battle and would be won by faith in God's power and grace. The plan, the timing, and the results were part of God's meticulous design.

On the Jericho Road

I. INTRODUCTION

Mission Possible

*T*hose who have had experience in business or in nonprofit organizations of one kind or another, or even perhaps in the church, understand the importance of mission. Too many mission statements read like platitudes—they either say everything or they say nothing. Or perhaps they are written in such a boring manner that no one can get excited about what they say. We read a lot about "high quality" and "excellence" and in church or mission board statements about "fulfilling the Great Commission." But usually mission statements are weak and in some cases, nonexistent.

In an article in *University Business* (July/August 2001), Gerald H. B. Ross offered four tests of a mission statement, the first of which is *the breath test*. Can you state your mission in one breath? That's how brief it should be, how specific and terse. Ross argues that if you can't state it in one breath no one will ever remember it. The second is *the motherhood test*. If your mission statement is so agreeable that no intelligent person could argue the contrary, it raises some questions about the distinctiveness of the statement and whether it really describes your organization. For example, if you are a Christian school that claims to produce "high-quality students," it is highly unlikely that you would find another mission statement from a school that wished to produce low-quality students.

Ross's third test is *the substitution test*. This is similar to the last one except it simply says, "If your mission statement would work just as well for you competitor as it does for you, it doesn't say anything about your institution" (Ross, 31). And finally, *the would-it-get-you-out-of-bed-in-the-morning test*. This has to do with the excitement, the drive, the vision, and the enthusiasm of the statement.

Joshua 6 does not contain a mission statement as such, but it clearly describes a mission and a strategy for fulfilling that mission. And it passes every test, particularly the last one. The Israelites were more than happy to get out of bed on this day for which they had waited so long. And even without a specific mission statement, they understood the mission—to conquer Jericho and make it their first foothold in the promised land.

Robert Moffat was a missionary to Bechuanaland, but all his work had netted few converts. In those days mail to and from his homeland of Scotland would take six months. One year his church wrote inquiring about what they could send him as a Christmas present. Although he didn't have a single convert, Moffat asked for communion supplies. He gave a shout of victory before there was a crack in the wall. By Christmas, there were Christians who joined him in putting that gift to use.

What is your communion service? What is your Jericho wall? Are you willing to step out to tear it down by faith in God's presence and God's promise? Are you willing to tackle the mission, to obey him daily until he brings down the wall?

II. COMMENTARY

On the Jericho Road

> **MAIN IDEA:** *The attack on Jericho's walls required prayer and faith. It involved obeying God and depending on him to fight for Israel. It meant they must step out in faith even before they saw any cracks in the walls or any visible signs of victory.*

A Strange Battle Plan (6:1–14)

> **SUPPORTING IDEA:** *The delay in victory was designed to allow God to overcome the Israelites as well as the Canaanites.*

6:1–5. What if preachers were more like heavyweight boxers? "I'm going to pound this sermon into you and have you feeling convicted by the second point. I dare you to sit there and listen to me. You'd better watch out because I'm starting now and soon heads are going to roll. I'll pound this pulpit until the wood splinters!"

I confess to having heard that kind of preaching, but I hope I've never done it. That is certainly not what God accomplished at Jericho. Seven days of trumpets and marching. Was he posturing? Trying to intimidate the Canaanites? Working up his power? Why did God choose this military strategy for the first battle in the promised land?

We all know God could have spoken the word and Jericho would have vaporized. The real battle with Jericho was not with the Canaanites but with the Israelites, not with the wall of a city but with human hearts.

The first verse of the chapter has a rather ominous sound to it. The Canaanites were afraid and were hoping their walls would protect them. But the Israelites had to wonder too. This place was shut up tight. How could they ever hope to take Jericho?

Not a big city but certainly a strong fortress, Jericho represented the necessary first step for Israel's conquest of the land. By taking Jericho and Ai the Israelites would control the central ridge from which they could hold the high ground to attack both north and south. We'll deal with the seven priests and seven days in "Deeper Discoveries." Here let's notice that the divine commander had promised supernatural destruction of Jericho, so conventional weapons were unnecessary. Furthermore, the execution of this command in absolute silence except for the trumpets could not but produce ridicule among the enemy and would certainly stretch the discipline of humiliation for the Israelites. In some ways these six days demonstrated as great a faith as we have seen this far in the history of Israel.

In the future Israel would fight most of their battles in conventional fashion, but this battle would be different. No battering rams, siege ramps, or scaling ladders. No bows, arrows, or spears. God gave specific instructions to Joshua that were to be obeyed to the letter—marching, trumpets, priests, ark, and a loud shout—along with the promise of God. The promise of verse 2—**I have delivered Jericho into your hands**—is a prophetic perfect tense verb, a future event as good as accomplished because God said it would happen. Although Joshua had been given the whole plan, it seems he gave instructions to Israel only one day at a time—a great test of national faith.

And these were no ordinary trumpets but rather jubilee trumpets, according to the Hebrew text used in connection with Israel's feasts to proclaim the presence of God (Num. 10:10). It may be worth remembering that trumpets appear again in connection with the Second Coming of Christ. Throughout this six-day exercise, Israel incarnated Psalm 108:12–13: "Give us aid against the enemy, for the help of man is worthless. With God we will gain the victory, and he will trample down our enemies."

This was not the first time Israel waited seven days for God to do something. Moses stayed on Mount Sinai for seven days before God spoke to him (Exod. 24:16). Later in their history the armies of Syria and Israel stood against each other for seven days before engaging in battle (1 Kgs. 20:29). Presumably long before this date at Jericho, Job's friends sat with him seven days before they began to speak (Job 2:11–13).

Sometimes we think the entire nation marched around the city, but that task fell only to armed men. The women, children, and livestock remained in the camp at Gilgal.

From these verses we assume the priests blew the trumpets continuously on the march around the city, but at the **long blast** all the marchers gave a loud shout on the seventh day. Again, it is unlikely the people knew this plan in advance. The end result described in verse 5 is rather dramatic. Madvig says, "This passage is telling us that from their positions around the city, the Israelites were able to go directly in—though not necessarily in a perfectly straight line—so that the city would be attacked in every corridor at the same time" (Madvig, 278).

6:6–14. A clear strategy. First an armed guard marching ahead of the priests, then seven priests with seven trumpets, then the ark and the rear guard following the ark. Trumpets playing all the time but no speaking whatsoever. What was the purpose of all this? Clearly to test Israel's faith and to show that the battle was in God's hands. God sent a message to his people. These ram's horns called them to worship, not to war, and the ark in the middle of all the activity indicated God's presence. This became God's battle in every way. And remember, the walls didn't crack a little more each day to give them encouragement. Even on day seven after seven times around, nothing had yet happened. They seemed no closer to bringing down those walls than when they started. The second day they did the same thing, and the text sums up the rest of the first six days by a simple sentence: **They did this for six days** (v. 14).

Every day they received their instructions; every day God tested their faith. Marching again? In silence except for the seven trumpets? What will this prove? What's Joshua waiting for? What if they come over the walls and attack us? The whole scene has an ominous mystery about it. The text does not tell us whether the activity threw greater fear into the inhabitants of Jericho or whether they relaxed their defenses and went back to business as usual. In any case, it didn't make any difference—the outcome had been pre-determined.

They had to march by faith, play trumpets by faith, walk out each day by faith, and then eventually shout a victory cry by faith. Hebrews 11:30 tells us, "By faith the walls of Jericho fell, after the people had marched around them for seven days." The first battle in the promised land was a battle for faith.

We all have Jericho walls that stand in the way of our spiritual victory. Anger, bitterness, lust, fear, unforgiveness, selfishness, pride, materialism, and indifference, to name a few. Paul reminds us in 2 Corinthians 10:3–4: "For though we live in the world, we do not wage war as the world does. The weapons we fight with are not the weapons of the world. On the contrary, they have divine power to demolish strongholds."

An unknown poet once wrote,

> Compass the frowning wall
> With silent prayer; then raise—before the ramparts fall—
> The victor's song of praise.
> It shall be done! Faith rests assured;
> Challenge your mountain in the Lord!

B Strategic Battle Timing (6:15–21)

SUPPORTING IDEA: *In God's battles all the spoils of war belong to him. This principle of firstfruits reminded Israel (and should remind us) that all the promised land belonged to him and he gave it to them as stewards.*

6:15–16. The battle plan changed for the seventh day as the Israelite warriors marched around Jericho seven times. This time when the trumpet blast sounded they were to **Shout!** Campbell embellishes the text realistically:

> And what a shout that was, as the Israelites gave release to their repressed emotions and stifled voices. It was a shout that reverberated through the hills around, startling the wild creatures in their dens and terrorizing the dwellers of Jericho in their homes. At that moment when the air was rent, the wall of Jericho, obeying the summons of God, toppled into ruin (Campbell, 53).

What was this city like? Just a six-hour hike on foot from Jerusalem, Jericho loomed like a tropical paradise, three thousand feet lower in altitude at eight hundred feet below sea level. Summer is hot, and the winter months are warm and pleasant, but the battle took place in the spring. Not the largest city in Canaan, Jericho was located strategically—hence attacked first. It was already an ancient city by the time Joshua arrived, well fortified with walls possibly twenty feet thick and over twenty-five feet high. From the top of these walls military guards could see for miles. Against its natural enemies in the Dead Sea plain, Jericho seemed a safe refuge. Against the supernatural power of God, it had no chance.

6:17–19. Here we encounter a new concept and a key word that appears three times in our passage—**devoted** (see "Deeper Discoveries"). In the same breath that we talk about God's mercy, we also address judgment. When the hammer fell, it fell hard on Jericho. The city was burned, all living things were killed, and all articles of gold, silver, bronze, and iron were **devoted** to the Lord and put into his treasury. The Israelites could not keep anything for themselves. Why?

Two reasons surface. First, God told Israel to wipe out the unrepentant Canaanites here and elsewhere in the promised land because Israel needed to be pure and separate from their pagan religion. The corrupting influence of Canaanite religion with its prostitution and infant sacrifice would make pure faith and worship to Yahweh very difficult. But the principle of firstfruits also surfaces here. God gave the victory; God received the spoils. What an important lesson for us. Everything God gives us belongs to him. Anything we have we hold in trust for him. We are stewards of his possessions and money. Our time and talents and all we have must be given over to God for his use.

We might also ask how long it took the Israelites to walk around the city. Archeology indicates approximately a nine-acre mound, so a person could easily walk around it in fifteen or twenty minutes. The simplicity accentuates the essential faith of the first six days. The Hebrew word *herem* (**devoted**) means something separated or banned from ordinary use. In Leviticus 27:21 it was a field and in Numbers 18:13 the firstfruits. The actual practice of *herem* was important but not nearly as important as its theological meaning. God wanted Israel to be a separated people, set apart from the evil Canaanites. He made clear that this was not possible if they began to assimilate Canaanite culture into their own nation and religion. Once again, this is a great lesson about worldliness in our day.

No new warning here. Deuteronomy 20:16–18 says:

> However, in the cities of the nations the LORD your God is giving you as an inheritance, do not leave alive anything that breathes. Completely destroy them—the Hittites, Amorites, Canaanites, Perizzites, Hivites and Jebusites—as the LORD your God has commanded you. Otherwise, they will teach you to follow all the detestable things they do in worshiping their gods, and you will sin against the LORD your God.

That's the warning; Joshua 6:18 offers the threat: **Otherwise you will make the camp of Israel liable to destruction and bring trouble on it**.

Rahab, of course, was the exception for reasons we have already seen. Furthermore, in keeping with the promise of the two spies, **all who are with her in her house shall be spared**. The **treasury** of verse 19 can hardly refer to some specific building or place of worship for a people on the move in a strange land. Obviously, it means that everything taken should be set aside for the worship of God and not used as part of the general fund.

6:20–21. Here we have a terse and compelling statement of how the battle took place, picking up the story line from verse 16. Why not a more detailed account of this slaughter? Because that is not the point. Any emphasis on what the warriors of Israel accomplished in Jericho would detract from the fact that Jericho was God's gift to the nation and this victory was not achieved by the efforts of Joshua's army.

Redpath observes:

> God forgive us that we are attempting today to fight spiritual enemies by carnal means. It cannot be done. May he forgive us when we seem to think that by planning, publicity, advertising, campaigning, and working we will attain something, whereas, in point of fact, we achieve nothing. Have we not understood that the weapons of our warfare are not carnal? (Redpath, 97).

Specific Battle Results (6:22–27)

SUPPORTING IDEA: *In the midst of a story of judgment and destruction and death, we have a shining example of mercy and salvation and life. Not only was Rahab's life spared; she also gained a whole new identity among the Israelites.*

6:22–23. We have already studied the amazing response of Rahab in chapter 2, so we know why she was spared. Unlike the rest of the Canaanites in Jericho, she took what she knew about the Israelites and their God and turned it into faith. Because she and her family trusted God, trusted the spies, and stayed in her house with the red cord, the miracle of the falling wall got even better because one part of that wall did not fall—the part with the scarlet cord. Rahab experienced God's mercy, became a part of God's chosen nation, and became a part of the lineage of Christ.

What a beautiful picture of what God does for us as well. When we come to him in faith, he saves us from the judgment all around us, plucks us from the crashing walls, and places us into his chosen family. Surely it must have been difficult for Rahab to watch her city being burned even though she and her family remained safe. It was all she had known, and now it would be left behind. Sometimes we have trouble letting go of our sin and past life. But God wants us to move forward and take up a new life that he provides as he did for Rahab. They had to be placed **outside the camp of Israel** for a period of cleansing before they could join the assembly of the Israelites.

6:24–25. The Israelites obeyed God's will to the letter as **they burned the whole city and everything in it** but saved the precious items for the treasury of the Lord. Our narrator appends an interesting phrase to the end of verse 25 when he says about Rahab that **she lives among the Israelites to this day.** Howard points out:

> At first glance, this last statement would suggest that the Book of Joshua was written within a few years after the events described in the book, and that very well may have been the case. However, the reference to "Rahab" living among the Israelites "to this day" could have referred to her *descendents*, in the same way that the reference to "David" in Hos. 3:5 indicates David's descendents rather than David himself (Howard, 176).

6:26–27. Not only was Jericho destroyed; it was **cursed before the LORD.** We will look at this curse in greater detail in "Deeper Discoveries," but the point here is that the city of Jericho would be an object lesson of God's great victory for Israel. Furthermore, God issued no curse against resettling the Jericho area, simply against rebuilding it. We see Jericho occupied again in Judges 3:13–14 and as well in 2 Samuel 10:5.

The chapter ends on a glorious note: **So the LORD was with Joshua, and his fame spread throughout the land.** Not because he fought the battle of Jericho as the old spiritual indicates but because God fought it. Not because he designed a great battle plan but because he followed God's strategy. Joshua and the Israelites learned some great lessons that day. God wanted their faith, and if they trusted him God would fight their battles. Consider the following poetic rendering by Joseph Parker that applies the battle of Jericho to our own spiritual lives.

> I'm more than conqueror through his blood,
>
> I rest beneath the shield of God,
>
> I've got a kingdom to obtain,
>
> I shall through him the victory gain.
>
> Before the battle lines are spread,
>
> Before the boasting foe is dead,
>
> I win the fight though not begun
>
> I'll trust, and shout, still marching on.
>
> I'll ask no more that I may see,
>
> His promise is enough for me,
>
> Though foes be strong and walls be high,
>
> I'll shout, he gives the victory.
>
> Why should I ask a sign from God?
>
> Can I not trust the precious blood?
>
> Strong in his Word, I meet the foe
>
> And, shouting, win without a blow.

MAIN IDEA REVIEW: *The attack on Jericho's walls required prayer and faith. It involved obeying God and depending on him to fight for Israel. It meant they must step out in faith even before they saw any cracks in the walls or any visible signs of victory.*

III. CONCLUSION

"Battle Hymn of the Republic"

In December 1861 the times were dark and bleak. Julia Ward Howe, a leading humanitarian and pioneer in women's suffrage, visited the federal battlefields on the Potomac. Somewhere along the way she heard the troops singing the old folk song, "John Brown's body lies a-mouldering in the grave" and wondered whether there might be more fitting words put to this fine tune. At the urging of her pastor, she wrote the words that have become popular as a patriotic hymn.

We have no idea what biblical text may have been in her mind at the time of the writing, but certainly the hymn connects with Psalm 2:6–7: "I have installed my King on Zion, my holy hill. I will proclaim the decree of the LORD: He said to me, 'You are my Son; today I have become your Father.'"

When singing this historic hymn, we should not think only of the Civil War, the abolition of slavery, or even the freedom of all people under God. The regular repetition of the last line lifts our eyes to God's rulership of his world, from the battle of Jericho to the present hour, and directs our attention to Christ's ultimate kingdom. Even in times of great difficulty we can know and sing, "Our God is marching on."

> In the beauty of the lilies Christ was born across the sea,
> With a glory in His bosom that transfigures you and me;
> As He died to make men holy, let us live to make men free,
> While God is marching on.

When you feel discouraged about national or international events, remember the words of the Lord in Psalm 2—and remember the battle of Jericho.

PRINCIPLES

- All the marching and horn-blowing in the world means nothing unless the Lord brings the victory.

- When we come to God in faith, he saves us from the judgment all around, plucks us from crashing walls, and places us into his chosen family.
- We often sorrow over loss even though we know it is for the best. But God wants us to leave the past behind and move on with him.

APPLICATIONS

- List victories God has won in your life.
- Take time to thank God for his faithfulness in what seemed impossible situations.
- Trust God for the challenges you face today.

IV. LIFE APPLICATION

Perfect Melody

When he was a young man, Andrew Lloyd Webber expressed interest in writing music for the theater. His father played a certain song for him, "Some Enchanted Evening," from *South Pacific* by Rodgers and Hammerstein. He told young Andrew, "This is a perfect melody. If you ever write anything like that you'll have really accomplished something." Later in his life after Webber became one of the most celebrated musical playwrights of all time his dad said, "You've equaled 'Some Enchanted Evening.'"

Some will argue whether "Some Enchanted Evening" is a perfect melody, but no one could challenge the productivity of Richard Rodgers, who is unrivaled by any other twentieth-century composer. He was more prolific than George Gershwin and more popular than Steven Sondheim, publishing more than nine hundred songs during a career that spanned more than five decades, a treasury of golden classics from America's musical stage. Along with Hammerstein he put together the score and lyrics for *Oklahoma!, Carousel, The King and I,* and *The Sound of Music.* Every year an estimated four thousand revivals of Rodgers's musicals are produced around the world.

It's hard to imagine what the priests' trumpets sounded like on those seven days, but for God's purposes they were indeed a "perfect melody." And we should consider the other audience of those seven days—the citizens of

Jericho. According to Rahab's report in chapter 2, these Canaanites had heard about the Red Sea and the battles Israel had won east of the Jordan, and they were afraid. But only Rahab had pleaded with the spies for mercy.

As Israel marched and played the rams' horns, what if the people of Jericho had run out on day seven and said, "Please don't destroy us; have mercy on us; we repent of our sins and we believe in your God!"? Would God have relented? He did for Rahab, and he did for Nineveh, and he would have for Sodom and Gomorrah. We have every reason to believe that he would have done the same for Jericho. We read in 2 Peter 3:9, "The Lord is not slow in keeping his promise, as some understand slowness. He is patient with you, not wanting anyone to perish, but everyone to come to repentance." So the "perfect melody" of seven horns for seven days accompanied by marching feet and a great shout could have been a call to repentance—never answered by the people of Jericho.

How many times has God marched around us waiting for us to repent and seek his forgiveness and mercy? He is patient with us, but eventually the seventh day comes. Teachers often give a "grace period" for finishing a paper or project, but eventually it has to be dealt with. God employed his marching tactic so Israel would have a chance for faith and perhaps so the Canaanites would have a chance for mercy.

V. PRAYER

Father, thank you for fighting our spiritual battles for us and equipping us for spiritual warfare. May we always leave the strategy and the outcome in your hands. Amen.

VI. DEEPER DISCOVERIES

A. The Number Seven (6:4)

The number seven, used no fewer than fourteen times in this chapter, is the number of divine perfection or completeness. We have seven priests, seven trumpets, seven days, and seven trips around the wall on the seventh day. All of this is important for our understanding of the text. The number seems to relate to the judgment; seven priests bearing seven trumpets for seven days indicates that the judgment on Jericho would be complete.

The seven trumpets take on a symbolic meaning in later writings and become connected with prophetic messages. In the Book of Revelation, John uses the seven trumpets to describe the events of the last days. The first six trumpet blasts are followed by disaster after disaster (Rev. 8:7–8,10,12; 9:1,13). And finally when the seventh trumpet sounds, the battle is over. So this was not just some idiosyncratic choice at Jericho but a foundational symbol for the role of sevens and trumpets in God's future plans.

Hamlin observes:

> The trumpets also heralded the new age of God's kingdom. The victory at Jericho was set in the first month of the year when the trumpets sounded to announce the joyful celebration of the new year (Num. 10:10). Even today, the central feature of the Jewish Rosh Hashanah (New Year) services is the sound of the ram's horn trumpet. The seven days and seven trumpets also recall the "seven times seven years" (Lev. 25:8) marking the jubilee year, when the trumpets would sound throughout the land to "proclaim liberty" (v. 10) and restoration of rights of the poor, the slave, and the landless (vv. 13–55) (Hamlin, 50).

B. Devoted (6:17–18,21)

The RSV and NIV use the word *devoted* while the KJV chooses *accursed* and TLB says *destroyed*. They all translate *harem* (noun) or *haram* (verb) which could mean any of those English words. In the Septuagint the word *anathema* appears, which is not uncommon in English vocabulary even today. The word describes anything irrevocably devoted to God because it was hostile to the divine mind by having been associated with another deity (Deut. 7:25; 20:17).

The point is that things that belong to paganism could not be brought over into godliness and used commonly, although they were not always destroyed (e.g., the gold the Israelites took from the Egyptians at the exodus). Certain possessions or captured objects were banned and dedicated to sacred use in the sanctuary as in the case of the "silver and gold and the articles of bronze and iron" in Jericho. In the case of the inhabitants, however, the city and all its contents were completely devoted to Yahweh, and nothing could be considered loot for the invading army. The idea of the firstfruits indicates that all Canaan lay ahead as a gift from God, and there was no need to keep anything from this first battle.

We should not get the idea of pillaging here but strictly destruction for theological purposes. It must have been difficult for these fighting men, owning nothing throughout all their lives up to this point, to pass up all the wonderful weapons, pottery, and clothing they found in Jericho—but that was God's command.

C. Curse on Jericho (6:26)

The curse on Jericho was a prohibition against refortifying, not against inhabiting the site (Josh. 18:21; Judg. 3:13; 2 Sam. 10:5). The actual fulfillment of the curse occurred during the reign of Ahab when Hiel rebuilt the walls at the cost of his two sons (1 Kgs. 16:34). Garstang notes:

> The charge was apparently observed. Excavations at Jericho have disclosed four chief periods in the occupation of the city. Three of these we have examined; they cover approximately three separate but fairly continuous periods of two hundred years each, from 2000 down to 1400 B.C. But after that date the city lay in ruins with no appreciable population for some five hundred years. The first part of the Early Iron Age (1200–900 B.C.) is not represented at all in the archeology of the site: the stratifications representing the second phase of the Iron Age (900 B.C.) are found in general directly over the destruction layers of the late Bronze Age (Garstang, 147).

There is some question about what exactly happened to Hiel's sons Abiram and Segub. The text of 1 Kings 16:34 may indicate that he offered them as blood sacrifices in building the foundations for the city, following ancient pagan custom. Whether they became sacrifices, died mysteriously, or were killed outright by God, Joshua's curse against Jericho was carried out.

VII. TEACHING OUTLINE

A. INTRODUCTION

1. Lead Story: Mission Possible
2. Context: Joshua 6 is the first real test of the conquest of Canaan. Chapters 1–5 described preparations, but now the actual battles begin.
3. Transition: The chapter begins in verse 1 with a parenthesis introduced to explain the immediate situation of Jericho to the reader and then follows the actual orders to Joshua. Nothing in chapter 6 prepares us for the opening of chapter 7: "But the Israelites acted unfaithfully."

B. COMMENTARY

1. Strange Battle Plan (6:1–14)
2. Strategic Battle Timing (6:15–21)
3. Specific Battle Results (6:22–27)

C. CONCLUSION: PERFECT MELODY

VIII. ISSUES FOR DISCUSSION

1. In what ways does God make us be patient and wait for his timing in winning spiritual battles in our lives and churches?
2. Name at least three ways Rahab is an example for us in this chapter.
3. What are some examples of "devoted things" in our lives and experiences?

Joshua 7

Trouble in the Valley

*"O*ur sense of sin is in proportion to our nearness to God."

Thomas D. Bernard

GEOGRAPHICAL PROFILE: AI

- Means heap of stones
- Still lies in ruins today
- Located about two miles southeast of Bethel

PERSONAL PROFILE: ACHAN

- Son of Carmi and grandson of Zimri
- Member of the tribe of Judah
- Mentioned again in 1 Chronicles 2:6–7

IN A NUTSHELL

*A*fter their great success at Jericho, the last thing Israel expected was defeat. But sin by a person always harms the corporate body. The story of Achan is a continuing reminder that sin's consequences go far beyond the person who sins.

Trouble in the Valley

I. INTRODUCTION

How's That Again?

*T*he following newspaper headlines were gathered by Bob Reid in Delhi, India.

> Lingerie Shipment Hijacked—Thief Gives Police the Slip
>
> Patient at Death's Door—Doctors Pull Him Through
>
> Juvenile Court to Try Shooting Defendant
>
> Killer Sentenced to Die for Second Time in Ten Years
>
> Twenty-Year Friendship Ends at the Altar
>
> Cold Wave Linked to Temperatures
>
> Police Discover Crack in Australia
>
> Collegians Are Turning to Vegetables
>
> Caribbean Islands Drift to the Left

People don't always say what they mean, even in newspapers and magazines. And we know fuzzy communication is a problem in all kinds of human relationships. But in chapter 6 we saw the clarity and specificity of the Lord's words to Israel through Joshua. Look again at verse 18: "But keep away from the devoted things, so that you will not bring about your own destruction by taking any of them. Otherwise you will make the camp of Israel liable to destruction and bring trouble on it."

Achan heard every word of this pronouncement. He knew exactly what God wanted, and he knew exactly what the result would be if he violated God's will. But that's what the sin nature does, both in Achan and in us. It turns us against God's clear and specific will, leads us to violate God's authoritative word, and then makes us wonder why we have to pay the penalty.

This is a chapter about failure, sin, and punishment. It describes an event that shocked an entire nation. Achan had no confusing headlines to offer as an excuse for his behavior.

II. COMMENTARY

Trouble in the Valley

MAIN IDEA: *Sin, even when hidden from everyone but the sinner, corrupts the life of God's people. Joshua and Israel had to learn the hard way that the behavior of Achan and people like him could not be tolerated.*

A Failure Brings Humility (7:1-9)

SUPPORTING IDEA: *Just as Israel exercised faith and expectation of victory at Jericho, they had to exercise repentance in evaluating their defeat at Ai.*

7:1-2. It started when the walls of Jericho fell. What a victory. And everything happened just the way God said it would. Israel was on a spiritual, emotional, and military high. Taking the promised land was going to be a piece of cake. A little marching, blowing trumpets, some shouting—and every city in Canaan would be theirs.

They knew it wouldn't always be that easy, but they were full of confidence. Next stop, Ai—a small fortress city only two miles from Jericho but in a strategic position for the conquest of the land. The people there had probably heard the crashing of the walls of Jericho and were already packing their bags. But just to be sure, Joshua sent out spies again.

As the chapter opens, our narrator tells us something Joshua does not know—God was angry with Israel because of the sin of Achan regarding **the devoted things**. The location of Ai is not certain, but the importance of this defeat raises a huge flag in the text about God's attitude toward sin. Even the first word of the chapter gives us a warning—**but**.

Campbell spells it out:

> Though one might wish to give credit to the discipline of Joshua's forces because only one of his soldiers gave in to temptation, even this one did not escape God's notice. God saw Achan's sin in taking some of the devoted things, and because of it God's wrath burned against the entire nation. He considered them collectively responsible and withheld his blessing until that matter was made

right. In fact it is apparent that Israel's history would have ended here if God's anger had not been turned away (Campbell, *BKC,* 343).

We see the same principle appearing in the New Testament where Paul warns that sin in the church can contaminate the whole assembly: "Don't you know that a little yeast works through the whole batch of dough?" (1 Cor. 5:6). How interesting that Beth Aven (house of wickedness) should be so close to Bethel (house of God). You will find more on the location of Ai in "Deeper Discoveries." Here we note only that this vast number of people faced a significant climb from Jericho to Ai, from eight hundred feet below sea level to twenty-five hundred feet above.

7:3–5. Suffering from overconfidence, displaying no evidence of prayer before the battle, and operating with unknown disobedience in the camp, the Israelites had no chance in this battle. They were riding a positive high from the experience at Jericho. After all, Ai was much smaller and could muster only a few thousand warriors. But the text is clear: **they were routed by the men of Ai, who killed about thirty-six of them**. They chased them downhill to the **stone quarries**. The result when the report came back to Joshua was that **the hearts of the people melted and became like water**.

What could have happened here? They figured Ai was no bigger than Lake Woebegon and probably didn't even have a Wal-Mart. No need to take up a large group; three thousand troops could easily handle this one. Joshua's spies were surely growing in their confidence, and he trusted them explicitly. He hadn't received any battle plans from God, but the job sounded easy nevertheless. Perhaps this was small enough that God would let them do it by themselves. But Joshua learned that self-assurance can be dangerous. We are most vulnerable to spiritual defeat right after a great spiritual victory.

The stone quarries to which the Israelites fled are identified as *shebarim,* meaning "broken places." Archeologists identify them with the next gorge north of the famous one at Michmash. The Israelites were ignominiously routed as they tried in panic to reach the descending trail on the south rim of the wadi.

Obviously the blame in this chapter goes to Achan, but Joshua seemed to make an error in judgment as well. He had at his disposal possibly as many as one-half million troops (Num. 26:51) including the forty thousand armed men from the two and one-half Transjordanian tribes (Josh. 4:13). They had no military excuse to treat this conquest lightly. The whole thing was a disaster. "The wordplay involving 'melting' here—recalling Rahab's and the spies' statements in 2:9,11,24—is obvious: because of Achan's sin, Israel had now become like the Canaanites, alone, without any true God to protect them and melting away with fear" (Howard, 190).

7:6–9. Failure brought humility not only to the nation but especially to their leader, who **tore his clothes and fell facedown to the ground before the ark of the LORD, remaining there till evening.** God's words to Joshua in chapter 1 about being courageous and unafraid seemed to have melted along with the hearts of the people. Days before his faith had been strong, but this defeat at Ai hit him so unexpectedly that he crashed. He lost his perspective; he forgot God's promises; and worst of all, he began to doubt God's plan. Joshua seemed more concerned about Israel's reputation as a nation (and his own reputation as a leader) than he was about God's reputation and name. Imagine. He lost only thirty-six men out of three thousand with thousands yet in reserve, but he was ready to turn tail and run back across the Jordan River.

Spiritual defeat can be devastating, even for God's chosen leaders. No matter how strong we may consider our faith, we are not immune to discouragement and doubt. Joshua's greatest fear seemed to be the revival of hope among the Canaanites and what they might do if they united all their forces against the invading Israelites. Redpath warns of the dangers which come in the flush of victory:

> There is no moment so perilous as when, for the first time in his Christian life, the man of God has experienced deliverance from sin. At such times we begin to take pride in ourselves, and to boast that our own arm has saved us. We so easily imagine that because we have achieved victory once, God has imparted to us some new strength which will see us through all our earthly journey (Redpath, 116).

It may be worth noting that the **elders of Israel** appear here for the first time. These may be the same as the officers mentioned earlier in the book or a different group of spiritual leaders appointed for this time of conquest.

While we want to lift up the heroic and faithful side of Joshua and the book certainly does that repeatedly, let us understand that failure brings such humiliation and despair that even a leader like Joshua can be driven to blaming God for what happened. Madvig says, "In self-piety Joshua charged God with capriciousness. Though Joshua could not be expected to know about Achan's sin, confidence in God's faithfulness should have made him look elsewhere for the reason for Israel's defeat" (Madvig, 285).

Ⓑ Failure Requires Accountability (7:10–18)

SUPPORTING IDEA: *God would not allow sin to go unchecked among his people. He demonstrated his omniscience and required the Israelites to exercise discipline.*

7:10–12. God wasted no time in responding to Joshua, and his language was less than gentle. The problem was not God's abandoning Israel as Joshua presumed but sin in the camp. How often we try to blame God for our own problems and then realize they have arisen from our own failures and sins.

Now God told Joshua what he doubtless would have told him if Joshua had prayed earnestly about how to approach Ai. The law of the **devoted things** had been violated (see Howard for a complete discussion of this terminology in Joshua). Stealing and lying had made an entire nation **liable to destruction**. God's threat was downright frightening: **I will not be with you anymore unless you destroy whatever among you is devoted to destruction**. The **covenant** had been violated. According to Howard,

> The word "covenant" refers to many different dealings of God with his people at different times, but here the specific reference appears to be to the portion of the covenant he had made with his people through Moses that referred to the annihilation of the Canaanites (Deut. 20:10–20) (Howard, 194).

7:13–15. Why didn't God just tell Joshua who was guilty so he could take care of Achan and get on with the war? Why this whole process involving tribes and clans and families? Part of the answer lies in the fact of the collective sin of the group. Just as God's blessing could be removed from a church in which one or two people are sinning, so God's blessing was removed from an entire nation in which one man was guilty. All Israel needed to search their hearts and learn from this tragedy. Not a person was allowed to stand by without feeling the fear of God's pointing figure—tribe by tribe, clan by clan, family by family. And the word **takes** could be rendered "catches." This was a manhunt pure and simple, and the whole nation watched the process.

Joshua also realized that perhaps God was giving the guilty an opportunity to repent. As the people consecrated themselves, or even as lots were being cast, the guilty could confess and plead for forgiveness. But no one knocked on Joshua's door that night or the next day.

7:16–18. Finally it came down to the tribe of Judah, the clan of the Zerahites, the family of Zimri, and Achan himself. All this was done by the sacred ritual of drawing lots, perhaps inscribed potsherds from a jar (1 Sam. 10:20–24; 14:41–45; Prov. 16:33). This was also the method used in apportioning the land among the tribes (Num. 26:55). This slow, deliberate, and agonizing process stands in contrast to the constant failures of human courts in which the guilty often go free and the innocent are detained, sometimes even executed. The family came forward **man by man, and Achan son of Carmi** was caught. God had demonstrated omniscience, and it was time for discipline.

Ⓒ Failure Demands Punishment (7:19–26)

SUPPORTING IDEA: *Through the common Old Testament system of lots, God singled out Achan and his family as those who were responsible for the defeat at Ai.*

7:19–21. As Achan stood before Joshua, God's leader knew he deserved a chance to explain. So he said, **Tell me what you have done.** Then Achan explained the sin in its progress—he **saw**; he **coveted**; and he **took.** In this amazing scene God received glory through the public confession of sin. We should not miss the marginal note in the middle of verse 19 which indicates that **give him the praise** could be translated "and confess to him." In this case they constituted one and the same. Achan's loot consisted of three items: **a beautiful robe from Babylonia, two hundred shekels of silver and a wedge of gold weighing fifty shekels.**

With Achan's confession, why didn't he receive forgiveness? Because there was no evidence of repentance and because the confession was forced, not volunteered (Ps. 32; 1 John 1:9). All during the long process of casting lots he had hardened his heart. Only when Joshua looked him straight in the face and commanded his confession did he admit his guilt. Madvig says, "His confession is not indicative of repentance because he would not have confessed if he had not been caught. True confession goes beyond the admission of what one has done. It includes recognition of guilt and true remorse" (Madvig, 288).

Amazingly, the same three verbs that we found above—*saw, coveted, took*—appear in the story of the fall in Genesis 3. What happened to Adam and Eve had now happened to Achan. But in the case of Adam and Eve, punishment fell only upon the guilty and their progeny; here an entire nation suffered. Schaeffer poignantly applies Achan's experience to our lives:

> While it is wonderful to have an infinite God, this means we must take his omniscience into account in our daily lives. There is nothing we do that God does not know. There is no night so dark, no coal mine so deep, no astronaut so far out in space that God does not know it. God knows every single thought, every single action. He knew when Achan first coveted, and he knew when he carried out his covetousness.

> Achan expressly said, "I coveted them." Sin always begins in the mind. As a work of art begins in the mind, and then is externalized, so also does sin. It is from the heart, Jesus said, that sin comes. The last commandment of the Ten Commandments is "do not covet" because coveting comes before every other sin. Before we break any of the other nine, we have coveted internally something either of God's or of another man's. Then we externalize the sin. Achan coveted; then he stole (Schaeffer, 110–11).

7:22–23. Joshua's messengers ran to uncover the loot and found it exactly where Achan said it was. But this sin would not remain hidden any more than its public effects had been hidden. They brought the stolen items to the center of the camp **and spread them out before the Lord.** Why all this fuss about a petty thief? Because an important principle was at stake here. Verse 15 talked about "a disgraceful thing in Israel," a phrase used elsewhere in the Old Testament only to describe violation of sexual ethics (Gen. 34:7; Deut. 22:21; 2 Sam. 13:12; Jer. 29:23). Hamlin says:

It seems clear that the Teacher wished to establish some connection with the sexual liberties practiced by the Canaanites. He is suggesting that the sin of Achan would certainly lead to participation in the fertility rights and the destruction of family life, and could thus be termed "a shameful thing in Israel" (Hamlin, 62).

7:24–26. We must not forget for a moment that everything in Jericho was under the ban; all the loot and plunder of the city belonged to God, not to Israel. They had been warned by God not to take anything, but Achan disobeyed God and ignored that warning because he wanted something for himself. He didn't trust God's provision, and he didn't believe God's warning. He coveted, stole, hid the plunder (proving he knew it was wrong), and then lied by his silence until exposed.

Rather than viewing his judgment harshly, we should see that God extended his grace by giving his people a warning in advance and by giving Achan time to come forward earlier. But he did not—and many others were stunned and even killed by the consequences of Achan's sin.

Now Joshua took everything to the Valley of Achor—Achan, the plunder, **his sons and daughters, his cattle, donkeys and sheep, his tent and all that he had** and destroyed them. The man who had brought **trouble** experienced disaster himself. A pile of rocks memorializing the horror of the execution as well as the defeat at Ai became the Valley of Disaster. Even those who agree that Achan should have been stoned for his crime wonder about the extent of the punishment to his sons and daughters. We can only conclude that since Achan buried the treasure in the tent, the family was in complicity with the theft. At any time any of them could have come forward during the casting of lots. But along with their father, the whole family remained silent while the silver, the gold, and the robe burned in their hearts even as it lay buried in their tent.

Howard links the pile of stones in the Valley of Achor to the stones piled up in chapter 4:

The connection between this pile of stones and the earlier set of twelve memorial stones that Joshua erected on the banks of the Jordan River is hard to ignore. The reason for each one was different, but both piles of stones remained in their place "until this day" (4:9; 7:26; see also 10:27). The first set was specifically to be a reminder to Israel of God's presence with them (see 4:7). The pile of stones over Achan is not infused with the same meaning, but the very fact that it remained "until this day" shows us that it was a reminder to Israel of the story of Achan and the consequences of sin (Howard, 199).

The place where Achan was killed and buried is so significant as the valley of trouble that in 1 Chronicles 2:6–7 Achan's name appears as Achar—the man and his doom blend into one down through the years of Israel's history.

> **MAIN IDEA REVIEW:** *Sin, even when hidden from everyone but the sinner, corrupts the life of God's people. Joshua and Israel had to learn the hard way that the behavior of Achan and people like him could not be tolerated.*

III. CONCLUSION

Hidden Costs

No one, certainly not Achan, had any idea of the ultimate cost of his sin. He probably thought a little gold here and a little silver there could hardly make any difference, since the whole land of Canaan would eventually yield up its riches to the conquering army. There must have been loot lying everywhere around Jericho during and after the battle; certainly God did not need it all.

It reminds us of the hidden costs of government and how little we know about the way Washington spends money. For example, the federal budget for 2003 is more than two trillion dollars, an incomprehensible number so big that even mathematicians don't use the word. Here is what one trillion looks like: 1,000,000,000,000.

No person reading this has lived a trillion seconds. In fact, this country has not existed for a trillion seconds. Western civilization has not been around for a trillion seconds. One trillion seconds is approximately 31,688 years ago.

If we stacked the 2003 budget in dollar bills, the pile would stretch nearly 144,419 miles, two-thirds of the distance to the moon or more than five laps around the earth at the equator.

Hidden costs. Pork-barrel dollars going here and there completely unknown to the people who pay their taxes unless Tom Brokaw happens to mention it on his "Fleecing of America" segment some night. Imagine how many churches try to seek God's blessing and move forward while hidden costs hamper their spiritual and numerical growth. Imagine how many congregations have an Achan in the camp with some sin buried deep in his tent, some Babylonian robe stashed in the depths of her closet. This chapter deals with sin, punishment, failure, and how the omniscient God knows about all of it. I cannot fathom a trillion dollars, nor could I ever spend it. But I know that God knows every dime, just as he knows my every thought and holds me accountable for my violation of his Word and his will.

PRINCIPLES

- Nothing done privately escapes the vision of an all-seeing God.
- Outward defeat brings inner turmoil, and a life of unrest brings a heart of disquiet.
- We can never minimize the truth, and we can never minimize sin; in many cases the sin of one becomes the sin of all.

APPLICATIONS

- Ask God's Spirit to examine your heart in light of this chapter from God's Word.
- Don't make it necessary for some legitimate official to confront you with sin; initiate repentance and restitution on your own.
- Trust God's promise that if we confess our sins, he is faithful to forgive our sin and cleanse us from all unrighteousness.

IV. LIFE APPLICATION

A Very Personal Surgery

Chuck Swindoll tells the story of Dr. Evan O'Neill Kane, the chief surgeon of Kane Summit Hospital in New York City. Practicing his specialty for thirty-seven years, Kane became convinced that general anesthesia was too risky and local anesthesia could bypass some of the problems he had seen in his practice arising from general anesthesia.

He wanted to prove his theories, but he couldn't find a patient willing to go under the knife with eyes wide open. Everybody he talked to was afraid of waking up during the surgery, feeling the pain and the sharp end of that probing scalpel.

Kane had performed appendectomies thousands of times, so he decided on that particular procedure when he found a subject. The patient was prepped and brought into the operating room and the local anesthesia was administered to the area as the surgery got underway. The surgeon came to the right side of the abdomen, made a cut across the narrow section, and went in. He tied off the blood vessels, found the appendix, excised it, and finished with a neat but simple work of suturing the incision.

Actually the patient felt very little discomfort and was up and about the next afternoon. This whole story is quite remarkable since it happened in 1921 when people who had appendectomies often stayed in the hospital for a week. The medical world considered it a milestone. But it was also a milestone in courage because the patient and the doctor were one and the same—Dr. Kane had operated on himself.

Oh, if Achan had only done the same thing. True, he should not have taken the plunder in the first place. But once the process began and the defeat at Ai had people on their knees, it was time to operate on himself whatever the danger, whatever the pain.

V. PRAYER

Father, forgive us our sins. We admit that we fail you frequently and too often try to hide the failures. We know that you see us and know us, and we ask

that you will make us holy people who avoid sin if possible and confess it when-
ever we stumble. Amen.

VI. DEEPER DISCOVERIES

A. Breach of Trust (7:1)

As our chapter begins, we learn that the Israelites literally "committed a breach of faith in regard to the devoted portion." This was a crime against the covenant law, a transgression against the *herem* on Jericho. Gridlestone says of this type of sin:

> The word *ma'al* probably points to the unfaithfulness and treach-
> ery of sin, and represents wrong-doing as a breach of trust, whether
> between man and man or between man and God. It is rendered tres-
> pass about thirty times, transgression fifteen times, and falsehood in
> Job 21:34. . . . In Josh. 7.1, 22.20, it is used of Achan's sin (Gridle-
> stone, 82).

We will see this sin again in Joshua 22 when we read about the building of the altar on the eastern side of the Jordan River, and the Old Testament also applies it to Uzziah (2 Chr. 26:18), Ahaz (2 Chr. 28:22), and Manasseh (2 Chr. 33:19). It describes the people who married heathen wives in Ezra 9:2 and Nehemiah 13:27. Finally it is found in Proverbs 16:10: "The lips of a king speak as an oracle, and his mouth should not betray justice." In every case God takes it very seriously, primarily it would seem because the viola-tors were persons of privilege and authority. It was also true of the nation of Israel, especially after the victory at Jericho. God's people were on their way toward a clean sweep of Canaan when a breach of trust got in the way.

In its broadest sense, sin can be identified as lawlessness and the ulti-mate "man of sin" is called the lawless one. After analyzing all the Greek and Hebrew words for sin, Ryrie concludes:

> Sin may properly be defined by using all these descriptive words
> for its various forms as recorded in the Old and New Testaments.
> Such a definition would be accurate though lengthy. Indeed, it might

be a good idea to define it thus: sin is missing the mark, badness, rebellion, iniquity, going astray, wickedness, wandering, ungodliness, lying, lawlessness, transgression, ignorance, and a falling away (Ryrie, 212).

B. Location of Ai (7:2)

French excavations in the 1930s at et-Tell, the site usually identified with Ai, revealed a gap of some eight hundred years in its occupation. Many believe that the evidence from et-Tell better fits Beth Aven (house of idolatry), because pagan temples stood on its summit in the third millennium. Hosea applied the name Beth Aven to nearby Bethel (4:15; 5:8; 10:5). Archeologists believe that the scattered ruins of Ai may lie under the present village of Deir Dibwan just southeast of et-Tell.

The word *Ai* means "the ruins" since in Hebrew it is always accompanied by the definite article. Possibly this was not even the name of the city, since a term like that could apply to any ruins. The reference that it lay near Bethel and Beth Aven helps place the site with greater specificity. Campbell claims:

> The geography of the area fits perfectly with the details found in Joshua 8. So perhaps the king of Ai was the leader of forces mobilizing for the battle which occurred at a place that was *already* a ruin rather than a city. Some archeologists, however, are looking for alternative locations of Ai and excavations are underway at the nearby site of Khirbet Nisya (Campbell, *BKC*, 343).

VII. TEACHING OUTLINE

A. INTRODUCTION

1. Lead Story: How's That Again?
2. Context: No sooner has chapter 6 ended with a curse against the rebuilding of Jericho, then chapter 7 opens with a curse against Israel brought about by the sin of Achan. No sooner does chapter 6 end with Joshua's fame spreading "throughout the land" then chapter 7 opens with Joshua "facedown to the ground before the ark."

The text clearly portrays the distinction between the chapters and the stark contrast between the narratives of victory and utter defeat.

3. Transition: The Ai story does not end with chapter 7. With Achan buried beneath his pile of rocks, the nation will once again attack Ai and this time will be victorious, a record which awaits in chapter 8.

B. COMMENTARY

1. Failure Brings Humility (7:1–9)
2. Failure Requires Accountability (7:10–18)
3. Failure Demands Punishment (7:19–26)

C. CONCLUSION: A VERY PERSONAL SURGERY

VIII. ISSUES FOR DISCUSSION

1. In Joshua 7:7–9 Joshua asks three questions. How did God answer Joshua's questions?
2. What examples of sin as seeing, coveting, and taking might we identify in our modern world?
3. What is repentance, and how does this word relate to confession?

Joshua 8

Snatching Victory from Defeat

GEOGRAPHICAL PROFILE: MOUNT EBAL AND MOUNT GERIZIM

- Stand like twin mountains some three thousand feet above the Samaritan plain
- Site of the renewal of Israel's covenant under Joshua
- In New Testament times, Mount Gerizim served as the center of Samaritan worship (John 4)

IN A NUTSHELL

After a crushing defeat at Ai, Joshua regrouped, having dealt with Achan's sin, and organized a second and successful attack according to God's plan and pattern.

Snatching Victory
from Defeat

I. INTRODUCTION

People Can Change

*W*hen Joey Barrow was a teenager, he was labeled the class sissy. While other kids played sports, Joey took violin lessons. One day Joey had all the teasing he could handle, so he hit one kid over the head with his violin. Joey's friend Thurston McKinney also had enough and began taking Joey to the gym with him. Joey would always bring his violin and pay fifty cents to put it in a locker while the boys boxed. Thurston was already a Detroit Golden Gloves champion, but Joey flattened him in their first match.

By the time he was eighteen, Joey had long since abandoned the violin and now spent every day at the gym. When he turned twenty-three years old, he was the heavyweight champion of the world. Mamma Barrow never learned about all this until some years later because Joey had changed his name so she wouldn't know the newspapers were talking about her son when they applauded Joe Louis, "the brown bomber." People can change. Leaders are not born; they are made. Leadership is learned behavior.

As the Book of Joshua opened, we had an image of a somewhat timid Joshua called to courage by the Lord. Then we saw a victorious and confident Joshua after Jericho, and a broken and discouraged Joshua in chapter 7. Now the message of chapter 1 returns—"do not be afraid; do not be discouraged"—and Joshua will go up to Ai once again.

A friend of mine recently completed the manuscript of a new book in which he develops the idea of what he calls "positional thinking," the idea of living in the light of all that Christ means to us and in us, a biblical alternative to the more humanistic idea of "positive thinking." Excellence is possible in leadership because the Excellent One lives in us and makes it possible. First Peter 2:9 tells us, "But you are a chosen people, a royal priesthood, a holy nation, a people belonging to God, that you may declare the praises of him who called you out of darkness into his wonderful light."

In New Testament times that description applied to believers in Jesus Christ, the body of Christ, the church. In Old Testament times it applied to the people who were to march again on Ai and this time in God's power to defeat it.

II. COMMENTARY

Snatching Victory from Defeat

> **MAIN IDEA:** *Israel should have learned by now that when they get things right with God, he often offers second chances. Here he gives them an additional opportunity to do things his way. When Joshua conquered Ai, God told him he could keep the spoils of war. If only Achan had waited a few days, God would have given him all he wanted.*

A The Careful Plan (8:1–9)

> **SUPPORTING IDEA:** *Just as with Jericho, God's plan for the battle at Ai, executed in God's pattern and power, results in victory.*

8:1–3. Joshua's week did not end in the valley of trouble. Once Israel had purged the sin from the camp, God sent them back to Ai. This time they followed God's plan. Joshua sent out troops to set an ambush for Ai from behind and led the rest of the troops toward Ai. The plan was to run when attacked. The numbers seem somewhat confusing in this chapter, and Madvig attempts to set them straight. Using the ratio of fighting to nonfighting personnel from the Transjordanian tribes, he concludes:

> Using the same proportions the Twelve Tribes could have mustered an army of two hundred thousand to attack a city of twelve thousand counting both men and women. Does it seem reasonable to suppose that if Joshua had come against the city with a massive force of two hundred thousand men he would have been able to lure the inhabitants into attacking him? . . . [probably] the thirty thousand in v. 3 is the size of the whole army whereas the five thousand in v. 12 is the number of troops who were to lie in ambush. The rest of the army would have been held in reserve (Madvig, 290).

An ambush requires deceit, one of the tactics of warfare Joshua would see reinforced in chapter 9. This time God agreed to lead Joshua because the general was willing to listen to God's plan. It might be worth noting that some interpreters have suggested a different allocation of troops than Madvig proposed above. They observe that the word *eleph* translated "thousand" could also mean "officer." The troops in ambush would therefore be thirty selected chief warriors or officers carrying out a commando mission. We should not be troubled about these ideas, since in all of Joshua's battles the numbers are unimportant. God gave these victories, not the strategy or the strength of the troops.

8:4–7. As we noted in verses 1–3, the strategy of the spoils had been changed. Having purged the nation of Achan's sin, God now allowed people to keep plunder and livestock for themselves. Also there were no daytime marches around the city; this time the warriors were stationed at night. The main forces were located north of the city with the ambush force quite likely to the west. The people of Ai would charge out and chase the Israelites down the hill as they had done in chapter 7. This time, however, it was a trap. The key phrase of this section, indeed of the entire chapter, appears in the latter part of verse 7: **The Lord your God will give it into your hand**.

8:8–9. After the city had been captured and plundered, it was set on fire because this was what the Lord had commanded. The warriors went off to their places, **but Joshua spent that night with the people**.

> The ridge track, so helpful to the setting of the ambush, approached the west of Ai from the south. Clearly Joshua's further plan would be to gain the north side of the city from a different direction, and there to take up such a position that the first light of morning would disclose the hosts of Israel to the inhabitants. Secrecy was not so essential as their arrival at the appointed hour (Garstang, 157).

B The Clever Diversion (8:10–19)

SUPPORTING IDEA: *The nation of Israel learned a great lesson at Ai: Never underestimate the enemy and never be overconfident about the results. Here they commit all available resources to the battle—and win.*

8:10–13. Good news in verse 11: **The entire force . . . was with him.** The force of the army and the force of God make the scene quite dramatic. Ai was perched on the hill to the south. Israel set up camp on a ridge to the north **with the valley between them and the city.** The plan now turned into action. On a modern television drama, we would call this a "flashback." If we take the text at face value, Joshua, located with the main force on the ridge to the north, went by himself into the valley at night, presumably to make further spiritual preparations for the battle, perhaps to pray on the battleground itself.

8:14–17. Surely the **this** of verse 14 does not refer to the appearance of Joshua in the valley, because that took place at night (though it seems the logical antecedent). The writer of Joshua intends to convey that Ai saw the full force of Israel on the ridge across the valley and all they could think of was the easy victory in the previous encounter.

The Arabah of this verse describes the great Rift Valley which includes Jericho and the Jordan River, so the Aiites clearly had the high ground. In verse 15, however, we read that Israel drifted back **toward the desert.** Howard notes:

> The same phrase is found again in a similar context, where a coalition of Israelites set an ambush for the Benjaminites at Gibeah; and when they turned on the Benjaminites, they fled by "the way of the wilderness." . . . The phrase occurs again only in Exod. 13:18, referring to the route the Israelites took out of Egypt through the desert (Howard, 206–7).

We are somewhat surprised to see our narrator drop the name **Bethel** into verse 17. Taking the text seriously, we can only assume that the inhabitants of Bethel joined Ai in this expected rout of Israel. These may very well have been sister cities (Bethel was an important Canaanite city in its own right), and perhaps the Bethelites considered an attack on Ai an attack on them as well.

8:18–19. As far as we know, Moses never held anything more dangerous than a rod (which in itself proved lethal enough). Joshua, however, was a genuine general who was quite accustomed to holding a javelin that now pointed toward Ai as a symbol of God's judgment. But God did not give this city to the javelin; he gave it into their **hand.** After Jericho and Ai, only one other city is mentioned as being burned—Hazor in chapter 11. This javelin (or perhaps small sword) did not finish its task just as a sign to the ambush commandos. It remained held aloft until Ai was completed defeated.

C The Complete Victory (8:20–29)

> **SUPPORTING IDEA:** *Sometimes God not only gives victory but blesses his people with material things after the battle. Unlike the Jericho experience, Israel had access to valuable spoils of war.*

8:20–23. Two signals form part of the strategy here. When the ambush force saw the javelin, they rushed in and burned the city. When the main force saw the smoke from the burning city, they turned around and attacked the people of Ai, catching them in a vise maneuver—no place to run, no place to hide. They kept the king of Ai apart because God had said in 8:2, "You shall do to Ai and its king as you did to Jericho and its king." No Geneva Convention rules here; everybody was put to the sword.

8:24–27. Three killing places appear in the narrative—**the fields** . . . **the desert** . . . and the **city.** David Howard makes an interesting observation regarding the body count: "This is the only battle in the book for which a numerical total is given for the dead, consistent with the detailed description of all parts of the battle" (Howard, 209). We can only assume that all the warriors from Bethel were slaughtered at the same time, although the text makes no mention of them. The word **destroyed** in verse 26 is the Hebrew term *herem,* which means "devoted to the Lord." So this time the people were "devoted," but the goods and plunder were freed up for the taking. Like a wise parent God expects exacting obedience to his commands even though they might not make sense to the children.

8:28–29. Ai became **a permanent heap of ruins.** This phrase represents the common Hebrew word *tel.* Howard tells us that ancient cities usually were built on high points of land near water supplies; and when a city was destroyed, the new city was built on the same site, atop the packed and settled debris from the former city. Thus, over time, high mounds arose, topped by the current city. Ai was not rebuilt, and it remained a heap of ruins. This word is found only at Deut. 13:16 [Hb. 17]; Josh. 8:28; 11:13; Jer. 30:18; 49:2; and it survives in such place names in the Bible as Tel Abib (Ezek. 3:15) or Tel Melah and Tel Harsha (Ezra 2:59) (Howard, 210).

The defeat of Ai ended with the ominous words, **they raised a large pile of rocks over it, which remains to this day.** Two piles of rocks. One a reminder of God's faithful provision in bringing Israel across the Jordan River on dry ground. And the other a reminder of God's holiness and the terrible consequences of sin. And in between, a third pile of rocks raised up over Achan's grave.

Throughout this series of studies in Joshua, we think often of John Yates's famous and familiar hymn "Faith Is the Victory." He makes such a practical application to our spiritual warfare in stanza 2:

> His banner over us is love, our sword the word of God;
> We tread the road the saints above with shouts of triumph trod.
> By faith they, like a whirlwind's breath,
> Swept on o'er every field;
> The faith by which they conquered death is still our shining shield.

D The Covenantal Worship (8:30–35)

SUPPORTING IDEA: *The battle for Canaan was more spiritual than military warfare in nature. And all spiritual victories must culminate in worship according to God's Word and will.*

8:30. Israel had just conquered Jericho and Ai. It seemed like a good military strategy to press ahead and hit the enemy while they were still surprised and fearful. But instead, Joshua took the Israelites on a thirty-mile side trip. On a journey that would have taken the people several days to cover, the Israelites marched north on a road that ran over the top of the mountains, arriving in Shechem between Mount Ebal and Mount Gerizim. They apparently encountered no resistance along the way.

This place was significant for the Jews. Here Abraham had built his first altar to God. Here Jacob had dug a well. Here Joseph had searched for his brothers. And many years later Jesus would speak to a Samaritan woman at this well near Shechem. The two mountains are really one and one-half miles apart at the top but only about five hundred yards apart at the bottom. The valley between them formed a natural amphitheater for this historical gathering of the Israelites.

The initial loss and then subsequent victory at Ai had been a wake-up call for Joshua and the Israelites. They now realized that taking the promised land would be a spiritual journey, not just a military campaign. So they took time once again to be reminded of something we must never forget—heeding God's word is more important than fighting God's battles. They made this side trip because the covenant was more important than the conquest.

And while the people had two piles of stones over Achan and over the pagan king of Ai to remind them of the consequences of sin, here between the mountains they would see two more kinds of stones to remind them of their covenant with God.

8:31. Notice that Joshua built the altar on Mount Ebal, the mountain of curses. Why might he have done that? Perhaps this sent an important message since the altar served as the place of sacrifice for sin. Mount Ebal served as a reminder of the punishment that would come if the Israelites disobeyed God. But in the very same breath God illustrated his grace—a way for the people to come back to him and find forgiveness even when they sinned. Through the altar, the blood of the sacrifice, they could be restored to fellowship with God even if they found themselves in the mountain of curses. *The Nelson Study Bible* observes, "The unfinished stones would have contrasted with the finished stones found in many Canaanite altars. This was a reminder that, even in such rituals as offering sacrifices, the Israelites were to be different or distinct from their neighbors" (368).

But we find a spiritual picture here as well. These stones were not to have any human mark on them. No human intervention. No human effort. The altar stones were God's creation, not man's invention. The way of salvation and forgiveness is God's work, not man's effort. How did Paul put it? "For it is by grace you have been saved, through faith—and this not from yourselves, it is the gift of God—not by works, so that no one can boast" (Eph. 2:8–9). Sometimes we try to cut and shape stones for our own altars. We try to make excuses for our sin or rationalize our behavior. We try to be good enough so God will accept us, and some people even bet their eternal lives on their own self-righteousness. But the Ebal altar, placed as it was on the mountain of curses, reminds us of the futility of that position.

The offerings themselves were crucial to the Israelites. They brought burnt offerings for the forgiveness of sins, but they also sacrificed fellowship offerings. Moses had said that these offerings would help them rejoice and enjoy the presence of their God: "Sacrifice fellowship offerings there, eating them and rejoicing in the presence of the LORD your God" (Deut. 27:7). This altar was a place for confession but a place for celebration as well.

8:32. We need to go back to Deuteronomy to see more specifically what Moses said to the Israelites about this ceremony. Joshua followed his instructions precisely:

> When you have crossed the Jordan into the land the LORD your God is giving you, set up some large stones and coat them with plaster. Write on them all the words of this law when you have crossed over to enter the land the LORD your God is giving you, a land flowing with milk and honey, just as the LORD, the God of your fathers, promised you. And when you have crossed the Jordan, set up these stones on Mount Ebal, as I command you today, and coat them with plaster (Deut. 27:2–4).

Remember that the Israelites did not carry Bibles around with them. You couldn't get *the living law* in large print, a reference edition, or even the Moses Study Bible. These stones provided a public display of God's Word for everyone to see. Joshua may have put the entire law or just a portion of the law on the stones, but nevertheless they served as posters and bulletin boards—reminders of God's covenant with Israel. We can only speculate how much of the Mosaic Law was inscribed on these stones, although many interpreters suggest Deuteronomy 5–26. Campbell says, "Archeologists have discovered similar inscribed pillars or stelae six to eight feet long in the Middle East. And the Behistun Inscription in Iran is three times the length of Deuteronomy" (Campbell, *BKC,* 347).

8:33–35. As the officials stood around the ark near the altar midway between the two mountains and as the tribes occupied the slopes (Deut. 27:11–26), Joshua had the law proclaimed to the nation. This was in the heart of Canaan. God intended to have his Word set up in the heart of the country to become the law of the land. Ebal and Gerizim served as a place for the renewal of covenant vows to Yahweh.

We can hardly imagine this traumatic scene. One million Israelites on one mountainside and another million on the other. As they faced each other, they would look across at Joshua and the Levites beside the ark in the middle valley. The Levites read the blessings and curses from the law, and the people responded with "amens." Everyone was involved in this antiphonal object lesson. Schaeffer says of this event:

> We see in the reading of the blessings and curses not only a continuity of the authority of the written, propositional Scriptures but also an emphasis on the fact that bare knowledge is not enough. It was not that the Pentateuch gave these people knowledge, and that was the end of it. This knowledge demanded action. When Joshua took up his leadership, he was told the same thing. . . . The normative standard was the law of God; it was not an existential experience (as is often emphasized in the twentieth century), not a non-propositional religious experience (as is said by almost all contemporary liberal theologians). Not at all. What was involved was a propositional, written statement (Schaeffer, 129).

All this was done with **aliens and citizens alike**. This provoked Madvig to say, "The religion of Israel at its best has always been a missionary religion. From the time of the Exodus, aliens who chose to live with Israel and worship her God were assimilated into the nation as, for example, Rahab and her family" (Madvig, 294).

Why this side trip? Why this delay in Israel's military campaign? Why this spiritual interruption? We know it certainly wasn't for God's benefit. He didn't need to be reminded about his covenant with Israel. The covenant was for the Israelites' benefit, and this time-out reminder called the people back to God.

A coach calls a time-out not so the players can remind him of the game plan but so he can remind them of their assignments and can make adjustments in their execution of the game plan. This diversion was for Israel's sake. God rehearsed the game plan and reminded them of what would cause them to win or lose.

> **MAIN IDEA REVIEW:** *Israel should have learned by now that when they get things right with God, he often offers second chances. Here he gives them an additional opportunity to do things his way. When Joshua conquered Ai, God told him he could keep the spoils of war. If only Achan had waited a few days, God would have given him all he wanted.*

III. CONCLUSION

"Guide Me, O Thou Great Jehovah"

He was born William Williams, the son of a wealthy Welsh farmer, on February 11, 1717. Williams wanted to be a doctor, but God challenged him to enter the ministry. The Church of England denied him ordination because of his evangelical views, so he became a popular preacher for the Calvinistic Methodist Church and traveled around Wales for forty-five years. Williams wrote over eight hundred hymns in Welsh and another one hundred in English. But "Guide Me, O Thou Great Jehovah" is the only one commonly known today.

This great hymn reminds us of Psalm 48:1,14: "Great is the LORD, and most worthy of praise. . . . For this God is our God for ever and ever; he will be our guide even to the end." What a wonderful message both hymn and Scripture text provide. The Heavenly Father cares for his people throughout their lives. God never leaves us and never forsakes us. He doesn't require us to wander or depend on our own judgment but serves as our guide "even to the end."

> When I tread the verge of Jordan, bid my anxious fears subside;
>
> Death of death and hell's destruction, land me safe on Canaan's side.
>
> Songs of praises, songs of praises
>
> I will ever give to Thee, I will ever give to Thee.

The people of the Lord have relied on his guidance from Israel in the desert to the cyberspace age of our time. We can count on it for the tasks of every day.

God's guidance over Israel in building the altar and writing the law reminds us of the way we come to the cross for confession but also for celebration regarding our relationship with the living Christ and for rejoicing over the forgiveness we have in him. Even the mount of curses could be turned into a place of joy through the sacrifice. Do you regularly give a sacrifice of praise? Do you offer up your thanksgiving to God for his salvation in your life? For rescuing you from the curse of sin? When you find yourself on the mount of curses, in disobedience, remember to come to the altar to find forgiveness and to find the joy of restored fellowship with God. Then you can sing with gusto and confidence, "Guide me, O Thou great Jehovah."

We don't have an altar on a mountain, but we do see the cross on the mountain of the curse—Golgotha. God's own Son became the final, perfect sacrifice for our sin. He provides the only way out of the curse of sin and into God's forgiveness and grace. When we find ourselves in disobedience, living on Mount Ebal, we must look for the altar—the cross—and find our way back to God.

> I must needs go home by the way of the cross
> There is no other way but this.
> I shall n'er catch sight of the gates of light
> If the way of the cross I miss.

PRINCIPLES

- God is faithful with his justice and faithful with his goodness.
- Recovery of lost ground is only the beginning of a new experience with the God who has redeemed us from our sins through Jesus Christ.
- The prescription for the sacrifice in this chapter is so specific, it reminds us that we must worship the Lord only on his terms.

APPLICATIONS

- When was the last time God graciously restored you from a failure?

- We must never dress up our altars with Christian words and pious prayers while forgetting to get to the point at which we admit our sinfulness and put it on the altar.

- Take time to reflect on the fact that it is by Jesus' sacrificial death that we are restored to right relationship with God. What response does that bring from you?

IV. LIFE APPLICATION

Weather Alert

We've all had the experience. We're watching TV and suddenly we hear a beeping sound and a band of words begins to scroll across the bottom of the screen. A weather alert! We stop conversation or whatever else we may have been doing and watch to see whether a storm or tornado may be approaching our area. Even more disconcerting, a newsperson comes on the screen to say, "We interrupt our programming to bring you this special news bulletin." That really causes us to sit up and pay attention. We know this must be important to interrupt the ball game or some other favorite show.

Sometimes in our lives, God interrupts our routine to tell us something important. Sometimes he breaks into our busy schedules and says, "Time-out! I have something I want you to learn or consider."

It happens too frequently to people my age. Too often we find ourselves at someone's bedside watching death claim another friend. God interrupts our activities to remind us about the uncertainty and brevity of life. In the eighth chapter of Joshua, we have finally seen the Israelites moving into their promised land. They win some battles and progress in the conquest. But at the end of chapter 8, God breaks in with a special "weather alert" to remind Israel of their covenant with him.

We all experience those Ebal and Gerizim moments. At such times we need to choose a mountain. Or maybe we need to go to the altar as a way to get from Mount Ebal to Mount Gerizim. God has made a way. He has prepared the stones for the altar, and he wants both fellowship and celebration with us.

V. PRAYER

Father, thank you for the second chance at Ai and for the glorious victory you brought about for Joshua and the people of Israel. But thank you even more for the altar and the Word at the mountains of the covenant. May we be your sacrificing people who always remember to live according to the will and Word of God. Amen.

VI. DEEPER DISCOVERIES

A. Burnt Offerings and Fellowship Offerings (8:31)

As we look at the ritual between Gerizim and Ebal, we see immediately that both altar and ark signified God's presence; but there was a difference. The ark went with the people and represented God's constant presence with them. The altar stood in the middle of the land as a witness marking the holy place. And the purpose of the sacrifice on the altar was not to appease an angry God. God's anger had turned away after the death of Achan (7:26). Here we see relationship, the maintenance of solidarity between God and his people.

The burnt offerings were those in which the animals were completely consumed (Exod. 29:18; Lev. 1:1–17). These exemplified the total self-giving of the congregation and their total dependence upon God to take away their sin. In the New Testament sense, we find it in Romans 12:1–2:

> Therefore, I urge you, brothers, in view of God's mercy, to offer your bodies as living sacrifices, holy and pleasing to God—this is your spiritual act of worship. Do not conform any longer to the pattern of this world, but be transformed by the renewing of your mind. Then you will be able to test and approve what God's will is—his good, pleasing and perfect will.

The fellowship offerings (peace offering) had a different purpose altogether. As Hamlin puts it:

The peace offering (literally, that which makes for wholeness or well-being) included a meal together. The fat pieces of the animal were burned on the altar to symbolize God's part in the meal, while the meal itself both symbolized and created the solidarity, or *shalom*, of the group. With this mutual support and the assurance of divine blessing, the meal was naturally a time of rejoicing (Deut. 27:7) (Hamlin, 70).

B. Public Reading of Scripture (8:34–35)

The law was read for the whole assembly of Israel. The word *assembly* in Hebrew (*kahal*) takes the New Testament word *ekklesia* that becomes the New Testament word for *church*. Some consider that this refers only to the male adults of the nation, but the context of Joshua 8 suggests differently. This public reading of Scripture, so sadly neglected in the modern church of the twenty-first century, forms a basic foundation throughout Scripture. Campbell reminds us, "The huge natural amphitheater which still exists there made it possible for the people to hear every word and with all sincerity Israel affirmed that the Law of the Lord was indeed to be the Law of the land" (Campbell, *BKC,* 347).

We encounter something similar in Nehemiah 9:1–3:

On the twenty-fourth day of the same month, the Israelites gathered together, fasting and wearing sackcloth and having dust on their heads. Those of Israelite descent had separated themselves from all foreigners. They stood in their places and confessed their sins and the wickedness of their fathers. They stood where they were and read from the Book of the Law of the LORD their God for a quarter of the day, and spent another quarter in confession and in worshiping the LORD their God.

Four hours of Bible reading. Quite a contrast to today's church in which four minutes would seem intolerable to some people.

I'll let Redpath offer the spiritual indictment:

The whole trouble with many Christians today is that they are only playing at being Christian. They have never really gone in for a holy, dynamic Christian life, because they are afraid to pay the price. I tremble in my own soul at the shock many will get when they face our Lord and discover that the beliefs they have cherished, the doctrines they have embraced, and the Bible they have said they believe, have landed them in hell because their beliefs have never become actions, and the Bible has never become practice, and the lives have never been made holy. The law at the foot of the mountain of judgment has to be fulfilled, not *by* us, thank heaven, but *in* us by the Holy Spirit (Redpath, 129).

VII. TEACHING OUTLINE

A. INTRODUCTION

1. Lead Story: People Can Change
2. Context: Joshua 8 is a continuation and conclusion of chapter 7. As our title indicates, this is the record of how God allowed Israel to snatch victory from the jaws of defeat.
3. Transition: I find it fascinating that chapters 5, 6, and 9 of Joshua begin with the word *now* and chapters 2 and 8 begin with the word *then*. It shows the continuity from chapter to chapter as the story of the conquest unfolds.

B. COMMENTARY

1. The Careful Plan (8:1–9)
2. The Clever Diversion (8:10–19)
3. The Complete Victory (8:20–29)
4. The Covenantal Worship (8:30–35)

C. CONCLUSION: WEATHER ALERT

VIII. ISSUES FOR DISCUSSION

1. In your own words, describe how Christians move from defeat to victory in spiritual warfare.

2. Consider the location of the altar in Canaan described in this chapter. Why do you suppose God directed it to be placed at Shechem?
3. Think about the Ebal and Gerizim experiences in your own life. How can you spend less time on Ebal and more time on Gerizim?

Joshua 9

The Grunge Gimmick

I. **INTRODUCTION**
The Gullible Public

II. **COMMENTARY**
A verse-by-verse explanation of the chapter.

III. **CONCLUSION**
News Flash: God Knows the Future

An overview of the principles and applications from the chapter.

IV. **LIFE APPLICATION**
Expect the Unexpected

Melding the chapter to life.

V. **PRAYER**
Tying the chapter to life with God.

VI. **DEEPER DISCOVERIES**
Historical, geographical, and grammatical enrichment of the commentary.

VII. **TEACHING OUTLINE**
Suggested step-by-step group study of the chapter.

VIII. **ISSUES FOR DISCUSSION**
Zeroing the chapter in on daily life.

"*I*t is hard to make your adversaries real people unless you recognize yourself in them—in which case, if you don't watch out, they cease to be adversaries."

F l a n n e r y   O ' C o n n e r

GEOGRAPHICAL PROFILE: GIBEON

- Located about six miles northwest of Jerusalem
- Commonly associated with the modern village El Jib
- Located on the main road from Jerusalem to Joppa
- Later a site of the tabernacle in 2 Chronicles 1:3

PERSONAL PROFILE: HIVITES

- Descendants of Canaan, a son of Ham (Gen. 10:17)
- Possibly also known as Horites (see Gen. 36:2,20)
- One nation among the six common groups we often see listed as the Canaanites who must be driven out by Israel

IN A NUTSHELL

Having stumbled at Ai because of Achan's sin, Israel now finds itself in failure again because they did not ask God what to do about what seemed a simple situation. It becomes necessary for them to understand the cause, honor the commitments, accept the consequences, and expect the conciliation that comes from repentance after failure.

Joshua 9

The Grunge Gimmick

I. INTRODUCTION

The Gullible Public

*O*nce again the social sciences do their best to discredit Scripture and Bible miracles. Eric Altschuler of the sociology department at the University of California in San Diego has become a self-proclaimed Bible psychotherapist. In 2001 he gained media attention by diagnosing Samson with antisocial personality disorder and claiming the prophet Ezekiel suffered from temporal lobe epilepsy with symptoms such as extreme piety, fainting, compulsive writing, and the frequent inability to speak as well as aggression and delusions. Altschuler obviously has an obsessive compulsion to read modern psychotherapy back into the text of Scripture. We can't image what he might do with Peter, Stephen, and Paul, to say nothing of Jesus. Yet this is the kind of religion the public accepts and the kind of authority recognized regularly in the vast liberal wing of contemporary Protestantism.

The Barna Group also gives us some picture of the kind of public we deal with in our day when they tell us 82 percent of Americans who read the Bible regularly describe themselves as "at peace," but 58 percent of Americans who never read the Bible regularly describe themselves in that way. Yet 48 percent of American Protestant mega churches (more than 2,000) call themselves "evangelical." American religion today has become a vast river several miles wide and only a few inches deep.

Such a credibility problem also troubled our hero in the Book of Joshua. Too quick to believe the Gibeonites, he yielded to their deception and thereby took another step backward in the conquest. Once again, as in the case of Ai, God covered his tracks and reversed the error, but we are reminded of the gullibility factor almost every time we watch television or read a newspaper.

Or think about this chapter another way. You've just bought a used car. It was a beauty. Clean, low miles—and best of all—a great price. In fact, it was such a good deal, you didn't want to take the chance that someone else would grab it so you bought it on the spot. Normally you would have taken the car to a mechanic first, but there just wasn't time.

That was three days ago. Now you are having trouble with the car, and the mechanic has just explained the engine problems to you. It's bad news. The seller probably knew about it but deceived you. What do you do? Blame the mechanic? Obviously not. Demand your money back? Forget that; it won't do any good. Mope around griping and complaining that you got taken? Probably. But perhaps the best reaction is to try learning something from the mistake.

That very situation (with a potential enemy, not an automotive lemon) faced the Israelites, but with much more important spiritual ramifications. Missing God's will by making an honest but significant mistake, they were fooled by their enemies and had to live with the consequences. That's the story of Joshua 9.

II. COMMENTARY

The Grunge Gimmick

MAIN IDEA: *The God of Israel was so abundant in mercy that he could bring reconciliation in spite of sin and failure. When they looked for the good that God provided and quit resisting his discipline, they were able to enjoy the blessings he offered.*

A Understand the Cause (9:1–13)

SUPPORTING IDEA: *Common sense is not enough. To accept the concession of the Gibeonites was a breaking of the plan of God for Canaan. Trying to walk by sight, the Israelites failed to walk by faith.*

9:1–2. The Israelite army pressed westward to cut the country in half and then proceeded to tackle a southern campaign followed by a northern campaign. The victories over Jericho and Ai had spread out to **the hill country, in the western foothills**, and as far north as **Lebanon**. There would be no more taking of city after city because powerful confederations had formed. Furthermore, these western allies understood that Israel was not invincible since Ai had defeated them once. The sin of the Amorites had become full (Gen. 15:16), and God had hardened the hearts of Canaanite leaders against Israel individually and collectively.

But chapter 9 is not about these six kings but rather the fascinating "ruse" (v. 4) pulled off by the southern city of Gibeon.

9:3–6. You have to give the Gibeonites credit for their cunning and acting ability. They at least had enough faith in the reports they heard about God to come up with a plan to get themselves on his side in some way. And they knew enough about the Israelites' directives for taking the land to know that their lives were in danger. And somehow they knew that by pretending to be from far away they could receive mercy through a treaty. What they didn't consider is that they could have just asked for God's mercy as Rahab did.

This is the first mention of Gibeon in the Bible, though it later became a Levitical city (21:17). Its primary importance in the Bible appears right here in Joshua 9. We note here that if the Gibeonites' claim had been accurate, the treaties the Israelites made with them would have been acceptable (Exod. 34:11–12; Deut. 20:10–18).

But just a moment. Our narrator has made a geographical shift that we dare not overlook. We ended chapter 8 in Shechem at Mounts Ebal and Gerizim. Now all of a sudden we're back at home camp at Gilgal, and that's where the Gibeonites came. Howard doubts that to be the case and says:

> It seems more likely that this was a different place with the same name, somewhere in the vicinity of Mounts Ebal and Gerizim, where the covenant renewal ceremony had taken place (8:30–35). There are at least three different places called Gilgal in the Old Testament . . . it appears that the Gilgal here is . . . the same one that is mentioned in Deuteronomy 11:29–30, which was near Mounts Ebal and Gerizim and the oak of Moreh (Howard, 224).

Not all commentators agree, however. The casual way our storyteller drops Gilgal into the narrative certainly would lead innocent readers to believe this was the Israelite camp west of the Jordan River with which they had become familiar in earlier chapters. This seems especially true when we read the phraseology **in the camp at Gilgal**.

9:7–13. Now we learn that the Gibeonites were **Hivites**, one of the groups slated for destruction. Certainly we have to agree that the Israelites acted with some caution. At first they suspected this might be a ruse, but perhaps they were touched by the worn-out clothes and moldy bread. They had sympathy and compassion on the people. Our immediate reaction leans toward accepting this as a positive and peaceful response.

But they did not seek God's advice as we shall see in verse 14; they "did not inquire of the LORD." Literally the phrase is "the mouth of Yahweh they did not seek." One would think they had learned their lesson at Ai on a matter like this. But now so soon again after the altar experience at Shechem, they fall into another serious mistake. Perhaps they considered this a military and not a spiritual decision, but that never works when we recognize the total control God has over every aspect of our lives.

Perhaps the people were on another spiritual high after the Gerizim and Ebal experience and thought they could now discern things for themselves. Perhaps they thought this was too small a matter to take to God. Perhaps they assumed common sense was enough in this situation.

Joshua must have understood the cause of their mistake or it would not be recorded for us here. We also must realize that sometimes we lack spiritual wisdom because we have not prayed. James says, "If any of you lacks wisdom, he should ask God, who gives generously to all without finding fault, and it will be given to him" (Jas. 1:5). The Israelites should have asked for wisdom, and the Gibeonites should have asked for mercy. But neither group behaved correctly, and it caused trouble.

🅱 Honor the Commitment (9:14–21)

> **SUPPORTING IDEA:** *Having made a commitment to the Gibeonites, even though they were out of God's will to do so, the Israelites must honor the commitment.*

9:14–18a. We find it difficult to make our way past verse 14, which is laid out for us so clearly. They did the human thing—but not the divine thing. They did the earthly thing—but not the heavenly thing. They treated this decision as a matter of logic, not a matter of spiritual insight. Two major mistakes stand out. Joshua accepted highly questionable evidence, and he refused to ask God whether the evidence was valid and what decision should be made regarding the question before them.

In fact, the Canaanites lived only about twenty-five miles from Gilgal, right in the middle of Canaan and not some far country. Proverbs 12:19 says, "A lying tongue lasts only a moment." In this case the definition of *moment* was three days. The phrase **leaders of the assembly** in verse 15 attracts our interest as well. It appears four times in Joshua (9:15,18,19; 22:30) and five times in Numbers (4:34; 16:2; 27:2; 31:13; 32:2). The four cities mentioned here were located in a small area five to ten miles northwest of Jerusalem, apparently in some kind of loose federation not unlike that of the Philistines.

Some readers will recognize the name of Joe Gibbs, former coach of the Washington Redskins who is now involved with NASCAR. As the story goes (and I'm told it's true), Gibbs had a Labrador retriever and found the dog with his neighbor's rabbit in his mouth. Joe cleaned up the rabbit, blow-dried it, and sneaked it back in the cage that night. The next morning the neighbor appeared with the dead rabbit in hand. "We have a real sick person in the neighborhood," he complained. "My rabbit died three days ago and I buried it. Someone dug it up, cleaned it off, and stuck it back in the cage!"

Yes, there are sick people in the neighborhood, the community, and the world. Sick in sin and quite ready to lie about anything. The Bible tells us that the children of this world are wiser in their generation than the children of light. This ought to warn us not to assume we always know what's going on. We need to talk to God about everything. We need to ask him for wisdom regularly.

9:18b–21. Now the Israelites were in a pickle. They had sworn an oath to the Gibeonites **by the LORD, the God of Israel**. But what they had sworn to do would put them at odds with what God had commanded. Now what? We notice that the people grumbled against the leaders and apparently wanted them to retract the oath, but the leaders affirmed the requirement to follow through on their commitment. God's name and reputation were at stake. Even though their commitment was based on misinformation, to break the covenant would have compounded the sin. As we have heard all of our lives, two wrongs don't make a right. The Israelites were humiliated, but at least they maintained their integrity. Their commitment was tested in the very next chapter when they had to defend the Gibeonites in battle. And God helped the Israelites for honoring this oath. He also punished Israel years later because Saul abandoned this commitment and killed some of the Gibeonites (2 Sam. 21).

A Christian cannot say, "Oh, I was out of God's will to marry a person, and now it's not working out. Therefore God wants me to divorce this person so I can marry the right one." No, that's not the way it works. Even if we make foolish decisions without seeking God, he wants us to honor our commitments.

What if a man and woman disobey God by having sex outside of marriage and she becomes pregnant? Is abortion the answer? No. Their sinful choice involved a commitment to a child whom they should not abandon.

What if a person foolishly accepts a job without seeking God's counsel and it turns out to be a bad situation? If possible, he or she ought to remain in the situation and not quit because of personal foolishness. A commitment was made to the employer, and there is a principle at stake.

Why the decision to make them **woodcutters and water carriers**? Certainly this was a punishment of lifetime duration for an entire group of people. But, as Campbell puts it, "In order to keep the Gibeonites' idolatry from defiling the religion of Israel their work would be carried out in connection with the Tabernacle where they would be exposed to the worship of the one true God" (Campbell, *BKC*, 349).

Ⓒ Accept the Consequences (9:22–25)

SUPPORTING IDEA: *Repentance of their failure in being fooled by the Gibeonites did not end the problem. Israel now must learn to live with a constant visual reminder of their failure to consult God about a major decision.*

9:22–25. This principle of covenant-keeping can be difficult for us to accept. Even though the Israelites did the right thing by keeping their commitment, they still had to live with some consequences of their foolishness. And even though the Gibeonites responded to God, they also suffered consequences because they chose deceitful methods. They lived a life of slavery to the Israelites, and they accepted that lot.

For the Israelites the consequences were a bit more subtle. Israel would bear the burden of defending these people (ch. 10), and they would live with the embarrassment of their mistake by always having the Canaanites around in full view. Their daily practice of carrying wood and water would serve as a constant visual reminder to Joshua and Israel of this tragic mistake.

We pause for a moment at the phrase **the house of my God** since there was no such house at that point.

The "house of God" in later years signified the temple that Solomon built . . . or the temple rebuilt after the exile. . . . In Joshua's day, however, there was no temple and the "house of God" may have referred to the tabernacle or to a place such as Shiloh, where there was a house of God in the days before the temple was built (1 Sam. 1:7; cf. Josh. 18:1) (Howard, 230).

When our son Jeff was a little boy, his favorite stuffed animal was "monkey." No name, just a stuffed monkey called by that generic title. He didn't listen to his parents' advice and took monkey outside and left him in the rain, causing his stuffing to harden and clump. He was never the same. The results of Jeff's mistake could not be removed, but he kept monkey and never took him out again. The great joy here is that God can use negative results in our lives to bring about positive character. I think it was J. Oswald Sanders who once wrote, "God frequently allows the results of our compromises to run their natural course but uses them to serve our spiritual development."

𝔻 Expect the Conciliation (9:26–27)

SUPPORTING IDEA: *It is just like God to turn a curse into a blessing. The Gibeonites, constant reminders of Israel's sin, also become a blessing as they serve the nation and are exposed to the heart of Israelite worship at the temple.*

9:26–27. Obviously the deceptive Gibeonites received God's grace through Israel's protection. But there is a more subtle blessing here that comes out of their curse. In their servant roles as woodcutters and water carriers, the Gibeonites were right in the middle of Israel's daily offerings and cleansing ceremonies. They faithfully fulfilled their role. They could, if they chose, move to full acceptance of Israel's God. Years later when the Israelites returned from captivity, Ezra recorded descendants of the Gibeonites still serving in the temple.

Furthermore, this became a blessing to the Israelites who could now focus on military conquest of the southern and northern campaigns while the Gibeonites provided a much needed service to the whole community. My friend Don Campbell articulates the principle:

Such is the grace of God. He is still able to turn a curse into a blessing. Though it is usually true that the natural consequences of sin must run their course, the grace of God cannot only forgive but also overrule mistakes and often bring blessings out of sins and failures (Campbell, *BKC*, 349).

In Reese's Peanut Butter Cups commercials, the chocolate and the peanut butter come together by accident but end up tasting great. Many good recipes have been discovered that way. God takes our mistakes and sins, mixes them with his abundant grace, and creates a wonderful recipe for his glory. Yes, we must often live with negative consequences, but God is bigger than our mistakes and our problems.

> **MAIN IDEA REVIEW:** *The God of Israel was so abundant in mercy that he could bring reconciliation in spite of sin and failure. When they looked for the good that God provided and quit resisting his discipline, they were able to enjoy the blessings he offered.*

III. CONCLUSION

News Flash: God Knows the Future

At their meeting in Colorado Springs the week before Thanksgiving in 2001, the Evangelical Theological Society (ETS) affirmed God's foreknowledge. The statement read as follows: "We believe the Bible clearly teaches that God has complete, accurate, and infallible knowledge of all events past, present, and future, including all future decisions and actions of free moral agents." Amazingly, the resolution passed 253 to 66 with 41 members abstaining. In other words, over a hundred members of the ETS are not entirely comfortable with the full recognition that God knows the future.

Part of the reason for this is a longstanding discussion in that organization about "open theism," which emphasizes self-imposed divine boundaries. The position of the open theist argues that God has limited himself in dealing with human beings and given them free response that he neither predetermines nor foreknows. Many of the 253 who affirmed the resolution, however, argue that open theism contradicts the society's commitment to the inerrancy of the Scriptures that is the center point of the ETS doctrinal statement.

As reported in *Christianity Today* (1/7/02), former ETS president Wayne Grudem indicated that the resolution was "a serious encouragement to openness theists to change their minds—an encouragement that comes from the vast majority of their peers."

It is hardly within the purview of our discussion of Joshua 9 to debate open theism or even to discuss the difference between foreknowledge and predestination. Let us simply affirm scriptural reliability and emphasize again that God could have told Joshua exactly what the Gibeonites were doing and what they had in mind. This chapter offers a classic example of a good man with excellent training and the best of intentions falling into spiritual error because he depended too much on himself and not enough on God. Nothing in our lives is too small to bring before the Lord. Nothing in our lives is undeserving of spiritual consideration. Nothing in our lives represents an issue or a problem with which God is not concerned or on which he does not invite our sincere requests for wisdom.

But there is a higher New Testament lesson in this chapter, and Schaeffer spells it out.

> Let us remember that God insisted that the Israelites keep their oath, even though it was made because of the Gibeonites' deception. If God will not tolerate the breaking of an oath made in his name, how much more will he never break his own oath and covenant made to us on the basis of the shed blood and infinite value of Jesus Christ. How secure are we who have cast ourselves upon Christ as our Savior! (Schaeffer, 152).

PRINCIPLES

- As human beings we tend to think we have things under control and can handle our problems on our own.
- When we rely on our own understanding of a situation, we fail to seek the wisdom God has for us.
- When we make mistakes, sometimes God asks us to accept the consequences and live with them while we move on in obedience.

APPLICATIONS

- What are some occasions in which you have rushed ahead, failed to seek God's wisdom, and had to face the consequences?
- What are some of the experiences God has used to teach you a closer reliance on him in making decisions?
- Be faithful to your commitments and leave the problems to God.

IV. LIFE APPLICATION

Expect the Unexpected

Listen to the following dialogue between a husband and wife who had just returned from the funeral of one of their friends.

She: "Darling, if I died, would you remarry?"

He: "Deary, let's not talk about this; you won't die any time soon."

She: "But if I do, would you remarry?"

He: "Well, it's possible, but let's not talk about this; it's unnecessary."

She: "If you did remarry, would you let her live in this house?"

He: "Probably, it's paid for and comfortable, but let's not talk about this."

She: "Would you let her drive my car?"

He: "Well, you certainly wouldn't need it, so it's possible, but let's not talk about this."

She: "Would you let her wear my clothes?"

He: "Well, if they fit, I suppose she might want some of them, but let's not talk about this."

She: "Would you let her use my golf clubs?"

He: "Absolutely not! She's left-handed."

This less-than-subtle *entendre* reminds us that Christians need to be aware and alert at all times, expecting the unexpected. Joshua thought he was in a standard battle, and he looked for enemies who hid behind their fortified cities and concocted plans to attack the invading Israelite army. But this was a new kind of situation, and it looked harmless. Nevertheless, it was not harmless, and the consequences, as we have seen, became difficult on both sides of the error. Many great Christians have made many great mistakes: Paul (Rom. 6), Augustine, Martin Luther, John Wesley, and, to be even more specific, all of us. But we learn that God somehow usually lets us live beyond those mistakes (Ananias and Sapphira did not) and can turn our stupidity into service, our mistakes into ministry.

I close with the inspiring words of Alan Redpath, a deeper life theologian and former pastor of Moody Church in Chicago:

> I've discovered that the thing in which I have blundered, the sin that I have committed, the wrong that I have done, though the memory of it often haunts my life, is now what drives me daily to the Cross for cleansing, for forgiveness, for power. The wretched man who once was bound by sin discovers that the very sin which bound him is now the blessing which, more than anything else, brings him to concentrated service to his Saviour. What a wonderful Saviour we have! (Redpath, 145).

V. PRAYER

Father, keep us from dealing deceitfully and treacherously with other people, especially in spiritual matters, and give us the wisdom to consult you when there seems to be any possibility that others have treated us in such a manner. Amen.

VI. DEEPER DISCOVERIES

A. Joshua 9 and Luke 16:8–9

This New Testament verse seems to shine back like a beacon on our Old Testament chapter to remind us of our vulnerability on earth. People who are spiritually minded are clearly less focused on worldly and material things and therefore "sitting ducks" for those who approach them in a Gibeonite-like manner with deceit and treachery.

In this parable, a shrewd manager, though hardly the hero, teaches several basic lessons about our possessions. The parable has ended at verse 7 and the Lord's comments begin at verse 8 where he says:

The master commended the dishonest manager because he had acted shrewdly. For the people of this world are more shrewd in dealing with their own kind than are the people of the light. I tell you, use worldly wealth to gain friends for yourselves, so that when it is gone, you will be welcomed into eternal dwellings (Luke 16:8–9).

The first perspective is that of the rich man who acknowledges and even commends the manager's shrewdness. Again, we must not confuse shrewdness with stewardship. The Lord observes that worldly people show more shrewdness than Christians when it comes to "dealing with their own kind." Bishop Trench once said of this parable that we should learn "that the world is better served by its servants than God is by his."

The second perspective of these verses reflects the Lord himself as he suggests that worldly possessions can be used to prepare for eternity. Obviously this is not a reference to buying salvation (1 Pet. 1:18) but using "worldly wealth" for eternal goals. Shrewd businessmen constantly sacrifice comforts for future profits. Shrewdness in planning the Lord's work as well as one's life can certainly be taught from this passage.

The traditional rendering of the word here translates as "worldly wealth," but it actually refers to more than money, including influence and positions as well. Apparently the Lord felt the disciples did not handle their resources properly, and he wanted them to become more astute in their stewardship.

Let's remember that principle. The parable should strike a familiar chord in our day. What does Western culture value at the beginning of the twenty-first century? Money, fame, beauty, power, position, titles, strength, visibility, and self-assertiveness. Virtually everything our society lusts after and pays exorbitant prices to obtain stands in contradiction to the values of God's Word. This parable of possessions reminds us again of the classic and poignant sentence once penned by Jim Elliot in his diary: "He is no fool who gives up what he cannot keep to gain what he cannot lose."

VII. TEACHING OUTLINE

A. INTRODUCTION

1. Lead Story: The Gullible Public

2. Context: The defeat of chapter 7 which became victory in chapter 8 now becomes defeat again in chapter 9. Not as catastrophic as Ai, the experience with the Gibeonites nevertheless would set Israel back because of their failure to contact God and get his will on every matter.

3. Transition: Just as chapter 8 follows immediately the events of chapter 7, so chapter 10 will immediately follow the events of chapter 9. Here Israel makes a treaty with the Gibeonites, and in chapter 10 they have to make good on their promises.

B. COMMENTARY

1. Understand the Cause (9:1–13)

2. Honor the Commitment (9:14–21)

3. Accept the Consequences (9:22–25)

4. Expect the Conciliation (9:26–27)

C. CONCLUSION: EXPECT THE UNEXPECTED

VIII. ISSUES FOR DISCUSSION

1. Try to isolate the most important lesson we learn from this story about the Gibeonite deception.

2. In addition to the obvious example of marriage, what other commitments should Christians keep even when things go wrong or the commitment may be considered a mistake?

3. Name some ways God has brought blessing out of blunder in your own experience.

Joshua 10

The Longest Day

I. INTRODUCTION
The Bible According to College Students

II. COMMENTARY
A verse-by-verse explanation of the chapter.

III. CONCLUSION
Watch Yourself in the South

An overview of the principles and applications from the chapter.

IV. LIFE APPLICATION
Power of Prayer

Melding the chapter to life.

V. PRAYER
Tying the chapter to life with God.

VI. DEEPER DISCOVERIES
Historical, geographical, and grammatical enrichment of the commentary.

VII. TEACHING OUTLINE
Suggested step-by-step group study of the chapter.

VIII. ISSUES FOR DISCUSSION
Zeroing the chapter in on daily life.

Quote

"*It* is never enough to have pity on the victim of injustice if we do nothing to change the unjust situation itself."

John R. W. Stott

GEOGRAPHICAL PROFILE: JERUSALEM

- First mentioned in Genesis 14 where it is called Salem
- Conquered by Joshua but lost again to the Canaanites during the period of the judges
- Defeated by David and proclaimed his capital (2 Sam. 5:6–12)
- Became the focal point of the nation when Solomon built God's temple there

GEOGRAPHICAL PROFILE: GOSHEN

- Not to be confused with the Goshen in Egypt (Gen. 45–47)
- The area around Debir in southern Canaan
- One of eleven towns in the southern hill country of Judea

IN A NUTSHELL

In this chapter we find Joshua and his troops engaged in one of the most bitter battles of their lives. They face the enemies of the southern campaign. If not for one of the most amazing miracles in the Bible, they probably would have been defeated again. But God literally moved heaven and earth to bring about their victory.

The Longest Day

I. INTRODUCTION

The Bible According to College Students

*I*n the Book of Joshua, we read an incredible story about the sun standing still. If you think this is a wild story, have a look at some of these.

If the Bible had been written by college students . . .

- the loaves and fishes would have been replaced by pizza and chips.

- the Ten Commandments would have been actually five but double-spaced and written in large font so they look like ten.

- forbidden fruit would have been eaten heartily because it didn't come from the cafeteria.

- Cain killed Abel because they were roommates.

- Moses and his followers walked in the desert for forty years because he didn't want to ask for directions and look like a freshman.

- the Tower of Babel would be blamed on the foreign language department.

- instead of God creating the world in six days and resting on the seventh, he would have put it off until the night before it was due and then pulled an all-nighter and hoped no one noticed.

Before we're finished with this chapter, we will be looking at one of the most controversial stories in the Bible—the day the sun stood still. In preparation for how we treat that, let's remember that the author of this volume and the publisher of this series are committed to biblical inerrancy and the principle that one takes every Bible passage at face value, treating it historically and naturally while at the same time deriving spiritual applications as much as possible.

II. COMMENTARY

The Longest Day

> **MAIN IDEA:** *The central lesson of Joshua's southern campaign centers in persistence against bitter enemies and a willingness to keep commitments even to people who don't deserve faithfulness.*

A March—Even When You Don't Want To (10:1–15)

> **SUPPORTING IDEA:** *Bolstered by the promises of God, Joshua moves boldly forward to attack a coalition of five kings that marched on Gibeon—a people Israel had promised to defend.*

10:1–5. The conquest heats up. Joshua and the Israelites had taken control of the central plateau of Canaan, and the Gibeonites had tricked Israel into making a treaty with them. Now five kings of the southern region realized they were in trouble and banded together. Under the leadership of Adoni-Zedek, king of Jerusalem, the kings of Hebron, Jarmuth, Lachish, and Eglon invoked the old principle "the friend of my enemy is my enemy" and chose to punish the Gibeonites and challenge the Israelites. The Gibeonites, of course, called on Joshua to keep his promise to them.

If most of us had been in Joshua's shoes, we would have been tempted to let the Canaanites fight it out among themselves; that would save a lot of trouble. Furthermore, the Gibeonites had deceived us and deserved it. But Joshua had made a commitment and given a promise. Keeping that promise was part of his walking correctly before God. Campbell emphasizes the motives that goaded Adoni-Zedek into this military maneuver:

> The treacherous surrender of the Gibeonite cities completed an arc beginning at Gilgal and extending through Jericho and Ai to a point just a few miles northwest of Jerusalem. The handwriting was on the wall. Jerusalem's security was being severely threatened. If the advances of Israel's armies continued without challenge Jerusalem would soon be surrounded and captured (Campbell, *BKC*, 349).

These kings came from cities of the Amorites in Canaanite hill country. This forced Joshua for the first time to look south where the aggression was gathering momentum. Actually these united kings never successfully attacked the Israelites. They concentrated on Gibeon, and the initial confrontation began there.

Interestingly, Adoni-Zedek is similar to Melchizedek (Gen. 14:18), thus perhaps a title rather than the name of a Jezbusite king. In Joshua's time there were nearly twenty city-states in southern Canaan, including those we have already met—Jericho, Ai, Bethel, and Gibeon. Hebron lay some nineteen miles south of Jerusalem, Jarmuth sixteen miles southwest of Jerusalem, Lachish about twenty-seven miles southwest of Jerusalem, and Eglon about seven miles west of Lachish. This was definitely a regional conspiracy.

10:6–11. In reality this allied army gave Joshua a great opportunity. He had been picking off one city at a time. Now all the major kings of the southern region had gathered together just twenty-five miles away. So Joshua marched his army all night up a four-thousand-foot incline over difficult terrain and **took them by surprise.** But this was not like the first battle at Ai or the confused decision regarding the Gibeonites. The Lord had already said to Joshua, **Do not be afraid of them; I have given them into your hand. Not one of them will be able to withstand you.** Many were killed in the initial battle, and the rest fled west down the Valley of Aijalon. When the first miracle occurred, **the LORD hurled large hailstones down on them from the sky.**

God gave his seal of approval to Joshua's obedience, and once again he provided the encouragement Joshua needed. This was the largest army he had yet faced, and the march to the battle site must have been exhausting. The record of this battle shows the interplay between Joshua's obedience and God's faithfulness. Joshua attacked, but God threw them into confusion. Israel pursued the enemy, but God hurled the hailstones.

All of us have made commitments to ministry, to relationships, and to live for Christ. God expects us to keep those commitments. In my son's first church staff experience after college, a new pastor came to the church and was dead set on running off all the staff. They hung in as long as they could even though it was not an easy situation. Sometimes Christians must follow through on their commitments even when we don't feel like it. We must march even when we don't want to.

10:12–15. The victory was going so well that Joshua needed more time. So he prayed, openly and publicly, **in the presence of Israel.** And not a general prayer for victory either but a specific request for a longer day. The result was that **the sun stopped in the middle of the sky and delayed going down about a full day.**

This is one of the most amazing miracles in the Bible. Scholars throughout the centuries have argued about the nature of this miracle. We will treat it in more detail in "Deeper Discoveries." My inclination is to take it at face value. Joshua saw victory within Israel's grasp and asked God to lengthen the day so they could pursue their enemies and finish what they had started. Ironically, the Canaanites worshiped sun and moon deities, so once again God proved his supreme power and authority and answered Joshua's bold prayer with an awesome miracle.

The Book of Jashar is also mentioned in 2 Samuel 1:18 and apparently contained some record of the annals of heroics in the nation of Israel. Any serious Bible student knows that this passage is greatly challenged, and we must look at some of those challenges later. Here let me note Madvig's words on the subject:

> The final statement in this verse [13] clearly favors the notion that the sun stood still or that it slowed down in its course across the sky. In either event the problem for geophysics is so great that some other solution has been eagerly sought by scholars both liberal and conservative (Madvig, 303).

Verse 15 is a summary verse that seems out of place unless we see verses 12–15 as a unit referring to the quotation in **the Book of Jashar.** Obviously the battle continued as Joshua kept marching, engaging, and pursuing.

B Engage—Even When You Are Afraid (10:16–28)

SUPPORTING IDEA: *Joshua and his troops had learned an important lesson that appears again in these verses: press the battle according to God's plan and leave the miracles to him.*

10:16–21. Joshua's fear had dissipated a good bit by now after two strategic miracles, but the battle pressed on. The five kings were hiding in a cave at Makkedah about two miles northwest of Jarmuth attempting to reach that city. Joshua had marched twenty-five miles to get to Gibeon and had pursued the enemy another twenty miles southwest. So from their departure at Gilgal, they had now traveled forty-five miles on foot, fighting a good part of that way. The key here was not to kill the kings but to conquer the cities. So the kings were walled up in the cave at Makkedah while the cities were destroyed and the army returned to the cave and, quite unlike the twenty-first century, **no one uttered a word against the Israelites.**

10:22–26. Now it was time to take care of the kings, so Joshua brought them to subjugation as **army commanders** placed their feet on the necks of the kings and Joshua recited something he had been learning from God since chapter 1: **Do not be afraid; do not be discouraged. Be strong and courageous.** The killing of these five kings of major southern city-states was an example of what God would do in the future. The five joined the fates of the kings of Jericho and Ai.

10:27–28. Finally the sun set and the long day was over. The kings were cut down from the trees and thrown into the cave at Makkedah and another pile of large rocks was erected. Since Makkedah was one of the original five cities, we assume the killing of its king occurred in addition to the regular battle as a part of the southern campaign. No opposition remained in Canaan between a line across the east/west axis of the center of Palestine and all the countries south even to the Negev. Scattered cities still remained, of course, but for all practical purposes the battle was finished and it was mop-up time.

C Pursue—Even When You Are Tired (10:29–43)

SUPPORTING IDEA: *This section shows us that any serious opposition to Israel and the southern part of Canaan has now been eliminated. All the major cities have been defeated and any effective coalitions broken up.*

10:29–39. This section contains a great deal of repetition as we systematically follow Joshua through his pattern of victories from Makkedah to Libnah (not previously mentioned) to Lachish, Eglon, Hebron, and Debir. "The fact that there are exactly seven cities here—no more and no less—suggests that this may be a summarizing account, showing the destructions of representative cities and not intended to be comprehensive, detailing every city captured" (Howard, 256). Later in chapter 12 Geder, Hormah, Arad, and Adullam are taken still in the south, but the point of this chapter is to conclude that any serious opposition from the south has been taken care of.

Apparently this series of lightning-like raids against key Canaanite cities served the purpose of destroying the fighting ability of the inhabitants, not necessarily occupying the cities attacked. It was the task of the tribes to occupy the land; here we only deal with the conquest. Joshua broke the back of the resistance, but the text says nothing about burning the cities such as we read in Jericho and Ai. Consequently, most of these cities could quickly be resettled by Canaanites, perhaps even by some who fled from the cities in the wake of the advancing Israelite armies.

10:40–43. The geography of the southern campaign is summarized in these verses. We learn that **Joshua subdued the whole region, including the hill country, the Negev, the western foothills and the mountain slopes.** Goshen, in the mountains of southern Judea, is mentioned to identify the southern extent of this campaign. The single most important spiritual lesson of this last part of the chapter is one that we have often emphasized—God fought for Israel. As expert a general as Joshua must have been, he was not the victor in these battles. This was God's war, and these were God's victories.

Two secondary lessons loom large in Joshua 10. The first is the importance of perseverance. Joshua was so eager to do God's work he ignored the fact that they had already been marching all night and asked God for more time to finish the job. The second lesson is the power of prayer. What amazed Joshua about this event when he looked back to record it was not that the sun stood still, but that an almighty God would hear the prayer of a man. A radio station in Houston provides billboards and bumper stickers that read "God listens," the call letters, and its frequency. What a wonderful thought. He still listens.

Complete victory is the message that arises from the text of Joshua 10, at least in the southern campaign—the north was still ahead. When we march on God's side, we also can expect spiritual victory. We serve a very big God—and he is not just big when the hailstones fall and the sun stands still. He is big every day we need him.

MAIN IDEA REVIEW: *The central lesson of Joshua's southern campaign centers in persistence against bitter enemies and a willingness to keep commitments even to people who don't deserve integrity and faithfulness.*

III. CONCLUSION

Watch Yourself in the South

Joshua had no hesitation about rushing down to Gibeon's aid, and God won a great victory that day. Even though almost a century and a half lies between us and the American tragedy we call the Civil War, still at times the hostilities between North and South manifest themselves in stories circulating south of the Mason-Dixon Line. This one is a good example.

When a man in Macon, Georgia, came upon a wild dog attacking a young boy, he quickly grabbed the animal and choked it to death with his two hands. A reporter saw the incident, congratulated the man, and told him the headline in his newspaper the following day would read, "Local Man Saves Child by Killing Vicious Animal."

The hero, however, told the journalist he wasn't from Macon. "Well then," the reporter said, "the headline will probably say, 'Georgia Man Saves Child by Killing Dog.'"

"Actually," the man said, "I'm from Connecticut."

"In that case," the reporter said in a huff, "the headline will read, 'Yankee Kills Family Pet.'"

Nobody told any jokes about Joshua down in southern Canaan in those days. In fact, as we have seen, no one said anything. But the battles here, though very physical, represent the kind of struggles fought commonly in ancient times. Beers explains it well:

> In Joshua's day, there were no high-powered rifles, grenades, or fighter jets. In battle, each man looked his opponent in the eye and the more powerful man usually won. This was hand-to-hand combat, and even with the invention of chariots, soldiers still fought this way. When God was with Joshua's army, it made no difference how skilled the enemy was. But years later, the Israelites did not follow God with such enthusiasm, and ran into deep trouble when faced with war (Beers, 138).

Again, I let Redpath summarize the spiritual lesson of physical battle, the ever present theme of spiritual warfare:

Every gain I have made in Christian character will be resisted by the devil down to the end of life's journey, and there will be no personal experience of the power of Jesus Christ in victory until I declare war on sin. I ask you in the name of heaven, are you attacking on all fronts? Have you identified yourselves by declaring war on pride, on self, on tongue, and on criticism, by determining to attack and to conquer them in the name of Jesus? You have a constant attitude to maintain, and a victory to claim (Redpath, 155).

PRINCIPLES

- God is able to provide resources that exceed our expectations.
- Whether you are beginning life or coming to its close, you will be in situations where you need to call on God for help.
- When we call, God will listen, and he will fight for us.

APPLICATIONS

- When God gives you a task, a ministry, or a calling, pursue it with perseverance.
- Don't be afraid to make commitments to ministry, to relationships, and to live for Christ and to follow through on those commitments wherever they take you.
- Make sure your spiritual victories are complete even to the conquering of the "kings" of sin in your life.

IV. LIFE APPLICATION

Power of Prayer

The prayers of Joshua are important in this book and certainly in this chapter. I recall being present at the baptism of a ten-year-old girl by the name of Devan at a church in Austin, Texas, in August of 1994. Three children were baptized that morning, and each gave a brief testimony. Devan told about how she would pray as a child and said, "I was pretty little so I didn't know if the Lord was listening."

Yes, Devan, the Lord is listening and is eager to hear more from us—more prayer, more dependence, more expectation of victory that he will give.

Pastor Art Larson, formerly of Boca Raton, Florida, tells the story about a Mr. Genner in India who prayed for Larson when he was very sick and unable to preach during a campaign in that country. Larson recovered almost immediately and preached the service during which many people came to Christ. He later discovered that Genner carried a prayer book in which he listed the names of those for whom he prayed on a regular basis and every person saved in that evangelistic meeting had been named in Genner's book!

Often the insipid Christian living of Western culture understands nothing of the power of prayer like this. To write down the names of people and pray for them until they are saved. To pray for one of God's servants in illness and see the illness removed immediately. To pray that the sun would stand still so the battle could be fought for more hours in the day. These are the prayers of faith and the prayers of victory, the expectation that the God of the Bible watches over his people. When they are engaged in spiritual warfare and completely dependent upon him, he will hear their cries and answer their prayers.

V. PRAYER

Father, give us the grace to carry out the battle wherever you call and the faith to depend on you for the outcome. Amen.

VI. DEEPER DISCOVERIES

A. "The Sun Stood Still" (10:13)

This is admittedly one of the most difficult texts in Scripture to handle. I serve my readers best by giving them samples of what other commentators see here and then perhaps expressing a personal opinion in a most undogmatic way after we have looked at several options. Some see verses 12b–13 as a poetic fragment of the Book of Jashar and a summary statement rather than a literal prayer. Butler says, "The book does not encourage the people to retrace the steps of Joshua in totally demolishing all enemies so much as to trust Yahweh to fulfill his promise to his people and to do the necessary fighting for them, even against overwhelming odds" (Butler, 117).

The usual interpretation of the miracle here is that God prolonged the daylight about a whole day to enable the Israelites to complete their pursuit of the enemy. If the sunlight had been extended for several more hours (possibly as many as twelve), this would have been a more spectacular miracle than the crossings of the Red Sea and the Jordan River though it is only referred to once again in the Old Testament (Hab. 3:11). Consequently, some believe that what Joshua wanted was relief from the relentless sun of the dry season burning down on his pursuing troops already tired from their all-night climb. One commentator says, "For the sunshine to cease in the dry season would be miracle enough," meaning that cloudiness was the sum total of what we are to understand from these verses.

Howard does a masterful job of summarizing the options here, and serious students should consult his work. He indicates that five possible options present themselves, and I paraphrase freely to summarize his points.

1. *The earth stopped rotating.* We know the sun did not stop any more than it sets and rises in the common vernacular of the day. But if the earth stopped rotating, it would have given the appearance to Joshua that that's exactly what happened. Campbell adopts this view and says:

   The best explanation seems to be the view that in answer to Joshua's prayer God caused the rotation of earth to slow down so that it made one full rotation in 48 hours rather than in 24. It seems apparent that this view is supported both by the poem in verses 12b–13a and the prose in 13b (Campbell, *BKC*, 351).

Without fanfare, let me say that I tend to adopt this view as well, seeing in it the most natural reading of the text.

2. *The sun's light lingered.* This view allows for a refraction of light that produced more light so that the battle might be completed, achieving essentially the same goal. A spin-off of this view is that the light was defused because of a rain of meteorites, though the text says nothing about that.

3. *The sun's light was blocked.* I've already mentioned this view above, indicating that what Joshua wanted was not more light but less and therefore mist, fog, or at least low clouds allowed his men to fight on in relative coolness rather than the beating sun of the day. The problem here is that the same shade that relieved Joshua's men would have relieved the Amorites as well, so there does not seem to be much gain from adopting this position.

4. *A special sign was involved.* This view suggests that there was some kind of unusual alignment of the sun and moon and perhaps even the stars that served Joshua as an omen that God was with him and would continue to give victory. Such a view seems to stretch the text beyond the breaking point, especially in view of the fact that Joshua already had the direct promise of God that he would win the day.

5. *The passage is figurative.* Here these heavenly signs are viewed as figurative language that describes God's victory over the Canaanites by allowing even the sun and moon to participate in defeating them.

This is the position Howard himself takes:

If these points are valid, then the proposal with the least problems would seem to be that the words directed to the sun and moon were figurative, describing the battle in poetic terms but making no comment at all about any extraordinary positioning or movement of the sun and the moon. This approach has the advantage of dealing with the familiar, demonstrable phenomenon found in the texts of the Bible— the often figurative nature of poetry. It has the further advantage of the existence of several other poetic texts that use similar language, which can help in the interpretation here (Howard, 247).

And again two pages later, Howard says:

What do the words addressed to the sun and the moon mean, then, if not that the earth stopped rotating or shining (or something similar)? Simply this: that God was directing the sun and the moon to fight for Israel in the same way that the stars fought for Israel in Deborah's day (Judg. 5:20), or else that they were to stand amazed as he fought for Israel, just as they did in Habakkuk 3:11. We do not imagine that these statements in Judges and Habakkuk mean anything except that God's victory was total and that his majesty is awe-inspiring. Do we properly read these statements as involving universe-altering astronomical or geophysical phenomena? The issue is the same in Joshua 10:12–13. The suggestion offered here is that the language is similar to the psalmist's who urges the rivers to clap their hands and the mountains to sing for joy (Ps. 98:8), or the trees of the fields to sing for joy (Ps. 96:12), or when Isaiah writes that "the mountains and hills will burst into song before you, and all the trees of the field will clap their hands" (Isa. 55:12) (Howard, 249).

Let the reasonable reader study the text, allow the Holy Spirit to fill his or her mind and heart, and choose an interpretation that best fits the words and context of Scripture.

VII. TEACHING OUTLINE

A. INTRODUCTION

1. Lead Story: The Bible According to College Students

2. Context: Chapter 10 flows naturally from chapter 9 as the Gibeonite deception gives way to the necessity of vast battle activities to conquer the kings of the south.

3. Transition: We are now into the Joshua narrative that describes the southern and northern campaigns in that order. After returning to Gilgal at the end of the southern campaign in this chapter, Joshua will prepare to go out again in chapter 11, this time to the north.

B. COMMENTARY

1. March—Even When You Don't Want To (10:1–15)

2. Engage—Even When You Are Afraid (10:16–28)

3. Pursue—Even When You Are Tired (10:29–43)

C. CONCLUSION: POWER OF PRAYER

VIII. ISSUES FOR DISCUSSION

1. In your opinion, was Joshua right to pursue the five kings after they attacked Gibeon or was this carrying commitment just a bit too far?
2. After reading the Scripture and the evidence presented in this commentary, what is your opinion of the sun standing still over the Valley of Aijalon?
3. Name at least three important lessons for spiritual warfare that we can glean from Joshua 10.

Joshua 11–12

War and Peace

"God is active in the world at all times—

but God acts through people."

Gerhard Lohfink

Joshua 11–12

IN A NUTSHELL

Joshua's armies had cut a line from east to west across the middle of Canaan and then moved south to defeat the southern alliance. But now they face the northern alliance and the necessity of victory as well as annihilation of the paganism of Canaan.

War and Peace

I. INTRODUCTION

Mouse in the Pantry

*I*t happened at my son's house just a year or so ago—evidence of a mouse in the kitchen pantry. The whole family got excited, especially my grandson Brad, as they set out the little chunks of cheese in the traps and then waited day after day. For nearly a week they checked the traps with no success and then just lost interest and forgot about them. In about a month they came to the kitchen one morning and noticed a terrible smell. They couldn't figure it out at first. But upon tracing it to the pantry, they found the trap, the dead mouse, and the source of the unpleasant aroma. Now the job had taken on a new dimension. Getting rid of the mouse was joined by getting rid of the smell.

It's not enough to know you have a mouse in your trap; you must get rid of the mouse and, if necessary, the smell. That's the case with us. It's not enough to know we have a sin problem; we must get rid of the sin and, if necessary, the stench.

The Book of Joshua is about war and peace. It was not enough just to frighten, chase, or capture Canaanite enemies as Israel proceeded to conquer the promised land. God told them to eliminate the Canaanites. This was genuinely a holy war as Israel became God's tool of judgment on sinful nations and God's cleaning brush to eradicate idolatry from the land.

Readers will notice that we have dealt with no geographical or personal profiles at the beginning of this chapter. The reason is that much of Joshua from here on will contain a proliferation of personal and geographical references. We will deal with the important ones in the text and allow the rest to form the backdrop of our understanding of the story.

II. COMMENTARY

War and Peace

MAIN IDEA: *What seems like a bloody merciless war to us was really God's way of providing the environment most conducive for righteous living on the part of his people.*

A Description of Annihilation (11:1–11)

SUPPORTING IDEA: *When God's enemies harass God's people, they turn to him for protection and support.*

11:1–6. When word of Joshua's victory in the south reached the north, **Jabin king of Hazor** began immediately to put together a northern coalition to attack this enemy. The Jewish historian Josephus estimates this army at three hundred thousand soldiers, one hundred thousand cavalry, and twenty thousand chariots, by far the largest and best-armed force that Israel had ever faced. Hazor, the leading kingdom in this alliance, was the largest and best fortified city in Canaan.

It may be worth noting here that these chapters represent a preview summary of the handling of the promised land that includes a brief description of the conquered areas and a list of the defeated kings. By all standards this was an unwinnable battle. God had to come to Joshua again and say, **Do not be afraid**.

Twenty-four specific cities are mentioned, but this alliance was considerably stronger as Jabin contacted virtually everybody who had been untouched by the marching Israelites. His call reached as far north as the **mountains** to **the western foothills** and east to the Jordan.

As Howard notes:

> Here again, the enemy brought the attack to Israel. As we have noted earlier, only in the cases of Jericho and Ai did the Israelites initiate the conflicts. The Israelites were not to put their trust in military power: God again is given the credit for Israel's victory. . . . The reference to horses is the first time these are mentioned in the book, and it certainly shows a contrast between the Canaanite conduct of war and the model of leadership that Joshua exemplified and that Israel's kings were to exemplify: they were not to multiply horses for

themselves (Deut. 17:16), that is, not depend on their military might, but rather on God (Howard, 267).

But why hamstring the horses as God specifically instructed Joshua? Not only to cripple the enemy armies, but to make sure that Israel did not take over the horses and chariots and therefore copy the tactics of their enemies. Psalm 20:7 says, "Some trust in chariots and some in horses, but we trust in the name of the LORD our God." Even in David's day when horses were plentiful, the power for victory could not rest in the implements of warfare.

11:7–11. The battle took place at Merom a few miles northwest of the Sea of Kinnereth (Galilee), and the chase then went in two directions: northwest to Tyre and Sidon and northeast to the Valley of Mizpah **until no survivors were left**. We don't see hailstones or a long day in this battle, but the miraculous power of God was evident by the victory of an inconsequential minority force over a huge and superior enemy. Consequently we look back on God's words in verse 6, "Tomorrow I will hand all of them over to Israel, slain."

Only three cities were actually burned by the armies of Joshua—Jericho, Ai, and now Hazor, probably selected for such treatment because Jabin their king was the instigator of the northern rebellion. The flow of the Book of Joshua reminds us of Psalm 78:55: "He drove out nations before them and allotted their lands to them as an inheritance; he settled the tribes of Israel in their homes."

Hamlin describes the battle in a terse paragraph:

The divinely inspired (11:6) pre-dawn attack on the military camp caught the sleeping charioteers unawares. The attacking forces crippled the horses by cutting their rear leg tendons (hamstrings), and burned the chariots. Deprived of their military advantage, the Canaanite forces were badly beaten. This victory and its sequel opened the way for peaceful development of towns and villages in Galilee by the "Canaan generation" without fear of harassment or subjection to the pagan kings. In poetic language, "the people who walked in darkness" saw "a great light" (Isa. 9:2) (Hamlin, 102).

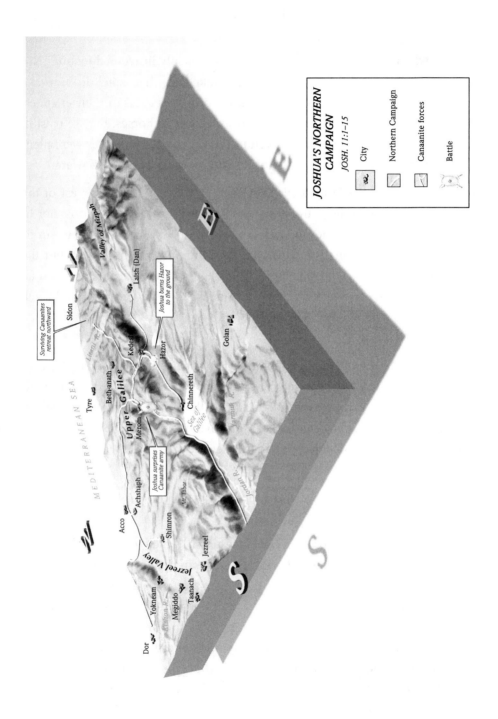

JOSHUA'S NORTHERN CAMPAIGN

JOSH. 11:1-15

City

Northern Campaign

Canaanite forces

Battle

Surviving Canaanites retreat northward

Joshua burns Hazor to the ground

Joshua surprises Canaanite army

MEDITERRANEAN SEA

Valley of Mizpah

Sidon

Laish (Dan)

Kedesh

Hazor

Golan

Tyre

Beth-anath

Upper Galilee

Chinnereth

Sea of Galilee

Yarmuk R.

Merom

Achshaph

Acco

Mt. Tabor

Shimron

Jezreel

Jordan R.

Jezreel Valley

Kishon R.

Yokneam

Megiddo

Taanach

Dor

N

E

E

S

S

𝔹 Purpose of Annihilation (11:12–23)

SUPPORTING IDEA: *God had hardened the hearts of the Canaanites because of their vile sin. In their rejection of his truth and his people, they brought the ultimate annihilation upon themselves.*

11:12–15. We must understand that all these Canaanites had the same opportunity as Rahab and the Gibeonites to respond to their knowledge of Israel and God with faith, repentance, and a plea for mercy. Instead they resisted God, and God hardened their hearts so they came out to make war against Israel. They chose battle rather than belief, fighting rather than faith. So the Israelites wiped them out, not because this was their idea or plan; it was God's.

Before they entered the land, God said, "In the cities of the nations the LORD your God is giving you as an inheritance, do not leave alive anything that breathes. Completely destroy them—the Hittites, Amorites, Canaanites, Perizzites, Hivites and Jebusites—as the LORD your God has commanded you" (Deut. 20:16–17). The Israelites were the instruments of God's judgment on these nations for their sin and idolatry.

And the principle carries through in the New Testament as well: "The wages of sin is death." God is not unfair; he demonstrated his justice and righteousness and holiness to show that sin cannot go unpunished. Many theme parks have a river rapids ride almost always with signs that warn "you will get wet!" And the sign is always true. As you watch, some people come off the ride smartly prepared with rain slickers, cameras and billfolds wrapped in waterproof carry-on bags, and only sandals on their feet. Other people dressed in slacks, sport shirts, and loafers didn't take the sign seriously, but they are no less wet than those who did.

From the time of creation, God has said that sin brings death. People who choose to take that ride will get wet. The first purpose of annihilation in the land of Canaan was to bring punishment for sin. As these verses show, all the plunder went to the victors.

11:16–20. The complete annihilation record continues, and though this reads rapidly, it was a long, drawn-out process. Judging by Caleb's age given in a couple of chapters, this conquest went on for about seven years. And this paragraph contains a key verse for the entire Book of Joshua: **For it was the LORD himself who hardened their hearts to wage war against Israel, so**

that he might destroy them totally, exterminating them without mercy, as the LORD had commanded Moses (v. 20).

This provides an example of what we call "judicial hardening." The Canaanites had exhausted their opportunities for grace and had continued in their sinful practices. So God hardened them against Israel in order that they would go against them in battle and then God could inflict his righteous judgment on them.

Campbell puts it well:

> The Canaanites' day of grace was gone. They had sinned against the light of God's revelation and nature (Ps. 19:1; Rom. 1:18–20), in conscience (Rom. 2:14–16), and in His recent miraculous works at the Red (Reed) Sea, the Jordan River, and Jericho. Now the sovereign God confirmed the hearts of these unrepentant people and their stubborn unbelief before judging them (Campbell, *BKC*, 354).

And that raises a second purpose in the conquest of Canaan and the annihilation—to bring about the purging of sin. We have already noted Deuteronomy 20:17, and here is verse 18: "Otherwise, they will teach you to follow all the detestable things they do in worshiping their gods, and you will sin against the LORD your God."

This process of total destruction was designed to cleanse idolatry from the land so Israel would not be tempted to sin in that way. We see here God's way of cleaning up the promised land so that it would be a safe place for his people. Good churches spend time cleaning nursery toys and furniture so they can provide a safe environment for children. In a much larger way, this is exactly what God was doing here.

11:21–23. Special attention is paid here to **the Anakites from the hill country.** We remember the Anakites. They were the giants who frightened the original spies into giving a doubtful report about the land of Israel, so they came in for special mention. We should also notice, however, that some Anakites were not annihilated. The text says **only in Gaza, Gath and Ashdod did any survive.** This is a verse David may have thought of when he stood across the field from Goliath of Gath, a descendant of these surviving Anakites. Please note that no criticism is given of Joshua here for allowing Gaza, Gath, and Ashdod to stand because these cities were apparently located outside Israelite territory.

The last sentence of our chapter reads almost like a sigh of relief. Finally there was some peace. This had been God's goal and purpose for Israel all along. They had to go through a war to experience peace. Madvig calls this last phrase "a profound declaration and a fitting conclusion for the first section of the book. It is prophetic of the 'rest' that will come when all evil has been conquered and Christ is made King of Kings and Lord of Lords (Rev. 11:15; 19:16)" (Madvig, 312).

How are we to understand the words **Joshua took the entire land** when just ahead in 13:1 we read, "There are still very large areas of land to be taken over"? Campbell says:

> To the Hebrew mind the part stands for the whole. It thus only needs to be demonstrated that Joshua took key centers in all parts of the land to validate the statement that he had conquered the whole land, . . . Included are conquered sites on the costal plain, the Shephelah (foothills), the central plateau, the Jordan Valley, and the Transjordan plateau. No area was totally bypassed. Joshua did indeed take the entire land, just as God promised he would if he followed the divine Word rather than human wisdom (Campbell, *BKC*, 354)

C Results of Annihilation (12:1–24)

SUPPORTING IDEA: *Israel becomes the tool of God's judgment against the barbarian behavior of the Canaanites as well as the peoples who lived east of the Jordan River.*

12:1–6. This chapter closes the first part of Joshua that deals with the conquest of the land by giving a summary of the battles won from Moses' victories east of the Jordan River to all the victories studied in Joshua. It offers a powerful reminder of God's faithfulness in fulfilling his promises to Israel to give them the land.

Two kings are selected for special mention: Sihon and Og defeated by Moses. It was essential in the Israelite trek north along the eastern coast of the Jordan River to defeat everybody who stood in the way of entering the promised land. Sihon had controlled land from **the Arnon Gorge** right about the midpoint of the Dead Sea all the way up to the Sea of Galilee. Og's territory stretched northward from there for about sixty miles to a point somewhere northwest of Damascus. Butler observes: "It is interesting that in giving the imprecise east-west boundary, the description extends the north-south boundary above the River Jabbok. The intention is to underline the completeness of Israel's conquest of the trans-jordan territory" (Butler, 135).

12:7–24. In this fascinating array of cities, the emphasis is on the destruction of the kings, but their names are not even mentioned. They were merely pawns, minor impediments in the way of God's providing victory in the promised land—**thirty-one kings in all** in addition to Sihon and Og.

But let's not lose the spiritual application in the list of nearly unpronounceable names. God's purposes in the conquest of sin are virtually the same as his purposes in the conquest of Canaan. No chariot, no sword, no arrow could bring total victory over sin. Though the Canaanites got what they deserved because of their sin, their deaths did not take care of the sin problem. God had to deal with that himself. Only the death of a perfect, sinless individual could pay the price for our sin and break the sin barrier between humanity and God. Jesus Christ died that death, took that punishment, and won the battle over sin.

Think of the extreme judgment on sin described in this chapter. Hundreds of thousands of people slaughtered. And think of God turning that judgment on his own Son so we could receive the grace and life that the Canaanites did not. Unlike Israel we do not have to exact God's judgment on sin. That judgment has already been absorbed by Christ. We need not strike ourselves or anyone else because of sin; Jesus has already borne our stripes. But as with Israel, God's purpose was more than judicial and judgmental. He also wanted to bring about a purging of sin as well as its punishment.

Though Christ bore the judgment for sin, he did not eradicate the problem of sin here on earth. Therefore, we must still enter into warfare as the Israelites did to cleanse our lives of the power of sin. This is the process of sanctification. The New Testament is filled with commands to "clean up," "take off," "put to death," "remove," and "get rid of" our sinful habits and ways. Paul makes clear in Romans 6:11–12: "Count yourselves dead to sin but alive to God in Christ Jesus. Therefore do not let sin reign in your mortal body so that you obey its evil desires."

Like Joshua and the Israelites marching through Canaan with swords drawn and slashing, we do battle with the areas of sin in our own lives. Not because we are under judgment for sin—God has already taken care of that—but because we need to purge the sin that will lead us astray and turn us against God.

> **MAIN IDEA REVIEW:** *What seems like a bloody merciless war to us was really God's way of providing the environment most conducive for righteous living on the part of his people.*

III. CONCLUSION

"A Mighty Fortress"

One should not confuse reformation with annihilation, but Joshua's heroic march through Canaan reminds us of Martin Luther's spiritual conquest of Europe. Samuel Coleridge once said, "Martin Luther did as much for the Reformation by his hymns as he did by his translation of the Bible." A bit of an overstatement perhaps, but the impact of hymns like "A Mighty Fortress Is Our God" cannot be taken lightly. This great hymn brings courage to Christians all around the world. Its first line in the German text (*Ein Feste Burg Ist Unser Gott*) is inscribed on Luther's tomb at Wittenburg.

Psalm 46:7–8 offers a joyful response from the people of Israel upon hearing the first six verses sung by the director of music and quite possibly a Hebrew choir: "The LORD Almighty is with us; the God of Jacob is our fortress. Come and see the works of the LORD." Few would question the assumption that Luther drew his hymn from the seventh verse of this psalm, which Joshua could have affirmed hundreds of years earlier and we can affirm today as we remind ourselves that the God of creation is with us every moment.

> A mighty Fortress is our God, a Bulwark never failing.
>
> Our helper He amid the flood of mortal ills prevailing.
>
> For still our ancient foe doth seek to work us woe;
>
> His craft and power are great and armed with cruel hate,
>
> On earth is not His equal.

Let us take great comfort in Luther's victorious words: "God's truth abideth still. His kingdom is forever."

PRINCIPLES

- In spiritual warfare, sometimes we have to endure war to experience peace.
- Our holy God still fights the battle against sin, and he still must punish sin to provide a safe environment for his people.
- Christ allowed himself to be made sin for us so we would not have to pay the price for our own sin.

APPLICATIONS

- Take some time to reflect on the total victory God has won over sin through the death of Jesus.
- Share with a friend or acquaintance the victories God has won in your life.
- What spiritual foes need to be purged from your own life?

IV. LIFE APPLICATION

Antlers Up

As I write this chapter, there is a story making the rounds about two novice hunters who were seen dragging a deer back to their truck. As another hunter came by, he said to them, "I don't want to interfere with what you are doing, but it is easier if you drag the deer in the other direction so the antlers don't dig into the ground." After he left, the two thought about it for a while and decided to try it his way. In just a few minutes one said to the other, "Man, that guy was totally right; this is much easier." "I agree," said his buddy, "but we keep getting farther and farther away from the truck."

Had Joshua attempted to conquer the promised land in his own way, he would have been dragging the deer with antlers down. One hardly wants to suggest that defeating an entire nation of heavily armed pagan Canaanites was "a piece of cake" or that Joshua was just playing out his role by allowing God to take care of things. Let's not forget that the central task here was not so much victory as what we might call "cleanup." Let me try a couple of different metaphors to make that point.

Suppose you were to hire me to trim some trees in your yard. What if I trimmed all the branches and then drove away, leaving your yard cluttered with debris? You would call me back to finish the job and wouldn't pay a dime until the yard was cleaned up.

Christ allowed himself to be trimmed and cut down to pay for our sins, but the cleanup job continues every day of our lives.

Or suppose you made another terrible mistake and hired me to come to your house and exterminate the cockroaches. I would tell you that you will have to go away for a few hours while I'm doing the treatment with some noxious chemicals, and when you return, you find dead bugs scattered all over the house; not one had been swept up. You might not consider cleaning up the bugs my job if all the cockroaches were now dead, but on the other hand you certainly wouldn't just leave them there and say, "Oh well, they're dead, and that's all that really matters." If I didn't clean up the mess, you would go about doing it immediately.

Christ died to exterminate our sin problem. But we cannot say, "Well, I'm a believer now, and that's all that matters. I'll just live with this mess in my life." No. We clean up that mess and try to keep the whole house spotless so other bugs will not be attracted.

In the same way God asks us to clean up our lives so sin is not attracted. To drive out the enemy so we don't begin to serve other gods. That's why we have to attack our problems of jealousy, anxiety, anger, depression, lust, or gossip. They are dead branches on the ground waiting to be cleaned up and cut up for firewood. They are dead bugs looking emaciated and ugly lying around the house or perhaps dead mice stinking up the pantry.

What is God's goal for us in all of this? The last phrase of Joshua 11, "The land had rest from war." We fight the war to achieve God's peace. When we obey him to do battle when he calls us to the front line, he gives victory and the glorious quiet and rest of his peace.

When my son and grandson wrestle on the floor, one will often call for "rest time." We need that kind of respite, and such rest is more appreciated after the effort of the fight. God is gracious. As he longed for Israel to live in their promised land in peace, so he longs for us to live in his blessings of peace.

Redpath says:

> If I always look within myself for this rest, what happens? I will start looking for an unscriptural experience of the Holy Spirit and I will think I am not saved because I haven't what some people call "the real baptism" and because I cannot speak in tongues. If I look within, I will become fanatical. If I look without and up to Christ without reckoning on the presence of the Spirit of God, I shall look in despair and say He is too far away, the prospect is too high, and I can never reach it. But if I look up to the Cross in the clearness of God's blue sky and know that it is empty because He who was crucified on it is sitting at God's right hand holding out all the inheritance of life and blessing for me—if at the same time I believe that He has shed into my heart the Holy Spirit to make it all real down here, then my soul will rest from war. I shall live above the noise, the clamor, the rush—above the dirt and the sin. I shall be resting in Christ, thankful that He has sent me the Holy Spirit to make His presence real to me (Redpath, 168–69).

V. PRAYER

Father, thank you for the victory, but thank you even more for the rest. Thank you that the sin which has so plagued our lives in the past is now behind us, and thank you that you still give victory over remaining sin whatever that might be. Amen.

VI. DEEPER DISCOVERIES

A. "Put to the Sword" (11:11)

The word *hereb* describes the short thrusting sword that served as the chief weapon of the Israelites. It had a bronze blade ten or twelve inches in length protruding from a hilt often fashioned like a lion's head with an open mouth. In Judges 3:16 we read about Ehud's sword which had two edges and an overall length of eighteen inches. Joshua's army also probably used the javelin (8:18), bows and arrows (24:12), and most likely the sling with stone balls in addition to a thrusting spear (Num. 25:7) and a hurling javelin (1 Sam. 18:10–11).

Israel used swords of bronze well into the time of David, since the Philistines alone knew the secret of forging swords from iron. In fact, when Jonathan gave David his sword (1 Sam. 18:4), he gave him a great gift because in all Israel only the king and his son had swords and spears of iron.

B. Hardened Hearts (11:20)

This is an expression revealing the sovereign working of God in confirming the hearts of unrepentant people in their obstinacy before judging them. (We see it in Exod. 4:21; 7:13–14; 9:12; 14:17; Isa. 6:10; John 12:40; and 2 Thess. 2.) The comparison between the Canaanites and the Egyptians (especially Pharaoh) cannot be overlooked. Howard says:

> Rahab and the Gibeonites were Canaanites who were spared, even if they were for different reasons. Those Canaanites who resisted Israel and its God, however, were shown no mercy and were annihilated. God's hardening of their hearts, then, was due, at least in part, to their own stubbornness and resistance of Israel's God. Had they been willing to react as Rahab (or even the Gibeonites) had done, undoubtedly the results would have been different (Howard, 274).

VII. TEACHING OUTLINE

A. INTRODUCTION

1. Lead Story: Mouse in the Pantry

2. Context: The switch from Joshua 10 to Joshua 11 is strictly geographical, a transfer of focus from the southern campaign to the northern campaign.

3. Transition: The last phrase of chapter 11 ends the description of the initial conquest in the center of Canaan, the southern conquest and the northern conquest. However, chapter 12 serves as a summary to

end the first section of the book. For now instead of fighting for land, Joshua will begin the division of the land.

B. COMMENTARY

1. Description of Annihilation (11:1–11)
2. Purpose of Annihilation (11:12–23)
3. Results of Annihilation (12:1–24)

C. CONCLUSION: ANTLERS UP

VIII. ISSUES FOR DISCUSSION

1. We have noticed that two purposes for the annihilation of the Canaanites were God's punishment of sin and God's purging of sin. Can you think of any others?
2. How does God harden people's hearts today and for what reasons?
3. Describe at least three qualities of spiritual rest that follows spiritual warfare. What is it like? How can you tell if you have it?

Joshua 13–14

Senior Moments

I. **INTRODUCTION**
Geezer Goof

II. **COMMENTARY**
A verse-by-verse explanation of these chapters.

III. **CONCLUSION**
Glorifying God Enough
An overview of the principles and applications from these chapters.

IV. **LIFE APPLICATION**
Doing Your Best
Melding these chapters to life.

V. **PRAYER**
Tying these chapters to life with God.

VI. **DEEPER DISCOVERIES**
Historical, geographical, and grammatical enrichment of the commentary.

VII. **TEACHING OUTLINE**
Suggested step-by-step group study of these chapters.

VIII. **ISSUES FOR DISCUSSION**
Zeroing these chapters in on daily life.

"*G*od has no larger field for the man who is not faithfully doing his work where he is."

A n o n y m o u s

GEOGRAPHICAL PROFILE: HEBRON

- The place where Abraham buried Sarah in the cave of Machpelah

- Once known as Kiriath Arba after the ancestor of Annakim

- Still exists today twenty-five miles southwest of Jerusalem

- Became the inheritance of Caleb in the division of Canaan

- Capital of Judah during the time of David and its largest city

PERSONAL PROFILE: ELEAZAR

- The high priest at the time of the entrance to Canaan

- Aaron's son and successor (Exod. 6:25; Num. 20:26–28)

- Carried out important duties in the wilderness (Num. 3:4,32; 4:16)

- Involved in the commissioning service for Joshua

PERSONAL PROFILE: CALEB

- Son of Jephunneh the Kenizite of the line of Judah

- One of the ten original spies

- A patient and faithful man who followed the Lord wholeheartedly

Chapters 13 and 14 serve as a transition point in our book. Here Israel moves from the conquest of the land to the allotment of the land, and we go from reading a war story to reviewing a land survey. Joshua's role changes from general to administrator.

Joshua 13–14

Senior Moments

I. INTRODUCTION

Geezer Goof

Leonard and Margaret, an elderly couple, were starting to have memory trouble so they developed the habit of writing everything down. One day as they were sitting in their family room, Margaret said to Leonard, "Would you mind getting me some ice cream?" "No problem," Leonard responded and slowly rose to head for the kitchen. "You better write it down or you'll forget it," Margaret called after him. "No I won't," Leonard replied, "it's ice cream. How hard can it be to remember that?"

A few minutes later Leonard walked back in the living room carrying a tray with eggs, bacon, coffee, cereal, and orange juice. Margaret sighed and whined, "Leonard, I told you to write it down. Now look—you've forgotten the toast."

These two chapters talk about men who did not have memory problems in old age. Working with senior leaders in our churches is becoming more of a reality, actually, a throwback to New Testament times when an elder was really an elder. Sometime in the mid-1980s the Social Security Administration listed over 32,000 centenarians on its rolls. As early as 1990 the U.S. Census Bureau counted 35,808 people at least one hundred years and older. Whatever else those numbers mean, they remind us that we live in an aging population.

Most church leaders find it impossible to project a ministry strategy for fifty years or even thirty, so let's pick the year 2020—less than a generation from the publication date of this book. True, we can't do any kind of specific long-range planning that far ahead, but we can anticipate what evangelical congregations should be doing to understand older adults.

Demographers project that in 2020 people sixty-five and over will make up 17.3 percent of the U.S. population, and pension and health-care payments will reach 11.8 percent of the gross national product. No wonder we hear cries out of Washington regarding the status of Medicare and the Social Security system. If these have been mismanaged, as some allege, the forthcoming needs will require every bit of competence we can muster. Already the retirement age has been increased by incremental levels, a decision of consequence to the church.

How do people feel about all of this? What primary concerns do they express? Even though nursing homes are opening in America at the rate of one a day, most older people report their health as good. Even among those eighty-five and older, fewer than half (45.4 percent) need assistance with everyday activities. That number drops to less than 10 percent among people between the ages of sixty-five and sixty-nine. Still health is a primary concern.

But not with the guys in our chapters. Our text opens with the line "When Joshua was old and well advanced in years," but we're only halfway through the book; there is still a great deal for him to do. And at the end of chapter 14, Caleb at eighty-five claims, "I'm just as vigorous to go out to battle now as I was then [when he was forty]" (v. 11).

I say all this not only to say that churches need to understand the issues and problems facing senior citizens but also to emphasize they can avoid geezer goof by making sure that mature, seasoned, veteran leaders not only have ministries that serve them but are greatly involved in major leadership decisions for the entire congregation the way elders should be.

II. COMMENTARY

Senior Moments

MAIN IDEA: *The conquest of the land was just the beginning. Now it is necessary to divide the land to the tribes in accordance with God's plan.*

A God's Message (13:1–13)

SUPPORTING IDEA: *Just as God took control over the battles, God also takes control over the rest and communicates specific plans for how he wants the land of Canaan divided.*

13:1–7. A few months ago I opened greeting cards for my sixty-seventh birthday. The experience was a combination of agony and ecstasy, since most of us don't like to be reminded that we are growing older. Joshua's reminder was special because it came from God himself. When God says you're old, you know you're old. Joshua was probably somewhere near a hundred years old at this point. We dare not forget that only he and Caleb remained of the generation that came out of Egypt. They were still alive because they brought a positive report about entering the land. Joshua was old, but the job wasn't finished.

As this staggering array of geographical locations unfolds for the rest of Joshua, some readers will find the change in story line a bit boring, but it was the most exciting time for Israelites. If we put ourselves in their sandals, we notice this was the first time in their history as a nation that they had their own land, their own cities, their own fields, and their own homes. Verses 2–5 describe the portion of land that had not yet been conquered. Essentially it consisted of Philistia, Phoenicia, and Lebanon (reading south to north), the southwest coastal region, and the far north territory.

This was no indictment against Joshua for having grown old before the job was completed, but it was a genuine reminder that there was more to be done. The Israelite army had done their part (11:16); now the remainder of the conquest was to be handled by the tribes on a town-by-town basis. So it was time for Joshua to divide the land. The allotting of the inheritance was intended to motivate the Israelites to finish driving out the Canaanites. How that could happen is clearly identified in verse 6: **I myself will drive them out before the Israelites**. As Joshua sent them to their portions of land, he could also provide this assurance of victory.

The division of the land was handled in a fair manner (Num. 33). The idea of **inheritance** was very significant for the Israelites. God gave them a place of their own that would remain the property of their tribes and families. They could finally put out their own mailboxes. For four hundred years they had been slaves in Egypt. For forty years they had been nomads in the desert. Now they were finally landowners in their own country.

The old movie *Gone with the Wind* contains a scene that communicates the importance of land, of inherited property. Scarlet picks up a handful of Tara dirt and vows never to let it go.

Do you remember your first house? Ours was a little three-bedroom, one-bath in Overland Park, Kansas. White with brown trim. It wasn't much, but it was ours. Our name on the deed and on the mailbox. Our address. Our dirt. Our mortgage. Our headaches.

And think of your attitudinal difference between renting and owning. We rented a small house the year before we lived in the one I just described, but we put nothing into that place. No paint; no planting; no pampering—because it wasn't ours. When we bought a house, we worked, sacrificed, sweated, and made personal investments in the place because it was ours. Allotment of the land would increase Israel's commitment to involve and invest themselves in completing the conquest.

But spiritually, we respond to the one who has guaranteed our future. Therefore, we serve him. Colossians 3:23–24 reminds us, "Whatever you do, work at it with all your heart, as working for the Lord, not for men, since you know that you will receive an inheritance from the Lord as a reward. It is the Lord Christ you are serving." But having a guaranteed inheritance can also be risky business.

Perhaps a note of intent would be useful here. Throughout the rest of Joshua as scores of towns and locations are scattered across the pages, we will try to stay true to the intent of this commentary series (user friendly) and focus on the spiritual impact of the book's message rather than wandering into geographical bypaths. For those interested in exploring each town in some detail, I recommend both Howard and Butler and particularly Howard's "Excursus: Identifying Geographical Entities" (284–86). I do need to say that this commentary rejects the notion that these lists reflect some later superimposition on the text. These lists represent accurately distributions of land made in Joshua's time whether or not they were added to the text at some future point.

On that note, here is a helpful paragraph from Howard:

> Many scholars believe that the author of the Book of Joshua was not responsible for producing the lists in chapters 13–21, and this may very well be true. The lists may have been independent records that the author incorporated into his work, just as the authors of 1–2 Kings, 1–2 Chronicles, and Ezra-Nehemiah used lists and sources in the course of writing their books. These lists undoubtedly came directly from Joshua, Eleazar (see 14:1), or someone else in the nation's leadership (or their scribes). At least some of the lists were produced by the twenty-one surveyors sent out from Shiloh to survey the territories of the seven remaining tribes of chapters 18 and 19 (see 18:1–10) (Howard, 294).

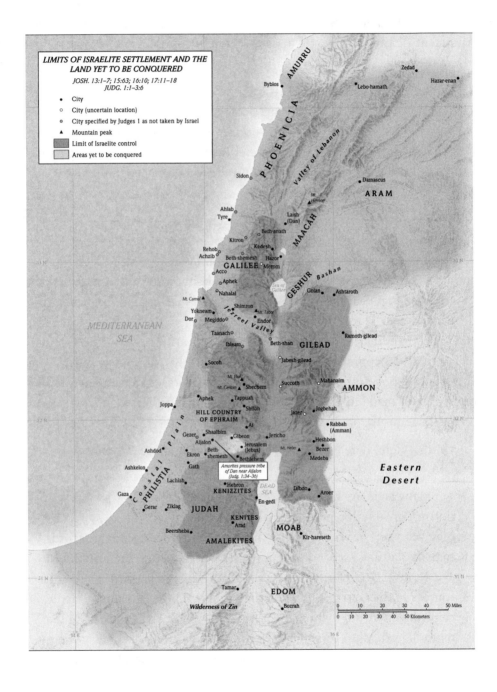

13:8–13. These verses describe the tribes east of the Jordan River who obeyed in helping conquer the land in Canaan but failed to finish the job in their own backyard. This is the first of many such statements in the Book of Joshua. No immediate crisis took place, but the Israelites paid for this later as God said they would.

Why didn't they complete the job? Laziness? Complacency? Dissatisfaction with where they were? Whatever the reason, they did not receive all that God had for them—a historical reminder of a spiritual condition in which many Christians live today. We should learn from these verses that God gives as we receive, he drives out as we stand up and fight, and he provides as we appropriate.

Some farms have a cattle trough designed to supply fresh water to cattle as they require it and at the same time limit waste in the time of drought. The trough is built in the center of a platform into which is built a strong steel spring. When the animal steps onto the platform, the spring is compressed. This opens a valve that releases water into the trough. As long as the animal remains on the platform, the water flows. When it leaves, the water stops. The supply of water is always available but only when appropriated. So it is with spiritual power in our lives, only available when we stand on the platform of God's promises.

William Penn befriended some Indians who offered him a gift. He could have all the land he could walk around in one day. Taking them at their word, Penn rose early the next morning and walked briskly all day until dusk. When he returned, one of the Indian chiefs said, "The pale face has had a very long walk today." But they were not displeased. He had honored their word, and they honored his trust. The land he encircled that day became the city of Philadelphia.

We wonder sometimes why we keep coming back to these Transjordanian two and one-half tribes, and Madvig has a suggestion: "The author was eager to uphold the unity of the Twelve Tribes in spite of the geographic separation and an undercurrent of feeling that only the land west of the Jordan was truly the promised land" (Madvig, 318). Incidentally, we will treat the strange development of how the half tribe of Manasseh came about in "Deeper Discoveries."

Moses surfaces again in this passage (we haven't seen much of him in the first half of the book) because he was responsible for leading the conquest east of the Jordan River and dividing the lands. An interesting verb appears in verse 8—**received** or *took* (*lqh*). Howard notes:

> The taking (*lqh*) of the land that the two and one half tribes did also sets the precedent for the rest of the tribes to do the same thing, although the only other time this verb is used in the book to describe taking of land, it again refers to the two and one-half tribes (18:7). Not once is it said that any of the tribes west of the Jordan took (*lqh*) their lands. The focus in the latter chapters is on God's and Joshua's *giving* of the land and their *possessing* it—and, sometimes, on the fact that the tribes *did not* dispossess the land's inhabitants (Howard, 308).

Let me say again that the tribes had not yet colonized their portions when these lists were drawn up. In actuality Dan did not permanently settle its appointed territory, Ephraim did not conquer or settle Gezer, and the Benjaminites never conquered or enjoyed sole occupation of Jerusalem although that city was assigned to them. Many of the cities and their villages listed in these chapters were not conquered by the Israelites for centuries to come.

Some of the town sites listed may then have been uninhabited by Canaanites and not settled by Israelites for a long time after the distribution of the land. None of that sets aside God's promise to give them precisely the lands described as we read them.

B Levi's Ministry (13:14–33; 14:4)

SUPPORTING IDEA: *Sometimes God calls certain people to specific tasks and places them in rigid boundaries. Such was the role of the Levites, whose call to minister is described in these verses.*

13:15–32. In this section we want to focus specifically on Levi, but we cannot bypass the bulk of the passage that describes the territory given to Reuben, Gad, and Manasseh. Once again the order reads south to north with Reuben occupying the territory immediately east of the northern half of the Dead Sea, dangerously bordered by Moab and Edom to the south and Ammon to the northeast. A simple glance at a settlement map shows Reuben in a most precarious spot. Just north of Reuben was the territory of Gad, west of Ammon and located right in the area where the Israelites gathered to cross the Jordan River. Towns like Adam and Zarethan that we have encountered earlier in Joshua fall into Gad's territory. Finally, the territory east of the Sea of Kinnereth (Galilee) belonged to the half tribe of Manasseh stretching from Ramoth Gilead in the southeast and reaching up toward Mount Hermon in the north. The famous Golan Heights so significant in modern Israelite military history are located immediately in the center of the ancient allocation to Manasseh.

In earlier chapters we have discussed whether the decision of the two and one-half tribes showed good judgment while at the same time acknowledging their faithfulness and integrity in marching across the Jordan River and into the land to assist their brothers. However, we cannot ignore the historical and even spiritual implications of this kind of a decision.

Campbell raises the point well:

> Was the request of the two and one-half tribes to settle in Transjordan a wise one? History would seem to answer no. Their territories had no natural boundaries to the east and were therefore constantly exposed to invasion by the Moabites, Canaanites, Arameans, Midianites, Amalekites, and others. And when the king of Assyria looked covetously toward Canaan, Reuben, Gad, and the half-tribe of Manasseh were the first to be carried into captivity by the Assyrian armies (1 Chr. 5:26) (Campbell, BKC, 356).

It would appear that the Transjordanian tribes had exchanged safety, security, and togetherness as a nation for vast amounts of land in known territory. They had exercised a well-known cliché: "A bird in the hand is worth two in the bush."

13:14,33; 14:4. It doesn't sound fair that the Levites would not receive their own land, but they were well taken care of. They had cities to live in and would receive food from their portion of the offerings. We pick up verse 4 of chapter 14 here to get a complete picture, though Levites will be described further in chapter 21. The most important thing here is that the Levites were a reminder of God as their true inheritance. Not just the land. Not an inheritance of gold or possessions. The Levites reminded everyone else of their dependence on God. A reminder to take their eyes off the inheritance and put them on the giver of the inheritance.

The situation of the Levites reminds us of Matthew 6:19–21:

> Do not store up for yourselves treasures on earth, where moth and rust destroy, and where thieves break in and steal. But store up for yourselves treasures in heaven, where moth and rust do not destroy, and where thieves do not break in and steal. For where your treasure is, there your heart will be also.

We need the same reminder on a continual basis. In his book *The Testament*, John Grisham describes a multimillionaire businessman writing his final will and testament. His fractured family and spoiled children care more about their share of the inheritance than they do about the relationship with their father. Throughout the book they fight and squabble over the money while growing in their hatred for one another.

How sad to think that we sometimes get more focused on our earthly "inheritance" than on our heavenly inheritance in Christ. For the Israelites, the land was nothing without their God. For us, all we have—job, family, house, land, car, clothes, possessions—is nothing without God.

Israel received a special inheritance. Not an heirloom to store in the attic, but a land to be used and worked. And God gave the Levites a spiritual inheritance that served as a central reminder of their focus and the nation's focus on him.

Nor was this a new idea.

> The landless state of the tribe of Levi is important in the book of Joshua, but it had its roots much earlier. It is mentioned here and in v. 33, as well as in 14:3–4 and 18:7. These passages hark back to the Lord's directives to Aaron in Num. 18:20–24, where their inheritance was to be the tithes that the Israelites presented to the Lord, and to Moses' words in Deut. 18:1–5, where they were to receive the choicest offerings that the people brought to the Lord (Howard, 310).

There is also a connection here with Paul's words in 1 Corinthians 9:13 where, in making a case for payment of people in ministry, he argues, "Don't you know that those who work in the temple get their food from the temple, and those who serve at the altar share in what is offered on the altar?" We could argue that two principles arise from these few verses in Joshua 13 and 14: (1) God's people are to take care of those who minister to them in spiritual leadership and that giving is a part of their worship; (2) people who serve the Lord in ministry positions are not to accumulate to themselves large wealth, fancy homes, huge pieces of property, and other earthly possessions. Certainly in the last two or three decades of the twentieth century we saw ample illustrations of how corrupt this can become.

Actually there are fourteen tribal lists when we consider all the passages in this book and focus on cities as well as land boundaries. That number drops to twelve, however, when we link east Manasseh and west Manasseh as one and recognize that Levi was not a participant in the division of the land.

Of course, there are thousands of Christians who have no earthly possessions but could hardly be considered as part of vocational ministry. So the principle of God himself being an inheritance stretches far beyond those professional boundaries. Once again Alan Redpath brings the spiritual dimension to keen focus:

> To some, God has given no inheritance in the land, no home, no earthly love, only a way which seems full of hardship and crushing burdens. Perhaps you have come to believe that God has been punishing you for all your failure and reminding you that you were disqualified forever from His service because you bear a stigma upon you.
>
> How different is the truth! The Lord God of Israel is your inheritance. Yours is the unique privilege of testing the preciousness of the abounding grace of His pardon and His love. His offer to you is a life of worship, a life of work, and a life of witness if, out of the darkness of wilderness days, you chose Him as your undisputed Lord. To imagine, for instance, that a person who entered into a marriage that has proved disastrous must carry all through his life the stigma of it, is to place a burden on him which is utterly contrary to the Book and which the grace of Christ can utterly remove.
>
> Thank God that in that moment when someone has been crushed seemingly beyond help, when the things that he has cherished most in life have crashed around him, and he is left in the scattered wreck of what once he thought was a home, the Lord Jesus

holds out His hand to aid. Thank God, He takes the clay that has been mired, the precious, soiled, broken life, and molds it again, now into a vessel unto honor, sanctified, and meet for the Master's use. And He says, 'From this moment onward the Lord thy God is thy inheritance (Redpath, 190–191).

🄲 Caleb's Mountain (14:1–15)

SUPPORTING IDEA: *Caleb demonstrates that we are never too old to serve the Lord. His faithfulness through many decades qualified him for special blessing from God and even renewed responsibilities in his declining years.*

14:1–5. Having put aside the two and one-half Transjordanian tribes for the moment and explained the inheritance of the tribe of Levi (mentioned again in this section), our narrator is prepared to turn his eyes westward across the Jordan River and into Canaan. Let's remember that the Transjordanian tribes did not live in Canaan, nor was that portion of land, though occupied by Israelites, ever considered Canaan. Just to make sure everyone understands this strange division, we learn again that Moses had commanded this and arranged it in detail, including the status of the Levites. Joshua was the administrator, but Moses had laid out the plan **so the Israelites divided the land, just as the LORD had commanded Moses**.

But Joshua had some help as we meet **Eleazar the priest**, co-agent with Joshua in dividing the land. We notice in the text that Eleazar is named before Joshua and therefore doesn't appear to be just an assistant. Indeed since he would have worn the ephod with the Urim and Thummin by which the will of God was determined, his role would have been predominant in the process. Eleazar was named in Numbers 27:21 and 34:17 as well. Nor did Eleazar and Joshua handle the administration alone; they were assisted by **the heads of the tribal clans of Israel**. This whole thing was a team leadership operation, and the method that was used was by lot.

Campbell notes:

> According to Jewish tradition the name of a tribe was drawn from one urn and simultaneously the boundary lines of a territory from another. This method designated each tribal inheritance. But blind chance did not decide the tribal location, for God was superintending the whole procedure (cp. Prov. 16:33). The inequities of

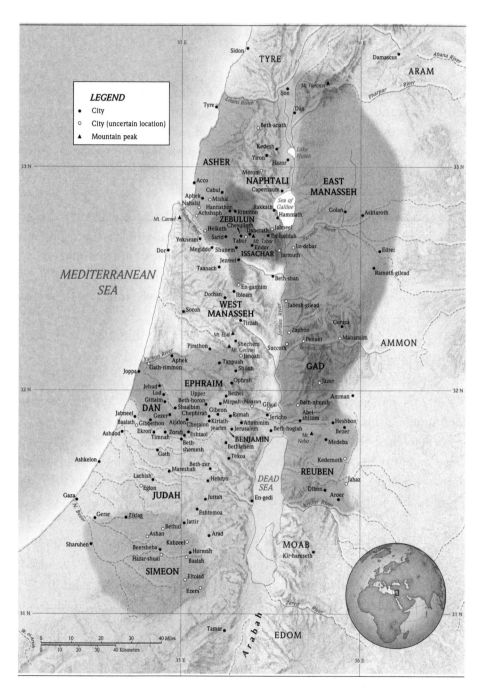

Tribal Allotments of Israel

assignments that existed and that caused some tensions and jealousies among the tribes should have been accepted as a part of God's purpose, not as something that was arbitrary and unfair (Campbell, *BKC*, 356).

14:6–9. But there was an exception to the lot process. Long before, Caleb the faithful spy had been promised the very portion of the land the ten spies went out to survey. Along with his buddies from Judah, he approached Joshua to remind him of what **Moses swore to me.** And he remembered the key word and offered it as an ongoing testimony: **I, however, followed the LORD my God wholeheartedly.**

Caleb was a Kenizzite. This means he was descended from Esau, not from Jacob, and was therefore outside the promised line. But somehow either before they went to Egypt or while there, Caleb's ancestors joined with the Israelites and the tribe of Judah. His name means "all heart," and he did have a great heart for God. When it came time for each tribe to pick a representative to spy out the land, the tribe of Judah selected Caleb, who was forty years old back then. Only he and Joshua came back with positive reports, Joshua's affirmation following Caleb's brave stand.

Nevertheless, for thirty-eight years Caleb had wandered in the desert because of the sin of the Israelites and for seven years he had fought faithfully under Joshua to conquer the land and defeat the thirty-one kings. The word **wholeheartedly** appears twice in this section, again in verse 14, all of these citations drawn from Deuteronomy 1:36. There's no gimmick about the word *wholeheartedly,* but it does become the flag and standard for the Caleb tradition. Butler says this concept of being totally loyal to Yahweh

> . . . is a rare expression in the Hebrew text, appearing to have its basic source in the Caleb tradition (Num. 14:24; 32:12; Deut. 1:36). . . . It is taken up only one time outside the Caleb tradition, that being in the Deuteronomistic judgment against Solomon (1 Kgs. 11:6), marking the beginning of Israel's downfall. The Deuteronomist thus appears to take the Caleb tradition as the prime example of how Israel should act. The writer thus restricts the language to Caleb's perfect example and to the moment when Israel began its irreversible trend in the opposite direction (Butler, 173–174).

This word *wholeheartedly,* so uniquely related to Caleb's life and ministry, is a nautical term that refers to a ship pushing straight ahead, no matter what. And, as we like to include occasional preaching and teaching tips, here's a little outline that shows three factors working against this kind of faithful commitment and dedication in Caleb.

1. He was dedicated *under pressure.* Even when ten spies spoke against him, Caleb stuck to his convictions. Even when the Israelites were ready to stone both Caleb and Joshua, they remained steadfast in their faith.

2. He was dedicated *under difficulties.* Caleb endured thirty-eight years in the wilderness for a sin he did not commit. He watched family members and friends die in the desert, and yet he remained true to God.

3. He was dedicated *under the shadow* of another leader. Though Caleb had impeccable character, he was not chosen to be the leader after Moses and "retire" as the head of his tribe but not as the leader of Israel. Nevertheless, Caleb followed and served faithfully in whatever position God called him to hold.

Is our dedication to God wholehearted? Do we follow him even when the crowd goes the other way? Even when things get tough? Even when we must accept our given positions in life? The excuses are all too easy: *No one else is doing it God's way. This is too hard and it's not my fault. It isn't fair; I deserve more.* But Caleb kept his focus on God in wholehearted devotion and laid down a historical model not only for Israel but for us.

14:10–12. Even after eighty-five difficult years, Caleb had a great attitude about serving God and fighting for him. He wasn't tired out; in fact, he was just getting excited. He didn't walk up to his old buddy Joshua to ask for a maintenance-free, energy-saving home. Preferably one with a large porch for his favorite rocking chair. No, he asked for the hill country still inhabited by giants. He wanted the very area that had intimidated the other ten spies— and the rest of the Israelites were probably glad to let him have it.

This is like getting into a pickup basketball game with a professional team and wanting to guard the biggest guy on the court. It would be like walking into a building that needed cleaning and volunteering to take the dirtiest and largest room there. Like a student choosing the toughest course offered by a college and then asking the hardest professor to give him the most difficult test.

But Caleb had such confidence and such a positive attitude about this conquest that he wanted the biggest challenge available. It reminds me of one of my favorite stories about a shoe salesman who was sent to a remote area of the world to sell shoes. He soon gave up dejected because no one in that area wore shoes. The company sent another salesman who quickly reported back enthusiastically, "Send lots of shoes; everyone here needs them!"

Like many of the other Israelites, our tendency is to want peace and prosperity as quickly as we can get it, and with the least discomfort and inconvenience. When we don't get our way, we tend to grumble and complain instead of seeing the benefit of challenge in our lives. Caleb didn't just accept the challenge; he asked for it.

A chronological note needs emphasis here. Caleb's mention of his age gives us the answer to the length of time it took for Joshua and his troops to conquer Canaan. Since Caleb was forty years old at the time of the spy mission and spent thirty-eight years in the desert, the fact that he was now eighty-five indicates that it took seven years to conquer Canaan (more about Caleb in "Deeper Discoveries").

14:13–15. If we only had the first half of verse 12, we might consider Caleb cocky and prideful. But the balancing factor is that his confidence was based on God's promise to help. Five times in those previous verses Caleb referred to God's promises—no wonder **Joshua blessed Caleb son of Jephunneh and gave him Hebron as his inheritance.** Caleb had a perspective that allowed him to see God as greater than any giant he might face. This faith had grown over his lifetime as he saw God fulfill promise after promise. We could say about Caleb that he had faith in the promises of God, in the presence of God, and in the power of God.

And just so we get the full impact of Caleb's request, our narrator reminds us that his land inheritance **used to be called Kiriath Arba after Arba, who was the greatest man among the Anakites.** Madvig suggests that the reappearance of the phrase **then the land had rest from war** "may be evidence that Caleb's conquest of Hebron actually took place as a part of the southern campaign. In Judges 1:9–10 the conquest of Hebron is credited to the men of Judah. Hebron is only one of many cities that had to be captured more than once" (Madvig, 325).

Like Caleb, as we walk in dependence on God and his promises and see him work, our faith grows stronger. Caleb had been on some wild rides in the wilderness and was confident that God would not let him down—and he didn't.

MAIN IDEA REVIEW: *The conquest of the land was just the beginning. Now it is necessary to divide the land to the tribes in accordance with God's plan.*

III. CONCLUSION

Glorifying God Enough

Caleb demonstrates that the purpose of excellence in our lives and ministries is to glorify God. Christian leadership must be measured qualitatively and not quantitatively or it's not Christian at all. I like *The Living Bible* rendering of 1 Peter 2:10: "Once you were less than nothing; now you are God's own. Once you knew very little of God's kindness; now your very lives have been changed by it."

My former boss was Dr. Don Campbell, third president of Dallas Seminary and a Bible scholar of significant dimensions. From his work on Joshua, we have gleaned numerous insights in this commentary. Campbell tells a story of a five-year-old boy hit by a car while playing in the alley behind his home. The injury required surgery to repair a broken arm. The boy woke up in the hospital quite surprised that he was not dead. In the ensuing conversation with his mother, he observed, "Mom, I know why I'm still alive." She stammered a bit at that statement and prodded him to explain further. "I'm still alive because I haven't glorified God enough yet in my life." Out of the mouths of babes—a distinct reminder to all of us of what God expects.

Caleb glorified God "because he followed the LORD, the God of Israel, wholeheartedly" (Josh. 14:14). Schaeffer makes the transfer from Caleb's situation to ours.

Back in Joshua's day when the master conquest was over God was the same, his promise was the same, his power was the same.

But the people did not possess their possessions because of their desire for peace and for tribute. We Christians stand in the same danger. It is all too easy to fail to possess the possessions God has promised because we either draw back out of fear of the troubles that being a Christian will bring us or we become caught up in the affluent society where people sail their little boats upon this plastic culture (Schaeffer, 162).

PRINCIPLES

- We have an inheritance and ownership in heaven. This assurance should motivate us to serve and sacrifice here and now.
- We dare not allow the promise of heaven and the assurance of our inheritance to lull us into sleeping through our Christian responsibility on earth.
- Israel only possessed as much of the land as they occupied; as they obeyed, God gave them more.

APPLICATIONS

- Have you known people who served the Lord wholeheartedly? What were they like? How have they impacted your life?
- Think about Caleb's example. What does this imply regarding God's plan for senior adults?
- What do you sense God wanting you to do in your senior years?

IV. LIFE APPLICATION

Doing Your Best

Former President Jimmy Carter likes to tell the story of his first interview with Admiral Rickover when Carter was a naval officer. Rickover asked Carter how he did at the Naval Academy, and Carter proudly responded, "Sir, I stood fifty-ninth in a class of 820." Rather than congratulating this outstanding student, the admiral scowled, "Did you do your best?" Carter, always the humble and honest gentleman, said, "No sir, I did not always do my best." Rickover sat silent for what seemed like several minutes, then snarled, "Why not?" Carter recalls those two words as a "question which I have never been able to forget, nor to answer."

Both Joshua and Caleb loom large in these two chapters as men who finished well, doing their best in the service of God. They exemplified excellence and made possible the passing on of their faith to their families. In fact, chapter 15 tells us about Caleb's daughter Acsah who came one day urging her husband Othniel "to ask her father for a field" (v. 18). In discussion with Caleb she acquired "the upper and lower springs" (v. 19). This is an interesting postscript for fathers. It seems that Caleb passed on his "we can take the promised land" faith to his daughter. She had the confidence in her earthly father that Caleb had in his heavenly Father—and that's the way it should work.

Parents, grandparents, our children should have confidence in us because we have put our confidence in God. They need to see wholehearted dedication to God, a positive and enthusiastic view of his work, and a lifelong dependence on his promises in us so they can follow in faith.

We have a great opportunity to leave an inheritance for our children. It might be only material (house, possessions, jewelry, clothes, stocks, money), but it can be a living legacy, an inheritance of love and relationship and principles and traditions and memories that our children and grandchildren can treasure forever.

You can *leave* an inheritance, or you yourself can *be* their inheritance. What's more important to you? A bank account and an attic of heirlooms or a life that's been impacted by your training and sacrifice? Will you teach your children to look for their inheritance here on earth, or will they know their inheritance is in heaven where rust and moth do not destroy?

Abraham Lincoln once said, "No one is poor who has had a godly mother." And we might add father, grandfather, and grandmother to that list as well. Like Caleb, we want to leave a godly inheritance for our children. We can be thankful to God for our inheritance in heaven and make sure we pass on that spiritual heritage to generations that follow.

V. PRAYER

Father, thank you for the great example that Joshua and Caleb provide us. May we follow the Lord our God wholeheartedly and trust your promises, presence, and power. Amen.

VI. DEEPER DISCOVERIES

A. Levi (13:14)

The ancestor of both Moses and Aaron, Levi was Jacob's third son by Leah. The name Levi may be derived from the Hebrew word for *attached*. Upon his birth Leah said, "Now at last my husband will become attached to me, because I have borne him three sons" (Gen. 29:34). Through Levi came the Levites, Israel's religious leaders and caretakers of the tabernacle (Exod. 32:25–29).

It may be worth noting that though all priests were Levites, not all Levites were priests. In later years at the temple most Levites did not enjoy the special privileges of priests but served by maintaining the building, providing music for worship, and aiding the priests at religious ceremonies. They were also in charge of the temple treasury. That is why upon the return from the exile Ezra told people to bring their tithes of crops to the Levites who, serving under the supervision of the priests, traveled from city to city to collect the tithe. Then they paid a tenth of what they received to the temple treasury to support the priests and help care for the poor.

In Exodus 13 the tribe of Levi is dedicated to stand in for all firstborn males dedicated to Yahweh. The whole tribe becomes a standing gift of people (Num. 8:16), and their cattle take the place of the people's cattle (Num. 3:45). Oehler offers a lengthy but useful paragraph regarding how the absence of specific land grants fit the spiritual and ministerial duties of the tribe.

> In order that the tribe of Levi might be withdrawn from ordinary labor,—which in the theocratic state was agricultural,—and might give itself completely to its sacred vocation, *no inheritance as a tribe was assigned to it* (Num. xviii.23). What Jehovah said to Aaron is in

Deut. x.9 applied to the whole tribe of Levi—namely, that Jehovah Himself would be their inheritance. The tribe is scattered among all the other tribes, in the territories of which it received forty-eight towns, with their suburbs, that is, pasturages. In this law, moreover, the priests are included along with the Levites. The thirteen special towns for the priests are first mentioned in Josh. xxi.4. Without doubt, this dispersion served the purpose of placing the Levites in a position where they could watch over the keeping of the law. The tithes were assigned to them *for their support*. . . . This was not an over-abundant endowment. Even when the tithe was conscientiously paid, it was no certain income (and, besides, it did not increase with the increase of the tribe). Moreover, if the people showed themselves averse to this tax (as was to be expected in times of falling away from the theocratic law), the tribe of Levi was subjected to unavoidable poverty. And thus Deuteronomy represents the Levites as placed in a position requiring the support of alms, and at standing in the same line with strangers, widows, and orphans (Day, 207).

B. Half Tribe of Manasseh (13:29)

If you are a pastor or a Sunday school teacher, you may assume that most of the people who hear you expound these chapters from Joshua have no clue why God allowed or even designed an east Manasseh and west Manasseh. It all goes back to a sin against Jacob recorded in the Book of Genesis.

Campbell tells the story well:

Centuries before the land was divided Jacob, when dying, had uttered prophecies regarding his sons. His prophecy about his firstborn Reuben was foreboding (cp. Gen. 49:3–4; 35:22). Though Reuben was the firstborn and entitled to a double portion (Deut. 21:17), neither he nor his tribe received it. Now after more than four centuries the punishment for Reuben's sinful deed was passed on to his descendants; the right of the firstborn passed over to his brother Joseph who received two portions, one for Ephraim and the other for Manasseh (Gen. 48:12–20) (Campbell, 356).

Furthermore, since it was necessary to maintain twelve tribes to keep that holistic Hebrew number, and since the Levites were not included in the number, the tribe of Joseph was divided into two tribes, Ephraim and Manasseh.

C. A Caleb Biography (14:6)

Unheralded and underrated, the son of Jephunneh the Kenizzite lived almost all his life in the shadow of Joshua. Even Alexander Whyte's famous *Bible Characters* includes Jepthah, Nabal, and Shimmei—but not Caleb. Yet in a time of outstanding human leadership, here is a man who still looked to the Lord and followed the Lord wholeheartedly.

He began his career with *service as a spy* at age forty, young by Old Testament Hebrew standards. When his fellow spies showed nothing but pessimism and fear, he exhibited the divine viewpoint and learned that criticism develops character. At no time did he allow himself to enjoy any competition with Joshua but constantly demonstrated a selfless spirit (Num. 13:21–33; 14:10,24).

But he also experienced *service as a survivor* (Josh. 14:6–11). Only two of the original Israelites were left out of two and one-half million, and Caleb was now eighty-five years old. He had seen it all—slavery, Egypt, the Red Sea, the golden calf, manna, the death of Moses, and the conquest of the promised land. In his patient waiting forty-five years to get the piece of property Moses had promised him, he shows us that there is no retiring from service for God and no looking back at problems or disappointments.

And Caleb also shows us *service as a senior citizen* (Josh. 14:11–15). He kept himself in terrific physical health that demonstrates a significant measure of God's grace along with human stewardship of his body. Since the number of people in the United States over the age of sixty-five increases by almost nine hundred a day, he shows us how to behave if you reach the age of eighty-five. Furthermore, he forms a bridge with the Book of Judges since Caleb's son-in-law Othniel, son of Kenaz, became the first judge. The fact that Othniel was also Caleb's younger brother (Judg. 1:13) indicates not only the common intra-tribal and family marriages of that era but Caleb's double influence on the first judge.

Let's not forget that Caleb's father was a non-Israelite who before the exodus had married a daughter of Hur of the clan of Kaleb in the tribe of

Judah (1 Chr. 2:9,18,50). She bore Jephunneh his first son and gave him the family name, Caleb. As a young man Caleb inherited the prerogatives of the clan and eventually became a chief of her tribe. Othniel is called a son of Kenaz in 1 Chronicles 4:13,15; the Kenazites were one of the tribes in the Negev and Mount Seir.

Caleb is an outstanding example of a godly believer because he wholly followed the Lord and claimed a glorious inheritance, the very land on which Abraham had lived and died. In capturing Hebron, Caleb rendered the whole nation valuable service and then later willingly yielded his city to the Levites and lived in the suburbs (Josh. 21:12).

Senior adults can offer the church knowledge, wisdom, unity, experience, and a constant awareness of the Lord's return. Caleb's goal in life was to know God's will and to do it; his badge in life was patient dependence upon God; and his legacy in life was a model of courage. For those of us called to serve in the shadows, let's remember that faithfulness, not stardom, is what counts.

VII. TEACHING OUTLINE

A. INTRODUCTION

1. Lead Story: Geezer Goof
2. Context: The second half of Joshua begins at chapter 13 as the division of the land gets underway. Interestingly chapters 12, 13, and 14 form the bridge with identical gates at each end—"then the land had rest from war."
3. Transition: The Caleb story of chapter 14 links the allotment of land to the Transjordanian tribes to the allotment in Canaan. Since Judah drew the first place, it seemed appropriate to our author to begin that description with the exciting record of the leader of the tribe, Caleb son of Jephunneh.

B. COMMENTARY

1. God's Message (13:1–13)
2. Levi's Ministry (13:14–33)
3. Caleb's Mountain (14:1–15)

C. CONCLUSION: GLORIFYING GOD ENOUGH

VIII. ISSUES FOR DISCUSSION

1. What did it mean for the Levites to receive the kind of inheritance they did?
2. Think of several senior citizens you know. In what ways are they like Caleb? In what ways are they not?
3. What would it mean to follow the Lord wholeheartedly in the twenty-first century?

Joshua 15–17

Israelite Cartography

I. INTRODUCTION
Spacious Skies

II. COMMENTARY
A verse-by-verse explanation of these chapters.

III. CONCLUSION
The Power of Positive Thinking

An overview of the principles and applications from these chapters.

IV. LIFE APPLICATION
The Man Who Discovered Britain

Melding these chapters to life.

V. PRAYER
Tying these chapters to life with God.

VI. DEEPER DISCOVERIES
Historical, geographical, and grammatical enrichment of the commentary.

VII. TEACHING OUTLINE
Suggested step-by-step group study of these chapters.

VIII. ISSUES FOR DISCUSSION
Zeroing these chapters in on daily life.

"*W*hen the heathen hear God's oracles on our lips they marvel at their beauty and greatness. But afterwards, when they mark that our deeds are unworthy of the words we utter, they turn from us with scoffing and say that it is a myth and a delusion."

Clement of Alexandria

Joshua 15–17

I N   A   N U T S H E L L

*A*fter the land was conquered, appropriate division according to God's plan became necessary. In these chapters we meet Caleb again and see the division of land to Ephraim and Manasseh.

Israelite Cartography

I. INTRODUCTION

Spacious Skies

The song began as a poem written by Wellesley Professor Katharine Lee Bates in 1893. Bates was head of the English department at the Massachusetts school. She wrote the words to "America the Beautiful" while teaching summer school in Colorado Springs, where she had fallen under the spell of the Rocky Mountains and Pike's Peak. It became a national favorite, but setting it to music proved tough. More than one thousand melodies were rejected before Bates's words were paired with an 1882 hymn by Samuel Augustus Ward, an organist from Newark, New Jersey.

Bates accepted no royalties for the song and claimed the poem almost wrote itself. She didn't feel she owned the song any more than she owned the spacious skies. According to Osbeck, Bates claimed, "We must match the greatest of our country with the goodness of personal godly living. If only we could couple the daring of the Pilgrims with the moral teachings of Moses, we would have something in this country that no one could ever take from us" (Osbeck, 164). Osbeck links the song to Proverbs 14:34: "Righteousness exalts a nation, but sin is a disgrace to any people," and says, "Each stanza is completed with an earnest plea for God's grace, God's healing, and his refining until we as a people achieve true brotherhood, law-abiding control, and nobility" (Osbeck, 164).

Certainly national pride swelled in the chests of the Israelites as they moved into their new land. There were plenty of spacious skies, though purple mountains were less likely. But they certainly could have sung, "Oh beautiful for pilgrim feet, whose stern impassioned stress a thoroughfare for freedom beat across the wilderness!"

These three chapters begin the parceling out of the land as Joshua releases appropriate sections to each of the nine and one-half tribes. These are admittedly difficult chapters to read, and there are more ahead. I have found it necessary to rededicate myself to the spirit of the Holman Old Testament Commentary series and not get caught up in long lists of cities but rather focus on the spiritual message, picking up lessons where we can find them. This is a ministry commentary, not an academic or scholarly work, though even those bog down when handling chapters like these. One frequently reads phrases like "the placement of this town and this location seems unclear" or "we have no idea of the sure site of this city." So we ask readers to understand again the purpose of the commentary series and not look for geographic detail but practical lessons.

II. COMMENTARY

Israelite Cartography

MAIN IDEA: *The settling of the promised land should have been an easy task after the seven-year conquest, but we find that the tribes lacked the initiative and courage to drive out the Canaanite inhabitants completely. This problem repeats itself throughout the second half of the Book of Joshua.*

🅐 Lion's Lair (15:1–63)

SUPPORTING IDEA: *During the conquest and the division of the land, Joshua and the Israelites had to learn that no matter how big their group or how strong their leaders, it was essential to follow God's commands down to the smallest detail.*

15:1–12. Many Christians have memorized Proverbs 15:1 to great profit: "A gentle answer turns away wrath, but a harsh word stirs up anger." But how about Joshua 15:1: **The allotment for the tribe of Judah, clan by clan, extended down to the territory of Edom, to the Desert of Zin in the extreme south.** I can't think of a person I know who could rattle off that verse if challenged to do so. We tend to pass quickly over chapters like Joshua 15–19 and for obvious reasons. Nevertheless, these are important texts that serve as land title documents for the tribes in their new land.

In fact, these chapters are the kind we always dreaded in Sunday school, reading impossible-to-pronounce names. But Joshua 15 takes us right back to Genesis 15 where in verse 7 God says to Abraham, "I am the LORD, who brought you out of Ur of the Chaldeans to give you this land to take possession of it." So as the fifteenth chapter of Joshua unfolds, the fifteenth chapter of Genesis becomes a reality. Although we may pass over chapters like this lightly, surely the Israelites listened with keen interest to this listing of their own cities, areas, and boundaries.

Matthew Henry once said of this part of Joshua, "We are not to skip over these chapters of hard names as useless and not to be regarded; for where God has a mouth to speak and a hand to write we should find an ear to hear and an eye to read; and God will give us a heart to profit." Furthermore, there is a hermeneutical principle at stake here, the principle of proportion. Simply stated, it means that God gives greater space to those things he considers more important. In chapter 14 we thrilled to the record of eighty-five-year-old Caleb wanting to march again into the hill country of the Anakites. But the Caleb portion of that chapter is only nine verses long. Now we face a sixty-three-verse chapter that lists towns one after the other.

But as I have said numerous times in the study of Joshua, there are direct parallels between Israel's conquest of the promised land and our spiritual conquest in the Christian life. Like the Israelites, God wants us to defeat an enemy with his help and to receive a blessing from his hand. In both cases God offers something that must be received or taken in some way. The Israelites had to fight battles and take ground to receive the blessings of the promised land. We fight spiritual battles and gain spiritual ground to realize the blessings of spiritual growth and maturity.

We should notice that the allocation of land started with Judah, probably because this was the largest tribe and its land portion exceeded that of any other. On his deathbed Jacob had prophesied that the Messiah would come from Judah's line (Gen. 49:10) and that Judah would essentially be the ruling tribe. Located in the southern portion of the land, Judah would always be subject to potential enemies, particularly Moab and Edom to the east and the Amalekites to the southwest. Jacob's promise also said about Judah, "He will wash his garments in wine, his robes in the blood of grapes" (Gen. 49:11), indicating that Judah would have land suitable for the planting of vineyards. Indeed, it was from this Judean territory (the Valley of Eshcol) that the spies cut down the gigantic cluster of grapes (Num. 13:24).

15:13–19. Meanwhile, back at the family of Caleb, we find him hurling Anakites out of Anak and dealing death to the folks at Debir. He makes a promise with an attractive offer: **I will give my daughter Acsah in marriage to the man who attacks and captures Kiriath Sepher** (Debir). A very interesting person takes up the challenge. He is listed in the NIV as **Caleb's**

brother, though some commentaries refer to him as a nephew. Whatever his previous relationship (Judges 1:13 refers to him as "Caleb's younger brother" so that would seem like the normal reading), he becomes Caleb's son-in-law, and together they decide on a wedding gift.

Once again, there is some grammatical question in verse 18 about who asked whom to approach Caleb **for a field**. In any case, the old gentleman was quite amenable to the request and provided **the upper and lower springs** so they could have water for the desert country they had acquired. It is not impossible that Acsah's first request for a field resulted in the land in the Negev and the second **special favor** (blessing) was the water to make the desert livable.

15:20–63. The descriptive boundaries of Judah describe a large piece of land dipping into the desert southwest at the southernmost point of the Dead Sea and sweeping all the way to the Mediterranean Sea. The northern boundary sweeps in from the Mediterranean Sea about halfway between the cities of Ashdod and Joppa, loops just south of Jerusalem, and reaches the northernmost point of the Dead Sea just south of Jericho. It encompasses the land given to Simeon that served as a concentric circle within Judean territory. Since the northern boundary of Judea later became (in rough lines) the boundary between Judea and Samaria, the name of this tribe became the name of the southern kingdom during the days of the divided monarchy.

The Israelites had traveled a long distance in their wilderness trek with God. They had enjoyed such great victories in the promised land conquest. But in some cases they didn't quite finish the race. They gave up and didn't go all the way in their obedience: **Judah could not dislodge the Jebusites, who were living in Jerusalem; to this day the Jebusites live there with the people of Judah** (15:63).

Did they just get tired? Or perhaps lazy? Or just weary of constant warfare? We don't know the reason, but we do know they didn't finish the conquest. It's like walking the last part of a hill. Sometimes we just get tired of trying to serve God and live for him and grow spiritually and we just give up before the race is over. We condescend just to "live with" negative issues in our lives.

This is the first "conquest motif" describing a tribe's failure to drive out the pagan peoples of Canaan from their territory. But this verse throws us off stride because the city of Jerusalem lay in Benjaminite territory not in Judah.

As Howard explains:

> Judges 1:21 is an almost verbatim repetition of this verse, except stating that *Benjamin* (not Judah) did not drive out the Jebusites. The reason for this dual assignment of the city undoubtedly is that Jerusalem sat astride the boundary between Benjamin and Judah, and it was not strongly identified with either tribe. On the one hand, Jerusalem was a Benjaminite city: in the Benjaminite tribal allotment, the boundary line runs "down the Hinnom Valley along the southern slope of the Jebusite city and so to En Rogel" (Josh. 18:16) and "the Jebusite city (that is, Jerusalem)" appears in the Benjaminite city list (18:28). On the other hand, Jerusalem also appears in the Judahite boundary list: the description in 15:8 uses almost the same language as is found in the Benjaminite list. . . . The solution to this difference in perspective lies in understanding that Judah's success [in driving out the Jebusites] may have been limited and temporary, while Benjamin's failure was total. In either case Jebusites and Israelites lived intermingled, according to Josh. 15:64 and Judg. 1:21, and the city was not taken decisively by Israelites until the time of David, ca. 1003 B.C. (2 Sam. 5:5–10) (Howard, 343–44).

B Joseph's Jurisdiction (16:1–10)

SUPPORTING IDEA: *In the case of Joseph, the blessing of God upon his family was more magnified in his children's children and therefore realized to a greater extent by future generations.*

16:1–10. Jacob gave his longest and most favorable blessing to his son Joseph. We cannot understand the allocation of rich, fertile land in central Canaan to Ephraim and Manasseh unless we review and understand that blessing.

In this blessing Jacob said:

> "Joseph is a fruitful vine, a fruitful vine near a spring, whose branches climb over a wall. With bitterness archers attacked him; they shot at him with hostility. But his bow remained steady, his strong arms stayed limber, because of the hand of the Mighty One of Jacob, because of the Shepherd, the Rock of Israel, because of your

father's God, who helps you, because of the Almighty, who blesses you with blessings of the heavens above, blessings of the deep that lies below, blessings of the breast and womb. Your father's blessings are greater than the blessings of the ancient mountains, than the bounty of the age-old hills. Let all these rest on the head of Joseph, on the brow of the prince among his brothers" (Gen. 49:22–26).

Now the allocation of land to **the descendants of Joseph** takes on a new meaning. Joseph was responsible for the survival of his family during the famine in Egypt and even prior to that was Jacob's favorite son. So rather than a specific and single blessing on Joseph, Jacob ordained that his sons Ephraim and Manasseh should be the heads and founders of tribes along with their eleven uncles. Side by side they occupied what later became Samaria with Ephraim on the south and Manasseh on the north. Ephraim's land included Shiloh, where the tabernacle would be located. Manasseh included both Mount Ebal and Mount Gerizim at the famous and sacred site of Shechem as well as Mount Carmel sticking like a knob out into the Mediterranean Sea.

Nevertheless, chapter 16 ends like chapter 15 by saying of Ephraim, **They did not dislodge the Canaanites living in Gezer; to this day the Canaanites live among the people of Ephraim but are required to do forced labor.** This was an alternate plan to God's command, and that is never a good idea.

Campbell writes:

> Motivated by a materialistic attitude, they chose to put the Canaanites in Gezer under tribute to gain additional wealth. That proved to be a fatal mistake for in later centuries, in the time of the Judges, the arrangement was reversed as the Canaanites rose up and enslaved the Israelites. In addition to the historical lesson there is a spiritual principle here. It is all too easy for a believer to tolerate and excuse some pet sin only to wake up some day to the grim realization that it has risen up to possess and drive him to spiritual defeat. It pays to deal with sin decisively and harshly (Campbell, *BKC,* 360).

One question remains in chapter 16. We know Manasseh was the first-born followed by Ephraim, and yet Ephraim's territory is mentioned first.

Perhaps that order reflects the ascendancy of Ephraim (Gen. 48:12–20) and the fact that in later years it would be the more important tribe. We might also note that the inheritances of these two tribes look different in the text because they contain no list of towns.

Manasseh Manor (17:1–18)

SUPPORTING IDEA: *Throughout its long and tumultuous history, Israel learned over and over again that complacency, compromise, and complaint always lead to failure.*

17:1–18. Let's not lose sight of the fact that all this distribution of land took place **according to the LORD's command** (17:4). Joshua expected that the people would also follow the Lord's command in driving out the Canaanites as they were clearly told to do, thereby following Joshua's example set in the first seven years of the conquest. But these three sins—complacency, compromise, and complaint—continually dogged the tracks of the tribes as they attempted to take over the land.

Here we find another conquest motif. Howard, working from the Joshua text and Judges 1:21,27–35, identifies nine conquest motifs in which the Israelites in general and eight tribes in particular (Judea, Benjamin, West Manasseh, Ephraim, Zebulun, Asher, Naphtali, and Dan) failed to drive out the Jebusites, the Canaanites, and the Amorites (Howard, 318–19). Here it is again in 17:12 where we read that **the Manassites were not able to occupy these towns, for the Canaanites were determined to live in that region.** They simply used the Gibeonite maneuver and made them forced laborers, a plan that backfired some years later.

But **the people of Joseph** also added complaint to compromise and complacency. The tribes of Ephraim and Manasseh were not content. They had a problem. They thought that because of their size they deserved more land. Joshua told them to clear some forest land and settle there. But they complained that the forest lands wouldn't work because this would put them too close to Canaanites with iron chariots. And we thought entitlement programs were an invention of the late twentieth century! These tribes didn't want to work or fight for their land. They wanted something given to them. Their complaining and fear got in the way of their blessing.

Have you ever complained to God that he is not doing enough for you? Lord Congelton once overheard a servant say, "If only I had five pounds, I would be perfectly content." He gave her five pounds and then heard her say, "Why didn't I ask for ten pounds?"

As Israel's military commander and chief executive officer, Joshua set a helpful example in the way he dealt with Joseph's people: "Clear the land and drive out the Canaanites and stop your bellyaching." We need to learn how to help ourselves and others when we get stuck in the spiritual mud of complacency, compromise, or complaint.

Let's drop back for a moment and look at verse 4 where Eleazar is mentioned again. Madvig has a helpful observation: "In the four incidents in this book where Joshua and Eleazar are mentioned together, Eleazar is always named first, perhaps out of respect for his crucial role as high priest in the casting of lots" (Madvig, 336). We should also not miss the reference to the daughters of Zelophehad, one of whom had the interesting name of **Noah**. In an early demonstration of the freedom and rights of women in Israel, **they went to Eleazar the priest, Joshua son of Nun, and the leaders and said, "The LORD commanded Moses to give us an inheritance among our brothers."** Joshua agreed and provided it.

This was an amazing event in Canaan where women were still considered property. Here again Madvig notes:

> Whether it was primarily the rights of the father or the rights of the daughters that were being protected, an unusual privilege and a remarkable measure of equality were granted to these women. In actual fact the daughters of Zelophehad had no "brothers" (cp. v. 3), which is why the inheritance was passed on to them. The Hebrew *ah* can refer to any male relative, and it should be understood as "kinsman" or "tribesman" here (Madvig, 336).

MAIN IDEA REVIEW: *The settling of the promised land should have been an easy task after the seven-year conquest, but we find that the tribes lacked the initiative and courage to drive out the Canaanite inhabitants completely. This problem repeats itself throughout the second half of the Book of Joshua.*

III. CONCLUSION

The Power of Positive Thinking

No, not the famous self-esteem book by Norman Vincent Peale, but the magnificent words written by Paul in Philippians 4:8: "Finally, brothers, whatever is true, whatever is noble, whatever is right, whatever is pure, whatever is lovely, whatever is admirable—if anything is excellent or praise-worthy—think about such things." Those attitudes largely marked the conquering Israelites for seven years. Then the entitlement programs began, and complacency, compromise, and complaint began to get the better of the day. In our spiritual warfare we might try combating those three negative C words with some positive T words—*think, try,* and *trust.*

Like the Israelites entering Canaan, we should not expect the surrounding culture to reinforce positive choices. A recent announcement by the University of California that it would no longer require SAT scores for admission is only one demonstration of the "dumbing down" of education in recent years. Among the boat builders on Britain's Clyde River there is a saying: "Once iron men came here to build wooden ships; now wooden men come to build iron ships."

Thinking is a key commodity, and the Philippians passage is extremely important. But *trust* teaches us that dependence is a key posture. We cannot lead unless other people trust, and we cannot lead unless we are completely dependent on the Heavenly Father for every resource essential for spiritual victory. One heresy that hinders Christians in their drive for conquest in spiritual warfare is the idea of prosperity gospel, the notion that God's blessing is measured by size or number. This carnal imposition leads to imperial leadership and self-glory, the exact opposite of Paul's praise for suffering.

I grieve to think of the millions of dollars wasted by evangelicals building enormous and elaborate places of worship while the Third World starves and mission boards struggle to keep their people on the field. Remember the words of C. T. Studd? "Some men die in ashes; some men die in flames. Some men die inch by inch, playing silly games."

And finally, instead of complaining, *try*—because perseverance is a key attitude. Outside Vancouver's Empire Stadium stands a piece of statuary commemorating a great moment in sports history. I once drove to the stadium just to photograph the statute. It dates back to 1954—Roger Bannister and John Landy in the "miracle mile." Landy led all the way but turned and lost stride as Bannister passed him and broke the tape. The statute captures that exact instant.

So many Bible characters provide examples of excellence for us to emulate. Then there is Demas, who started ministry and quit because the lure of the world was too great. We all need perseverance to finish our lives with excellence in spiritual warfare, and some need encouragement just to finish the next week. I implore you by God's grace and in the name of Jesus never to accept mediocrity in anything you do as a Christian. That was the problem with the tribes. The conquest was a howling success, but the occupation was soiled by mediocrity.

PRINCIPLES

- Spiritually we often do our own thing rather than waiting for God's best.

- We must always receive what God has for us without complaining that it's not enough.

- God never promised us that the Christian life would be easy or that spiritual growth would come quickly. Instead, we grow bit by bit, little by little.

APPLICATIONS

- Since we develop spiritually in increasing measure, we must be patient with the process and diligent in the effort at the same time.

- Let us recognize that the women among us have a legitimate claim to an inheritance in a portion of the ministry of any church.

- We must never allow the determination of the "Canaanites" around us to minimize or compromise our spiritual growth.

IV. LIFE APPLICATION

The Man Who Discovered Britain

In 300 B.C. after returning from a sea journey in the North Atlantic, the Greek explorer Pytheas said of Britain, "The island is thickly populated and has an extremely chilly climate." He also noted that the people seemed to be "unusually hospitable, and gentle in their manner." But no one believed him. And nothing remains today of Pytheas's once famous book *The Ocean*. In his day its pages were regarded as masterpieces of fabrication, and people wondered whether his discoveries were really discoveries at all.

But later scholars have decided that Pytheas was indeed the first Greek to visit and describe Britain and possibly to sail within sight of the Icelandic coast. At the time the northern waters of the Atlantic Ocean were unknown to the Greeks. Familiar only with the warm waters of the Mediterranean Sea, they could not believe he had seen chunks of ice floating in the sea. Stories of land that was entirely frozen and a place where the sun never set seemed like fabrications.

In fact, the voyage of Pytheas covered seven thousand miles. He circumnavigated Britain and went ashore several places where he saw people harvesting grain and tending cattle. He visited the tin mines of Cornwall and touched the coast of Denmark in his search for amber. Though his name is not well-known, he was one of the greatest explorers of his day.

In a very real way the tribes of Israel were explorers. They would never reach the coast of Britain or watch chunks of ice floating in the ocean, but they were seeing strange peoples in a new world which was now theirs. Like them we walk through strange territory and new experiences in our own lives. We face new challenges that require faith and courage never before used. Spiritual explorers, on a spiritual journey. For spiritual warfare we can trust God alone, and that is precisely what the tribes of Israel were required to do.

Recently I was reading some of the memoirs of Robert Murray McCheyne, that great man of God who passed on to glory when he was only thirty years of age and left behind him such a tremendous record of ministry and service. In his own prayer life McCheyne prayed, "Lord

Jesus Christ, let my heart and my mind enlarge together like brother and sister, depending the one upon the other. Let the capacity of my heart and the understanding of my mind increase as the years go by. That is blessedly true of Christian experience. Some people claim they are filled with the Spirit of God. My friends, that is a blessed truth, and I hope that all of us can say it sincerely, but we are filled only to the amount of our capacity. There is always more of His fullness as the years unfold, and you will never plum all the depths of the ocean of His grace and power (Redpath, 211).

V. PRAYER

Father, give us the courage to fight courageously and to conquer the spiritual territory you intend us to occupy. Amen.

VI. DEEPER DISCOVERIES

A. Judah (15:1)

Of the twelve tribes Judah could perhaps be referred to as the most important, certainly since it formed the lineage for the birth of Messiah. Judah was rather common in the days of Jacob, however, and the naming of Leah's fourth son was no outstanding event. We see his role in the selling of Joseph in chapter 37 and his shame with Tamar in chapter 38. After the death of his wife, he committed incest with his daughter-in-law who was disguised as a harlot. From their union came twins whom Judah called Perez and Zerah. From the line of Perez ultimately was born the Christ of Nazareth, God's gift to the world.

Once again we see how divine grace overcomes human frailty. Judah's Genesis 49 blessing is considerably different from that of Reuben, Simeon, or Levi:

Judah, your brothers will praise you; your hand will be on the neck of your enemies; your father's sons will bow down to you. You are a lion's cub, O Judah; you return from the prey, my son. Like a lion he crouches and lies down, like a lioness—who dares to rouse him? The scepter will not depart from Judah, nor the ruler's staff from between his feet, until he comes to whom it belongs and the obedience of the nations is his (Gen. 49:8–10).

The prophecy goes on, but we get the point. From the tribe of Judah came Elisheba the mother of all the priests; Othniel, the first judge; Bezaleel, the builder of the tabernacle; and all the pious kings from David on down. The tribe of Judah led the march into the promised land and, in the insurrection against David, stood alone in backing their king.

Perhaps the greatest reference to the figure of tribe as a lion appears in the last book of the Bible in John's vision of things to come. He looks up and sees the seven-sealed book, the opening of which no man could be found worthy. Finally, amid his tears, he sees one who comes from the root of David; he alone is worthy to open the book, and he is known in Revelation 5:5 as the Lion of the tribe of Judah.

B. The Purpose of These Chapters

The settling of the tribes was accomplished essentially in three phases. The first was the Transjordanian arrangement made by Moses for Reuben, Gad, and the half tribe of Manasseh. The second was done by Joshua at Gilgal, and then later arrangements were made at Shiloh. As we have seen, the Levites received no land as a capital possession, though they did have cities in which to live.

Howard offers a paragraph emphasizing the importance of this detail not only to the tribes themselves but to readers of the Old Testament:

> What is the importance of the mind-numbing detail of these lists? Why is it significant that there are certain patterns to them? There are several answers to these questions. First and foremost, as we have indicated, these lists are the heart of the book in that they "prove" to the Israelites and to the book's readers that God was being true to his promises. On one level, it was not enough simply to assert that God gave Israel the land, to state that he fulfilled his promises, and to ask the readers to take the author's word for it. For such promises as these, given so many centuries earlier, such simple assertions would have been profoundly anticlimactic. A deep sense

of satisfaction would come if the reader could actually trace the fulfillment of these promises, city by city, hill by hill, wadi by wadi, border by border. It is akin to a good book that a person becomes engrossed in, which he or she is reluctant to have come to an end. The reader wants every word and detail to count. So too here (Howard, 321).

VII. TEACHING OUTLINE

A. INTRODUCTION

1. Lead Story: Spacious Skies
2. Context: After the introduction of Caleb in chapter 14, the text proceeds to detail the allotment for Judah. The list will now unfold more or less in a south-to-north arrangement through the chapters that follow.
3. Transition: The one transition of importance here comes at the end of chapter 17 where the land grant office switches from Gilgal to Shiloh. But essentially chapters 15–19 form one piece of the Book of Joshua.

B. COMMENTARY

1. Lion's Lair (15:1–63)
2. Joseph's Jurisdiction (16:1–10)
3. Manasseh Manor (17:1–18)

C. CONCLUSION: THE MAN WHO DISCOVERED BRITAIN

VIII. ISSUES FOR DISCUSSION

1. Consider the issues of complacency, compromise, and complaint in the church today. In what form do these problems arise?
2. What are the spiritual parallels to the geographical distribution of the land in these chapters?

3. Note the request of the daughters of Zelophehad in chapter 17. What does your church believe about the leadership roles of women in the congregation?

Joshua 18–19

The Shiloh Settlements

I. **INTRODUCTION**
Strangers in a Foreign Land

II. **COMMENTARY**
A verse-by-verse explanation of these chapters.

III. **CONCLUSION**
"My Faith Has Found a Resting Place"

An overview of the principles and applications from these chapters.

IV. **LIFE APPLICATION**
Godly Leadership

Melding these chapters to life.

V. **PRAYER**
Tying these chapters to life with God.

VI. **DEEPER DISCOVERIES**
Historical, geographical, and grammatical enrichment of the commentary.

VII. **TEACHING OUTLINE**
Suggested step-by-step group study of these chapters.

VIII. **ISSUES FOR DISCUSSION**
Zeroing these chapters in on daily life.

Quote

"Peace is the deliberate adjustment of my life to the will of God."

Anonymous

GEOGRAPHICAL PROFILE: SHILOH

- Located halfway between Shechem and Bethel on a north-south axis
- Center of worship and home of the first permanent tabernacle location
- Twenty miles north of Jerusalem
- Served as Israel's center of worship for almost four hundred years

Joshua 18–19

IN A NUTSHELL

The last seven words of 19:51 sum up these two chapters: "And so they finished dividing the land." Three major things happen in these chapters: (1) the focus changes from Gilgal to Shiloh; (2) seven remaining tribes get their allocation of land; and (3) Joshua receives his city.

The Shiloh Settlements

I. INTRODUCTION

Strangers in a Foreign Land

A report from the headquarters of the denomination I serve (Christian & Missionary Alliance) tells about thousands of Africans who have crossed the scorching sands of the desert to the Mediterranean Sea on their way to Spain and a better life. Virtually everyone who makes the trip has a harrowing tale about the journey. Most made the trip for a better life and material gain. But many pastors joined them, struggling and persevering because they sensed that God wanted them to shepherd his people who were far from home.

One pastor languished in jail for eight months when his papers were stolen, surviving blistering heat and cold nights as he trekked on foot through the desert, only to be sent back again. On the second attempt it took him four years just to arrive at a place where he could cross the Mediterranean Sea into Europe. Another pastor, Jean Simon Bayekula Ngimbi, traveled from Congo, pastoring churches in two other countries on his way across Africa. He drank radiator water to stay alive and saw two friends die on the journey. Today he pastors one of the C&MA's new immigrant-based churches in Madrid. One of our missionaries in Spain, Gene Simillie, tells how these immigrant congregations cannot support their evangelists and pastors. These leaders survive by seeking employment, usually manual labor.

Africa is not the only continent from which immigrants are fleeing. Seventy thousand Ecuadorians have left their country to go to Spain because of economic crisis in Ecuador. And that number just counts the registered immigrants. Certainly many more have flooded into Spain from Ecuador, Colombia, Peru, and Argentina. Missionary Kathie Munro says, "Many immigrants believe that Spain will be the land of opportunity. Instead they end up working in menial jobs. Some come to understand that the abundant life doesn't come from a place or a situation but from a personal relationship with Christ" (*Missions Update,* February 2002).

The Israelites were also learning that the promised land was more than a place of conquest and settlement. As these two chapters open, we see a new focus on spiritual worship and the relationship of people to their God. Like the Africans, Ecuadorians, and Israelites, we find ourselves in a foreign land of pagan culture and must find our "Shiloh" to reconnect and stay closely related to our Lord.

II. COMMENTARY

The Shiloh Settlements

> **MAIN IDEA:** *Nearly halfway through the tribal settlement the real estate headquarters switches to Shiloh. Though these seven tribes had to wait longer than the rest to receive their allotment, there is no indication that they were less important than the other tribes.*

A The Meeting House (18:1–10)

> **SUPPORTING IDEA:** *Israel got stuck in the spiritual mud of complacency, compromise, and complaining. God sent them to the tent of meeting to get things right.*

18:1–10. Joshua had proved himself a motivator and an encourager in the way he dealt with the complaints of Ephraim and Manasseh. He affirmed their numbers and their strength in the fact that they could clear the forest and drive out the Canaanites. He played the role of cheerleader, but he still would not concede to their complaints or their negativism. He believed in them and in God's promise to them.

But perhaps the problems encountered in chapter 17 led to the move at the beginning of chapter 18. As tribes were sent farther and farther away from Gilgal, the necessity of a central place of meeting and worship became obvious. Furthermore, the complacency had settled over seven tribes who failed to take any action regarding their land allotments.

So in the early verses of chapter 18, Joshua faced a different problem. Seven tribes weren't complaining like Ephraim and Manasseh; they just weren't taking any action. They had the waiting down, but they didn't have the action to go with it. So Joshua organized them for action. Three men from each tribe became land surveyors who would describe, divide, and then report back to Joshua who would cast lots for the tribes. And it worked. The people needed someone to get them organized enough to get the job done.

The chapter opens with the setting up of **the Tent of Meeting** which, as Campbell says:

> . . . could remind the people that the key to prosperity and blessing in the land was worshiping and serving Yahweh. The dissatisfaction of the sons of Joseph with their allotment (17:14–18) was an ominous foreshadowing of the future disintegration of the nation because of self-interest. To counteract this tendency the tabernacle was set up in Shiloh to promote a sense of national unity (Campbell, *BKC*, 360–61).

This represents the fulfillment of God's last promise in Leviticus 26:11–12: "I will put my dwelling place among you, and I will not abhor you. I will walk among you and be your God, and you will be my people" (for more about the Tent of Meeting, see "Deeper Discoveries").

Verse 3 almost sounds like a bit of scolding on Joshua's part—and perhaps it was. The seven tribes just could not get organized, so Joshua stepped in to make things happen. Sometimes we need people like this in our lives. We need to recognize that organization is not anti-spiritual. Sometimes we need help in organizing our time, our resources, our finances, and our family lives so we can serve God better and live for him. Furthermore, if you are good at organization, teach or help someone else. Note how carefully these twenty-one surveyors did their work. Repeatedly in these verses there is reference to how they wrote down the details and brought them back to Joshua. Verse 10 brings closure to the whole process: **There he distributed the land to the Israelites according to their tribal divisions**.

Throughout these chapters Deuteronomy 7:22 is played out: "The LORD your God will drive out those nations before you, little by little. You will not be allowed to eliminate them all at once, or the wild animals will multiply around you." What we see, of course, with a number of the tribes (especially Dan) is an unwillingness to be patient with the details of the process.

𝔹 The Wolf Den (18:11–28)

SUPPORTING IDEA: *Both the military and spiritual progress related to the land acquisition in Canaan came about little by little. It also happened on the basis of God's appointment to places and positions where he wanted his people.*

18:11–20. Although Benjamin was a favorite son of Jacob, his allotment is one of the smaller ones in the entire promised land, indicating something of the size of the tribe. More important are the cities that fall within Benjamin's boundaries—Jericho, Bethel, Gibeon, Mizpah, Ai, and Jerusalem. Settled along the Jordan River with its western boundary reaching Kiriath Jearim and its northern boundary just north of Bethel, Benjamin was squarely positioned for a major role in Israelite history in the centuries ahead. We're reminded of Jacob's final prophecy in Genesis 49:27: "Benjamin is a ravenous wolf; in the morning he devours the prey, in the evening he divides the plunder."

We see the hand of God in the drawing of the lot for Benjamin. This tract of land between the Judahites and Josephites served to fulfill Deuteronomy 33:12 by placing the ultimate temple site in Benjamin and served to unite Israel by making Benjamin the link between the two most powerful tribal groups. We remember that it was Judah who offered himself as hostage in place of Benjamin (Gen. 43–44).

18:21–28. Though his tribal area is relatively small, Benjamin's city list is third longest of all the tribes, following only Judah and Levi. There is some adjustment in the boundaries as the seven tribes now fit into their territories along with the other five tribes who settled first. Borderline cities may have been dually occupied or may have fallen from one to the other. Note the list of Beth Horon that was also a levitical city now in the Benjaminite territory. Howard makes an interesting observation that "ten of the cities here never occur elsewhere in the Bible: Emek, Keziz, Avvim, Parah, Kephar Ammoni, Ophni, Mozah, Irpeel, Taralah, Zelah, and Haeleph" (Howard, 365).

We leave this chapter noting that the blessing of Moses upon Benjamin was considerably stronger than the blessing of Jacob. In Deuteronomy 33:12 we read, "About Benjamin he said: 'Let the beloved of the LORD rest secure in him, for he shields him all day long, and the one the LORD loves rests between his shoulders.'" We are not sure what to make of this metaphor except that Jerusalem, a Benjaminite city, would become the most holy city of Israel.

The Second Half (19:1–51)

SUPPORTING IDEA: *With half the tribes now settled, it's time to focus on the second half. Chapter 19 covers the land allotments for Simeon, Zebulun, Issachar, Asher, Naphtali, and Dan.*

19:1–9. Simeon's portion of land, as we have noted, lay within the border boundaries of Judah **because Judah's portion was more than they needed.** Simeon existed literally as a tribe within a tribe, occupying the cities of Beersheba, Hormah, and Ziklag among others. Once again Jacob's prophecy of Genesis 49 rises in importance as he says to both Simeon and Levi, "Cursed be their anger, so fierce, and their fury, so cruel! I will scatter them in Jacob and disperse them in Israel" (Gen. 49:7).

> Simeon was given land in the southern section of Judah's territory with 17 towns and their villages. But it was not long before Simeon was to lose her individuality as a tribe, for her territory was incorporated into that of Judah, and many of her citizens migrated north to Ephraim and Manasseh (cf. 2 Chr. 15:9; 34:6). This explains why after the division of the kingdom following Solomon there were 10 tribes in the north and only 2 in the south (Judah and Benjamin) (Campbell, *BKC*, 361).

19:10–16. Zebulun received a landlocked district in lower Galilee, including the New Testament town of Nazareth. Divine wisdom placed the Leah tribes, Zebulun and Issachar, to the north of the Rachel tribes in order to cement the union of all Israel. Judah, Issachar, and Zebulun had camped in the wilderness (Num. 2:3–7), and these ties persisted for centuries. Mary and Joseph, both of the tribe of Judah, lived in the old territory of Zebulun. The Zebulunites named one of their towns Bethlehem (19:15) after the town in Judah.

And what did Jacob say about his son Zebulun? "Zebulun will live by the seashore and become a haven for ships; his border will extend toward Sidon" (Gen. 49:13). No commendation; no condemnation. Simply geographical boundaries placing Zebulun due west of the Sea of Galilee though not actually on the coast. The Kishon River connected Zebulun to the Mediterranean Sea, a destination reached by passing through the territory of Asher.

19:17–23. The tribe of Issachar wandered for forty years in the desert, remembering Jacob's words about the good things their hard work would bring: "Issachar is a rawboned donkey lying down between two saddlebags. When he sees how good is his resting place and how pleasant is his land, he will bend his shoulder to the burden and submit to forced labor" (Gen. 49:14–15).

Issachar's territory included the Valley of Jezreel and from Mount Tabor on the west to the southern tip of the Sea of Galilee. Indeed, Issachar played such a small role in the future of Israel that the tribe is not even mentioned in the blessings of the tribes offered by Moses in Deuteronomy 33 except as a side note with Zebulun. Most notable in this allocation is the great battlefield Jezreel and the significance of Mount Tabor. Ultimately, of course, all the territory of Ephraim, Manasseh, Issachar, and Zebulun became known as Samaria.

19:24–31. Asher occupied the costal region from Mount Carmel north to Tyre and Sidon. Inscriptions from Seti I dated approximately 1310 B.C. and also of Rameses II contain references to a people called *Asaru* in a territory roughly corresponding to southern Phoenicia. This indicates that Asher had begun to settle by the end of the fourteenth century. Asher's blessing from Jacob was strictly culinary: "Asher's food will be rich; he will provide delicacies fit for a king" (Gen. 49:20). But Moses embellishes those words dramatically in a passage that includes one of the great verses of the Book of Deuteronomy.

About Asher Moses said:

> Most blessed of sons is Asher; let him be favored by his brothers, and let him bathe his feet in oil. The bolts of your gates will be iron and bronze, and your strength will equal your days. There is no one like the God of Jeshurun, who rides on the heavens to help you and on the clouds in his majesty. The eternal God is your refuge, and underneath are the everlasting arms. He will drive out your enemy before you saying, "Destroy him!" (Deut. 33:24–27).

A quick glance at a map will show that Asher's task was to guard the northwestern boundaries of Israel and to protect it from northern coastal enemies such as the Phoenicians. Asher shows up once in the New Testament when Anna the prophetess gives thanks for the birth of Jesus (Luke 2:36–38).

19:32–39. Running parallel north and south just east of Asher we find Naphtali stretching almost to Mount Hermon in the northeast and including the western side of the Sea of Kinnereth (Galilee). Much of the Lord's Galilean ministry in the New Testament took place within the boundaries of old Naphtali. Indeed, one of the great Christmas prophesies in Isaiah mentions this territory. We've all heard it sung many times in Handel's *Messiah*.

> Nevertheless, there will be no more gloom for those who were in distress. In the past he humbled the land of Zebulun and the land of Naphtali, but in the future he will honor Galilee of the Gentiles, by the way of the sea, along the Jordan—The people walking in darkness have seen a great light; on those living in the land of the shadow of death a light has dawned. You have enlarged the nation and increased their joy; they rejoice before you as people rejoice at the harvest, as men rejoice when dividing the plunder. For as in the day of Midian's defeat, you have shattered the yoke that burdens them, the bar across their shoulders, the rod of their oppressor. Every warrior's boot used in battle and every garment rolled in blood will be destined for burning, will be fuel for the fire. For to us a child is born, to us a son is given, and the government will be on his shoulders. And he will be called Wonderful Counselor, Mighty God, Everlasting Father, Prince of Peace. Of the increase of his government and peace there will be no end. He will reign on David's throne and over his kingdom, establishing and upholding it with justice and righteousness from that time on and forever. The zeal of the LORD Almighty will accomplish this (Isa. 9:1–7).

19:40–48. To further strengthen the union of Israel, God separated Dan from Naphtali and his wilderness campmate Asher. Dan was placed between Benjamin and the Mediterranean Sea, but part of that territory was lost to the Amorites in the Philistine Plain. Only once in these two chapters do we have a negative mention of a tribe unable to secure the boundaries that were allotted to it. That appears here where we read that **the Danites had difficulty taking possession of their territory, so they went up and attacked**

Leshem, took it, put it to the sword and occupied it. They settled in Leshem and named it Dan after their forefather.

So the Danites engaged in geographical apostasy, migrating northward and settling where they were not placed. The town they captured and renamed lay in the northeastern territory of Naphtali southeast of Mount Hermon. Notice that Dan's borders are not described; we see only mention of the towns. This strange behavior by Dan may have been tipped off in the ancient prophecy by Jacob: "Dan will provide justice for his people as one of the tribes of Israel. Dan will be a serpent by the roadside, a viper along the path, that bites the horse's heels so that its rider tumbles backward" (Gen. 49:16–17).

19:49–51. So all the tribes were settled. But one man remained to receive an inheritance—Joshua. Since he could not give himself his own portion, he received from the Israelites what they designated for him.

The specific command of God mentioned here that granted Joshua this inheritance is not recorded anywhere in Scripture, but God's word to the rebellious Israelites in Num. 14:30 were a general promise to Caleb and Joshua, the two faithful spies: "Not one of you will enter the land I swore with uplifted hand to make your home, except Caleb son of Jephunneh and Joshua son of Nun." Both spies not only entered the land, but they both also received special portions in it (Howard, 378).

Joshua found himself in Ephraim just eleven miles from Shiloh so he could worship comfortably at the tabernacle. This was Joshua's tribe (Num. 13:8), and he was buried in the city mentioned here (Josh. 24:30). Howard notes:

It would seem that Timnath Serah was Joshua's own personal possession because it does not appear in Ephraim tribal list (nor in any other list, for that matter). No other Israelite received any inheritance in this manner, that is, as a personal possession; even Caleb's city, Hebron, belonged to the tribe of Judah (15:13,54), and it was both a city of refuge (20:7) and a levitical city (21:11,13). This certainly contributes to the picture of Joshua as an extraordinary individual, one who demonstrated extraordinary faithfulness to God and who was a leader par excellence (Howard, 378).

MAIN IDEA REVIEW: *Nearly halfway through the tribal settlement the real estate headquarters switches to Shiloh. Though these seven tribes had to wait longer than the rest to receive their allotment, there is no indication that they were less important than the other tribes.*

III. CONCLUSION

"My Faith Has Found a Resting Place"

The conclusion of these geographical chapters shows us again Joshua's faithfulness. Although there is more to come, these chapters also provide a fitting resting point for the battles Joshua has faced since God first called him in chapter 1. Throughout all of this his courage and faith has been remarkable. We have seen him depending on God for victory and rest.

In 1 Peter 1:8–9 we read, "Even though you do not see him now, you believe in him and are filled with an inexpressible and glorious joy, for you are receiving the goal of your faith, the salvation of your souls."

Set to a beautiful Norwegian folk melody, the hymn "My Faith Has Found a Resting Place" proclaims the gospel more clearly than most of the hymns in any hymnbook. We know virtually nothing about Lidie Edmunds or the circumstances surrounding the writing of the hymn. It first appeared in *Songs of Joy and Gladness No. 2* in 1891, and the tune is the name of a town in Norway.

Every trusting Christian rests in the essential idea that there is no way to God apart from the cross. Jesus is the way, the truth, and the life. Nothing less than faith in his death and resurrection provides the way to eternal life. Not faith in faith, but faith in Jesus. All the verses of this wonderful hymn drip the sweet nectar of the gospel. I have found it particularly effective when sung during communion services.

My faith has found a resting place, not in device nor creed;
I trust the Ever-living One, His wounds for me shall plead.
I need no other argument, I need no other plea,
It is enough that Jesus died, and that He died for me.

PRINCIPLES

- The centrality of a place of worship is always important for God's people in any age and any place.
- Divided people can come together around a central place of worship like the Tent of Meeting at Shiloh.
- Sometimes people do not move ahead with their responsibilities unless a leader steps forward to show them what to do and how to do it.

APPLICATIONS

- In spiritual warfare, difficulty in taking possession of what God wants for us is no excuse for migrating elsewhere. Be faithful where God puts you!
- If we have carefully carried out our responsibilities before God, we don't have to be selfish or jealous about what we will get; God will take care of that.
- When God calls you to a place for ministry, be satisfied with what he provides and stay there until he moves you.

IV. LIFE APPLICATION

Godly Leadership

In John Gardner's book on excellence, he compares modern concepts of excellence to a Rorschach test—people may see anything they choose. But the Bible always measures excellence in relation to the absolute standard of God himself. Here is the *New American Standard Bible* wording of 2 Peter 1:3: "His divine power has granted to us everything pertaining to life and godliness, through the true knowledge of Him who called us by His own glory and excellence." For Christian leaders like Joshua, being is more important than doing, because what we are will determine what we do. Excellence in ministry begins with excellence in spiritual life. A comparison of the conquest of Canaan with spiritual warfare remains our central theme for the Book of Joshua. The text of 2 Peter 1 claims that salvation is not enough—that we must add to faith goodness, knowledge, self-control, perseverance, godliness, kindness, and love.

This symphony of grace God is composing in our lives shows up in the standards we set and follow for behavior in ministry. Our text tells us that "if anyone does not have them, he is nearsighted and blind, and has forgotten that he has been cleansed from his past sins" (v. 9). A. W. Tozer, one of the most insightful Christians of the twentieth century, applies all this to leadership in one tight sentence: "The true leader will have no desire to lord it over God's heritage, but will be humble, gentle, self-sacrificing, and all together as ready to follow as to lead, when the Spirit makes it clear that a wiser and more gifted man than himself has appeared."

I never place bumper stickers on my own car, but I enjoy reading them on other vehicles. Once I saw one that warned, "Jesus is coming—look busy." Few people today, even in ministry leadership, have any problem looking busy. The trick is not activity but *productivity*; not efficiency but *effectiveness*.

Even in Christianity we tend to acknowledge the flashy heroes and dynamic testimonies. People come out of the woodwork to see Christian bands under the lights; to watch well-known preachers on television or hear them on radio; to highlight famous athletes, business people, or politicians who are also Christians.

But today God is looking for people like Joshua. The faithful, durable servant. The patient, persistent, consistent, quiet warrior who will keep working to drive out the Canaanites, waiting patiently for God's timing in each victory.

V. PRAYER

Father, thank you for the tent of meeting—whether we think of that as our local churches or that spiritual sanctuary we have set up in our hearts where we visit with you on a regular basis. Amen.

VI. DEEPER DISCOVERIES

A. Tent of Meeting (18:1)

In order to centralize worship, the tabernacle was pitched at Shiloh, and the lots were cast there. For a common sanctuary the Israelites chose an abandoned Middle Bronze Age town site in Ephraim because of its central location among all the tribes. Shiloh lay ten miles northeast of Bethel and eleven miles from Shechem. The tabernacle acted as the focal point of Israel's organization before the establishment of the kingdom.

The tabernacle was a part of the law that God gave Moses providing for this beautiful dwelling place for the ark of the covenant and serving as God's house in the wilderness and in the promised land for many years. Fourteen raw materials were used to complete the tent of worship, including a variety of animal skins, acacia wood, and precious metals. Around the tabernacle was an outer court and inside the tent itself two rooms, the Holy Place where the priest entered each morning and the Holy of Holies which he entered only once a year. During the wilderness wandering, the court of the tabernacle was always the center of the camp with the tribes arranged around it, three on each side.

Beers describes the interior:

> The table of shew-bread was on the north side of the Holy Place. Twelve loaves of bread were kept here at all times. The golden candlestick or menorah was in the south wall of the Holy Place. It lighted the room. The altar of incense was in the center of the Holy Place, just in front of the veil which separated the Holy Place from the Holy of Holies. Each morning Aaron burned incense on the altar. Inside the Holy of Holies was the Ark of the Covenant, which contained the Ten Commandments (Beers, 118).

So these few verses at the beginning of chapter 18, though seemingly unimportant in the greater flow of geography in this part of the book, are very meaningful in the history of Israel. The only other reference to the tabernacle in Joshua occurs in 19:51.

VII. TEACHING OUTLINE

A. INTRODUCTION

1. Lead Story: Strangers in a Foreign Land

2. Context: Joshua 19 brings to a close the five-chapter section dealing with the cartography of Israel—the allocation of land for all the tribes. There is more designation to come, but it will have to do with cities rather than territories.

3. Transition: Throughout the Book of Joshua we have seen chapters leading into one another, and we've seen the ending of sections. There is no division between chapters 18 and 19, but at the end of chapter 19 we see a clear section conclusion with the words, "And so they finished dividing the land."

B. COMMENTARY

1. The Meeting House (18:1–10)

2. The Wolf Den (18:11–28)

3. The Second Half (19:1–51)

C. CONCLUSION: GODLY LEADERSHIP

VIII. ISSUES FOR DISCUSSION

1. In what ways is your local church like the Tent of Meeting and in what ways is it different?

2. Why do you think these final seven tribes were so slow in claiming their inheritance? How does this relate to the question of spiritual warfare in our own lives?

3. What specific leadership lessons can we learn from the behavior of Joshua in these two chapters?

Joshua 20–21

The Holy Cities

I. **INTRODUCTION**
Why All-Star Games Are Boring

II. **COMMENTARY**
A verse-by-verse explanation of these chapters.

III. **CONCLUSION**
Escape of the African Hornbill

An overview of the principles and applications from these chapters.

IV. **LIFE APPLICATION**
Title to Heaven

Melding these chapters to life.

V. **PRAYER**
Tying these chapters to life with God.

VI. **DEEPER DISCOVERIES**
Historical, geographical, and grammatical enrichment of the commentary.

VII. **TEACHING OUTLINE**
Suggested step-by-step group study of these chapters.

VIII. **ISSUES FOR DISCUSSION**
Zeroing these chapters in on daily life.

Quote

"*T*he eternal God is your refuge, and under-

neath are the everlasting arms."

M o s e s

Joshua 20–21

IN A NUTSHELL

*W*hy did God design cities of refuge? Perhaps he wanted to teach people that mercy is not universal in this world of sin and death. Salvation is found only in the place where God provides it—and that leads us to Christ.

The Holy Cities

I. INTRODUCTION

Why All-Star Games Are Boring

I don't like college football all-star games. Perhaps it's because the helmets don't match the uniforms. Other sports suffer the same problem, even at the pro level. At the NFL Pro-Bowl in Hawaii there's more action among the fans than on the field. The NBA All-Star Game is a shoot-out/dunking free-for-all, and the major league baseball All-Star game is a showcase for pitchers and heavy hitters. Yes, at the risk of sounding like Andy Rooney, I think all-star games are boring.

But the real secret can be found in the college "Grid-Iron Classic" and Senior Bowl games with their major network boycott and empty stadia. Sure, the players are showcasing their talents for pro scouts, but nobody else is interested. Nothing is at stake if they win or lose; even the rules change to dilute the competition.

But the bottom line in any all-star game is the absence of teamwork. One of the things that make any athletic team interesting is the ability of players to play with one another, maximize one another's strengths, minimize one another's weaknesses, and work together toward a common goal. Since all-star players have never played together before, for the most part, teamwork is lacking.

In these chapters we encounter a major team in ancient Israel—the Levites. By birth and by blessing they had been given special responsibilities, descended from Aaron the high priest. In Deuteronomy 33 Moses says of Levi, "He teaches your precepts to Jacob and your law to Israel. He offers incense before you and whole burnt offerings on your altar. Bless all his skills, O LORD, and be pleased with the work of his hands. Smite the loins of those who rise up against him; strike his foes till they rise no more" (33:10–11).

Yes, the Levites were a team. Scattered through forty-eight towns all across Israel, they had the responsibility for activities at Shiloh and the spiritual well-being of the people. We often think of Joshua as falling into that role, but we have just learned that he had his own city to take care of, and he had settled there. The spiritual formation and protection of the entire nation was in the hands of the Levites. They needed to play like a team to carry out that awesome responsibility.

II. COMMENTARY

The Holy Cities

MAIN IDEA: *The cities of refuge provided a demonstration of God's grace without detracting from his law. Everywhere these cities appeared across the land they showed that God provided for people who made big mistakes and needed mercy in their lives.*

Ⓐ Residences of Refuge (20:1–9)

SUPPORTING IDEA: *These cities were needed throughout Israel to ensure that justice, not personal vengeance, was carried out.*

20:1–6. Imagine yourself out for a summer picnic and a stroll through town. As you sit down with your ice cream cone, you notice some ominous dark clouds coming over the tops of the mountains. One of those pre-storm cool breezes whips against your face—obviously a storm is approaching. You can see the rain streaking down from the clouds coming toward you. You begin a brisk walk the few blocks to your car, watching the wind whipping the tops of the trees and the distant lightning closing in. Just as you climb into your car, the rain comes fast and furious, but you are safe in your metal refuge.

We've all had to run for cover one time or another. Running from storms or trouble to get to a place of safety. My son remembers being out on the playground in eighth grade and running from bullies who threatened to beat him up. A few of us have even literally had to run for our lives.

This chapter gives us a scenario just like that. It tells of the cities of refuge established in the promised land. Deuteronomy 19 provides an illustration of when a person might need a city of refuge and how it would work. This arrangement tells us much about God and Israel, but it also provides a wonderful illustration in foreshadowing the work of Christ.

From the very first murder when Cain killed his brother Abel to the first giving of the law when God said, "Thou shalt not kill," God made clear that he valued human life and that he would require a life for a life. Exodus 21:12 says, "Anyone who strikes a man and kills him shall surely be put to death." In the culture and family of the tribal system, it was the responsibility of the extended family to execute that judgment. But in the very next verse God also says, "However, if he does not do it intentionally, but God lets it happen, he is to flee to a place I will designate" (v. 13). The cities of refuge became those designated places.

This was not an escape from justice because the refugees still had to stand trial before the assembly and be proven innocent of intentional murder. Twice in verse 3 we find the emphasis—**accidentally** and **unintentionally**. And it appears again in verse 5, adding **without malice aforethought**. Discussion of the cities of refuge appears in Exodus 21, Numbers 35, Deuteronomy 19, and again here in Joshua. "According to Jewish tradition the roads leading to these cities were kept in excellent condition and the crossroads were well marked with sign posts reading, 'Refuge! Refuge!' Runners were also stationed along the way to guide the fugitives" (Campbell, *BKC*, 363).

The word **accidentally** (*segaga*) has to do with inadvertent killing such as negligence. **Unintentionally** has to do with knowledge of what was going on, basically ignorance that what the killer had done was wrong. The guilt is not in question here but the judgment.

Howard picks up on the idea of the blood avenger and connects it with the kinsman-redeemer concept:

> The idea of blood vengeance behind our passage here in Joshua 20 (and the related passages in Numbers 35 and Deuteronomy 19) is more limited than the broader idea of the "kinsman-redeemer." The "avenger of blood" was not free to take private vengeance: the Bible clearly reserves vengeance to God alone (Deut. 32:35; Isa. 34:8; Rom. 12:19). Numbers 35 states clearly that the avenger of blood was only free to kill someone who had killed another if (1) that person ventured forth from a city of refuge (Num. 35:26–28) or (2) that person was guilty of murder and not manslaughter (Num. 35:16–21). The avenger of blood had a legal status in society to carry out society's (i.e., God's) judgments and was by no means one who was to exact private vengeance (Howard, 385).

20:7–9. These six cities were strategically located to be available to anyone in Israel. Apparently the gates of the cities would remain unlocked so a desperate refugee could enter any time of the day or night. With their promise of justice and mercy, these cities were available to all Jews and even to the aliens living with them in the land. As we have noted, the roads were accessible and carefully repaired. Bridges were built where needed so an accused person did not have to run into a ravine but could go straight across, taking the shortest possible route to the city.

Only six specific cities in the whole nation qualified as cities of refuge. People could not run to any city and claim it as a refuge. Furthermore, the fugitive was only safe as long as he stayed in the city. The accused had to live in the city of refuge until the death of the high priest, at which time they could return to their hometowns. There was only one high priest, so when he died all refugees in all of these six cities would be freed at once. All across the country people would stream back to their homes.

What a day of freedom! But why when the high priest died? What was God's point? In human terms the high priest's death served as something of a statute of limitations ending the exile and giving an opportunity for freedom. Obviously two people who committed the same crime could spend significantly different times in exile in a city of refuge, possibly as great as twenty or more years to a few months.

But this must also be another one of God's dramatic pictures of redemption and atonement. In a sense, in God's eyes, the death of the high priest paid the debt for the freedom of those who were guilty of manslaughter. An accused person could not buy his own freedom; it could only be purchased with the life of a high priest. And forgiveness was forgiveness despite the intensity of the crime or the amount of time served in a city of refuge. Murderers and liars both go to hell if they do not trust Christ's salvation. But murderers and liars can also be saved in the same instant under the same conditions with no lingering spiritual consequences of the severity of their crimes.

The location of the cities put them in reasonable accessible distance and in significant population areas. Looking north to south on the eastern side of the Jordan River, there were Golan, Ramoth, and Bezer and north to south on the western side of the river were Kedesh, Shechem, and Hebron. A quick map study will show that every city of refuge also had a levitical city close by, with the exception of Shechem where the Levites would have lived at nearby Shiloh.

Some years ago at a Promise Keepers rally in Dallas, fifty thousand men sat in an open football stadium when a Texas storm blew in. As the sky darkened and the lightning flashed, they were instructed to file out of the stadium and across the parking lot to an indoor arena. Running through the rain, event organizers could be seen pointing and yelling, "This way to shelter! This way to shelter!" That is our role. To serve as signposts and shouters along the highways toward the cities of refuge, telling people where they are and directing them safely to shelter.

B Land for the Levites (21:1–8)

SUPPORTING IDEA: *The Levites were to serve God, so their earthly possessions were minimal. Nevertheless, God provided whatever they needed.*

21:1–8. Like Caleb, the Levites came to Joshua and Eleazar and the other land grant administrators in Shiloh to remind them of God's promise about land for Levites. This promise had been made in Numbers 35:1–8, and forty-eight towns were assigned, including the six cities of refuge. The allocations were made according to three main branches of the tribe which correspond to Levi's three sons—**Kohath**, **Gershon**, and **Merari**. To complete that family tree, let's notice that Kohath's sons included Amram, Izhar, Hebron, and Uzziel.

These cities with their pasturage were allocated in anticipation of complete subjugation of the land, some of which was not in Israelite hands until Solomon's reign. Nevertheless, most of the Levites had occupied their lands by the time of David (1 Chr. 13:2). This delay seems to be contrary to the original will of God. From everything we read in Joshua, God intended the conquest to be completed rapidly and for Jerusalem to be the seat of his sanctuary centuries before David came along. But Israel's repeated apostasy in the period of the judges prevented the execution of God's perfect will, including the proper allocation of the levitical cities.

Levitical towns were selected from every tribe, but they were not necessarily evenly distributed throughout the land. They did, however, seem to have been placed on the borders where spiritual protection from paganism could be provided. Notice for example Jahaz, Kedemoth, and Mephaath all

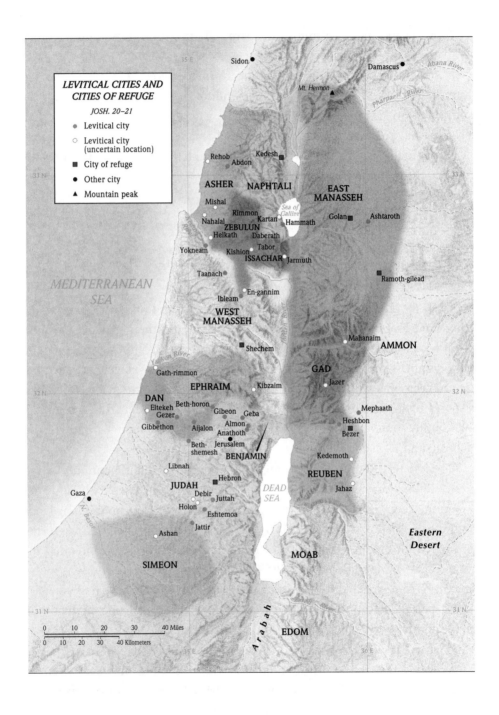

LEVITICAL CITIES AND CITIES OF REFUGE

JOSH. 20–21

- ◉ Levitical city
- ○ Levitical city (uncertain location)
- ■ City of refuge
- ● Other city
- ▲ Mountain peak

Sidon

Damascus

Abana River

Mt. Hermon

Pharpar River

35 E

33 N

Rehob · Kedesh
Abdon

ASHER · **NAPHTALI** · **EAST MANASSEH**

Mishal

Rimmon · Kartah · Golan · Ashtaroth
Nahalal · Hammath
ZEBULUN
Helkath · Daberath

Yokneam · Kishion · Tabor
ISSACHAR · Jarmuth

Taanach

Sea of Galilee

En-gannim

Ramoth-gilead

Ibleam

WEST MANASSEH

Shechem

Mahanaim

AMMON

GAD

Gath-rimmon

Jazer

EPHRAIM · Kibzaim

MEDITERRANEAN SEA

DAN
Eltekeh · Beth-horon
Gezer · Gibeon · Geba
Mephaath
Gibbethon · Aijalon · Almon · Heshbon
Anathoth · Bezer
Beth-shemesh · Jerusalem
BENJAMIN

Kedemoth

Libnah

REUBEN

Gaza

JUDAH · Hebron
Debir · Juttah · Jahaz
Holon
Eshtemoa

DEAD SEA

Jattir

Ashan

SIMEON

Eastern Desert

MOAB

Arabah

EDOM

31 N

32 N

32 N

31 N

36 E

0 10 20 30 40 Miles

0 10 20 30 40 Kilometers

clustered along Reuben's eastern border and Ashan and Jattir hunkered down at the northern border of the Negev even south of a line between Gaza and the Dead Sea. In Numbers 35 we learn that more than half a square mile of pasturage would be given to the Levites with each town.

According to Madvig:

> In as much as the temple would be built in Jerusalem, the towns of the high priest's family were conveniently located in the territories of Judah, Simeon, Benjamin. . . . The number of towns set apart for the descendants of Aaron is indicative of God's providence also. At the time of selection, there were only three or, at most, four generations of the descendants of Aaron; and they would scarcely have needed thirteen towns (Madvig, 350).

Ⓒ Pastures for the Pastors (21:9–42)

SUPPORTING IDEA: *The levitical cities were not monastic sites but places in which the Levites had specific duties from God and from which they would go out and serve the cities around them.*

21:9–19. The listing begins in the southwest with Judah and Simeon, although only one levitical city was located in Simeon (Jattir stood right on the border). And the count moves north to Benjamin. Actually one town from Simeon, eight from Judah, and four from Benjamin with no fewer than six levitical cities clustered around Jerusalem.

21:20–26. Ephraim provided four and West Manasseh two since the other two came from East Manasseh. In Ephriam we find the cities located in the extreme southern border and in West Manasseh just the reverse with Jokneam, Taanach, Ibleam, and En-Gannim all hugging the northern border.

21:27–33. Our historian jumps across the river to pick up the other half of Manasseh and then comes back to continue north with Issachar, Asher, and Naphtali where, in both cases, the cities are located in the southern half of the tribal area.

21:34–42. Finally we add Zebulun and cross the river to Reuben and Gad. And, as we noted earlier, the cities tended to lie on the eastern boundary almost as outposts against spiritual aggression from the Ammonites and Moabites.

The levitical distribution is summarized in the last two verses of this section (vv. 41–42). The emphasis here is on the exactness of the distributions and the fact that they were scattered throughout Israel. Verse 41 specifies the forty-eight cities, including the surrounding pasturelands, and it mentions that the levitical cities were to be found throughout Israel's territorial holdings. Verse 42 is somewhat obscure, but it focuses on the fact that each city was properly allotted. Nothing was left out, and nothing was left to chance (Howard, 395).

Someone has estimated that no one in Israel lived more than ten miles from one of the forty-eight Levite towns. Thus every Israelite had nearby a man well-versed in the Law of Moses who could give advice and counsel on the many problems of religious, family, and political life. And it was essential that Israel obey the Word of God in all areas of life because without this their prosperity would cease and their privilege would be forfeited. "But the final word is a sad one. The Levites did not live up to their potential; they did not fulfill their mission. If they had, idolatry and its corrupting influence might never have spread over the land of Israel" (Campbell, *BKC*, 364).

🄳 Possessing the Promises (21:43–45)

SUPPORTING IDEA: *Even though Israel failed frequently, God's promises prevailed, and they possessed the land he had promised long ago to Moses.*

21:43–45. These verses form a summary to tell us that land granting was over and God had kept his word about providing the promised land and all its special features. This, of course, did not indicate that every corner of the land was now in Israel's possession. As we have repeatedly seen, some of the territory awaited the conquest of David. Deuteronomy 7:22 indicated that the land would be overcome gradually.

Neither do these concluding statements ignore the tragedies that would develop during the period of the Judges, but those would be Israel's fault, not God's. Yet the unfaithfulness of Israel in no way impugned the faithfulness of God. Paul affirmed this fact in his words to Timothy, "If we are faithless, he will remain faithful, for he cannot disown himself" (2 Tim. 2:13) (Campbell, *BKC*, 364).

Let's be careful to distinguish between the allotments of land promised in Numbers 34 to ancient Israel and the ultimate messianic kingdom described in Genesis 15 to Abraham. Obviously any newspaper on any given day would indicate that Israel does not possess the land promised to Abraham nor for that matter even the land promised in Numbers 34. The Jews have gone through a long period of dispossession. But the promises of God prevail, and the Abrahamic land allotment of Genesis 15 will eventually be Israel's forever.

Some interpreters suggest that Joshua 21:43–45 is the key passage of the book, emphasizing the theme of God's faithfulness in keeping his promises to Joshua (1:5–9). In harmonizing these general statements with Israel's failure to subdue Canaan, we must remember God's provision for taking over the land gradually (Exod. 23; Deut. 7).

> **MAIN IDEA REVIEW:** *The cities of refuge provided a demonstration of God's grace without detracting from his law. Everywhere these cities appeared across the land they showed that God provided for people who made big mistakes and needed mercy in their lives.*

III. CONCLUSION

Escape of the African Hornbill

When an African hornbill chick of the genus *Tockus* enters the world, it must break out of its shell and then demolish a walled-up entrance to its special nursery. The female hornbill lays between one and six eggs in a tree trunk cavity and blocks up the entrance from the inside with cement made from clay and saliva. The bird leaves a hole just big enough for her mate to be able to feed her. The eggs are incubated for five weeks. When they hatch, she breaks through the wall, leaving her brood behind. But then the bird repairs the damage of the wall, often helped by the chicks on the inside. There they stay until they are strong enough to attack the wall with their beaks from the inside and emerge to the outside world.

The tribes of Israel faced enormous hardships on their trek through the desert, as they crossed the Jordan River and captured the promised land. Indeed, these struggles go on. But the chapters on the cities of refuge and the levitical towns remind us of what was waiting on the other side of the mud wall of struggle. Decades would pass until the land was actually occupied, but allocation had been made and God's promises fulfilled. All that remained now was faithfulness on the part of Israel.

There are several spiritual lessons in these chapters about Christ our refuge. God cares about the sanctity of human life. But he cares even more about our eternal spiritual life. We deserve to die for our sins because the wages of sin is death. But God does not want us to suffer spiritual death for our sin even though that would be perfectly just. He wants to show us mercy, so he has made a way of escape for us. He has provided a refuge, not an escape from justice, but a place of refuge within his just plan.

The execution of convicted killer Gary Graham in Texas a few years ago refueled the debate on the capital punishment issue. As a society, we are desperately trying to find the balance of justice and mercy. Appeals went out to the governor and the Supreme Court, but all were denied. Graham ran out of refuge and was executed. Our civil government will continue to wrestle with this because the only proper foundation for universal law and justice is the character of God. When one leaves that out of the picture, only shifting relative opinions remain.

It's also worth noting here that there are not multiple roads to heaven. There is only one way that God has designated: "Salvation is found in no one else" (Act 4:12). Christ is the only city of refuge. Being in Christ makes much more sense when we think of him as our city of refuge. Paul promised, "Therefore, there is now no condemnation for those who are in Christ Jesus" (Rom. 8:1). But 1 John 5:12 tells us that "he who does not have the Son of God does not have life." Outside of Christ is certain death.

In the movie *The Perfect Storm*, the story centers on a fishing boat and crew out at sea when the storm hits. They attempt to bring in their big catch of fish and head through the storm to their only place of refuge, a harbor on the coast. But out on the open sea there is no refuge, no shelter from the punishing winds and waves. Helpless outside their harbor, they are destroyed without mercy.

So it is with us. There is no other way, and there is no other place but Christ.

When we think about the levitical towns and the relationship of the priestly class to all Israel, we are reminded of Hebrews 2:17: "For this reason he [Jesus] had to be made like his brothers in every way, in order that he might become a merciful and faithful high priest in service to God, and that he might make atonement for the sins of the people." Christ became our high priest and died to set us completely free. The cities of refuge were temporary shelters under the law, but they foreshadowed the coming of the high priest who would set us free forever.

In our world today there are often needs for refuge. When trouble brewed in Kosovo, people streamed out of that country looking for refuge in nearby Albania and other places. Refugee camps are intended to be temporary places. Imagine the joy of any people when the gates are opened and they are free to return to their own homes.

PRINCIPLES

- God's law makes a distinction between accidental killing and murder.
- The cities of refuge demonstrated God's balanced but absolute character of justice and mercy.
- God made clear that his plan of mercy would be available to anyone who might need it.

APPLICATIONS

- We need to assess our motives when the impulse to vengeance arises within us.
- Take some time to reflect on the meaning of a refugee's being free when the high priest dies.
- As rescued refugees, we must tell others how to enter the place of safety.

IV. LIFE APPLICATION

Title to Heaven

Some of the most singable hymns we use were set to existing folk melodies which people already knew and loved. We sing the words to "When I Can Read My Title Clear" written by Isaac Watts to the tune "Pisgah," an early American folk song heard most commonly in the South. It appeared in the book *Kentucky Harmony* in 1816 and three years later in *Tennessee Harmony*. The hymn focuses on heaven, and Watts originally titled it, "The Hopes of Heaven Our Support Under Trials on Earth." Imagine trying to sing that!

Although not exacting in its theology, this hymn expresses the sentiment of being finished with this world's trials and ready for heavenly rest. As we sing or hum it, we can grasp the Lord's words to his disciples in John 14:1–2: "Do not let your hearts be troubled. Trust in God; trust also in me. In my Father's house are many rooms; if it were not so, I would have told you." One hymnist calls this song a "golden hymn which has made Isaac Watts a benefactor to every prisoner of hope."

> When I can read my title clear to mansions in the skies,
> I'll bid farewell to every fear and wipe my weeping eyes;
> And wipe my weeping eyes, and wipe my weeping eyes,
> I'll bid farewell to every fear and wipe my weeping eyes.

We praise the heavenly Father who gives strength for today and hope for life eternal. We praise him for our title of life that grants us entrance into heaven. But we also praise him for earthly mercies. Certainly the ancient Hebrews had every reason to thank God for these magnificent cities of refuge, a precursor of life in Christ and expectation of heaven.

But Francis Schaeffer points out two important distinctions between the cities of refuge and our relationship to Christ. First, the cities of refuge protected only the innocent. They existed for a person who killed by mistake. But Christ welcomes even the guiltiest sinner into his saving grace. And second, Christ is nearer than any city of refuge—no one need run ten miles to come to the Savior. Schaeffer emphasizes:

> We are not like a man who runs to a city of refuge and is acquitted after a trial because he is innocent. We are guilty. If you are still a non-Christian, run to Christ, for God's own promises say, "Refuge! Refuge!" If we are Christians, we should take Christ as our sufficient refuge in bringing specific sins under the work of Christ and in all the vicissitudes of life, this moment and moment by moment through the whole of our lives (Schaeffer, 200).

V. PRAYER

Father, thank you for the eternal city of refuge we have in the Savior. We have run to him for salvation; may we run to him for safety and security in all the problems of our lives. Amen.

VI. DEEPER DISCOVERIES

A. What About Intentional Sin? (20:3)

We have emphasized the words *accidentally* and *intentionally*. This is the principle on which the cities of refuge were based. But what did the Old Testament say about the atonement for intentional sins that were committed with "malice aforethought"? Some would say there is no sacrifice for deliberate sin, especially murder, and therefore the capital punishment system of today requires the execution of criminals found guilty of first degree murder. Numbers 15:30–31 complicates the problem further: "But anyone who sins defiantly, whether native-born or alien, blasphemes the LORD, and that person must be cut off from his people. Because he has despised the LORD's word and broken his commands, that person must surely be cut off; his guilt remains on him."

The word *defiantly* literally means "with hands raised in rebellion against God." We all know that Christ's sacrifice covered flagrant sins like this, but what about the Old Testament levitical law?

The difference, of course, is whether or not there is confession and repentance. The burnt offering of Leviticus 1 was propitiatory to make spiritual atonement, even though the physical punishment might not be expiated. Howard points out that Numbers 5:6–8 shows that a person who is

> . . . unfaithful to the LORD must confess his or her sin and also make restitution and then the sins can be forgiven. . . . It is also used with reference to Achan's sin in Josh. 7:1. The key here is the confession of sin. It would appear then, that the sin committed "with a high hand" in Num. 15:30–31 was a deliberate rebellion against God in which there was no confession; rather the sinner was standing defiantly before God, with an upraised fist, not humbly, with a broken spirit and

broken and contrite heart. . . . This would be the Old Testament equivalent of the blasphemy against the Holy Spirit of which Jesus spoke (see Matt. 12:31; Mark 3:29; Luke 12:10) (Howard, 384).

We see the same thing in the case of Ananias and Sapphira. Even though they were believers, earthly judgment was still carried out against them.

B. Were the Cities of Refuge Ever Used?

There is no record in the Old Testament of the cities of refuge actually being put to use. Some interpreters offer the argument that this proves the text was written much later and the cities of refuge were a post-exilic provision, but that does great damage to the text of Joshua. Others argue that the cities were never occupied until the time of Christ. Campbell proposes:

> In the face of such shifting arguments it is better to recognize the historicity of these accounts and to explain the silence of the record by the obvious fact that the Scriptural authors were selective about what they recorded. Once the provision was made, it was apparently not important to document specific cases of its use (Campbell, *BKC*, 363).

VII. TEACHING OUTLINE

A. INTRODUCTION

1. Lead Story: Why All-Star Games Are Boring
2. Context: Connected well together, the chapter on the cities of refuge and the chapter on the levitical towns properly fall after the allocation of the land is completed at the end of chapter 19. Contextually, the only correct place to include them is right here after the land is allocated and the eastern tribes return home.
3. Transition: There is no break between chapters 19 and 20. The word *then* at the beginning of chapter 20 indicates that God is moving to another phase of his plan. The same word opens chapter 22, but here we sense

that the book is winding down since the eastern tribes head back across the Jordan River and we get ready for Joshua's final farewells.

B. COMMENTARY
1. Residences of Refuge (20:1–9)
2. Land for the Levites (21:1–8)
3. Pastures for the Pastors (21:9–42)
4. Possessing the Promises (21:43–45)

C. CONCLUSION: TITLE TO HEAVEN

VIII. ISSUES FOR DISCUSSION

1. The commentator implies that though we see great lessons in the cities of refuge leading us to our position in Christ, the cities are not a type of Christ. What is your opinion on this question?
2. Name some ways Christians point people to Christ as a city of refuge in our day.
3. How can we say "not one of all the LORD's good promises to the house of Israel failed, every one was fulfilled" (21:45) when we know that large portions of the land had not yet been settled by the tribes to whom they had been given?

Joshua 22

Where to Worship

I. INTRODUCTION
No Laughing Matter

II. COMMENTARY
A verse-by-verse explanation of the chapter.

III. CONCLUSION
Baptist Knees

An overview of the principles and applications from the chapter.

IV. LIFE APPLICATION
Caution: Engage Brain Before
Opening Mouth

Melding the chapter to life.

V. PRAYER
Tying the chapter to life with God.

VI. DEEPER DISCOVERIES
Historical, geographical, and grammatical enrichment of the commentary.

VII. TEACHING OUTLINE
Suggested step-by-step group study of the chapter.

VIII. ISSUES FOR DISCUSSION
Zeroing the chapter in on daily life.

Quote

"*W*orship is not a text but a context; it is not an isolated experience in life, but a series of life experiences."

Gary Gulbranson

PERSONAL PROFILE: PHINEHAS

- Son of Eleazar and grandson of Aaron
- Priest who headed the delegation to the eastern tribes
- Zealous for God's honor (Num. 25:11)
- Assigned to leadership by Moses as well (Num. 31:6)
- Succeeded Eleazar as high priest (Judg. 20:28)

Joshua 22

 I N   A   N U T S H E L L

*S*ometimes messages can get mixed up. In this chapter the Is-raelites argue over an altar. This argument arises from a misunder-standing that almost caused a war. Fortunately, cooler heads prevailed, and the tribes remained united.

Where to Worship

I. INTRODUCTION

No Laughing Matter

A Christian businesswoman did a lot of traveling by air and always took her Bible with her, often reading it on the plane. One time she was sitting next to a man who gave a chuckle and went back to what he was doing when he saw her pull out her Bible. In a few minutes he turned to her and asked, "You don't really believe all that stuff in there do you?"

She replied, "Of course I do. It is the Bible."

"Well, what about that guy who was swallowed by the whale?"

"Oh, Jonah. Yes, I believe that; it is in the Bible."

"Well, how do you suppose he survived all that time inside the whale?"

"I really don't know. I guess when I get to heaven I will ask him."

"What if he isn't in heaven?"

"Then you can ask him!"

Heaven and hell are no laughing matter. Neither is worship. Right worship and wrong worship shape eternal destinies. This question of right worship was the key question for Israel. They had taken possession of the promised land. Now we read about a wonderful expression of God's faithfulness in keeping his commitment to them. God did everything he said he would. Every promise fulfilled. Every enemy defeated. God had been completely faithful.

Now came the test. Would God's people respond in similar faithfulness? Would they keep their promises? Would they fulfill their part of the relationship covenant? Would they worship only the Lord God and only in the ways he had designed?

II. COMMENTARY

Where to Worship

> **MAIN IDEA:** *The nation of Israel, now divided by the Jordan River, had to learn there would be no variation in the singularity of their worship. They also had to learn not to criticize the worship of their brothers and sisters.*

A Call to Commitment (22:1–9)

> **SUPPORTING IDEA:** *One of Joshua's major tasks was to call God's people to commitment and worship. It was their responsibility to listen and respond.*

22:1–5. This chapter presents the first test case in Israel's collective and corporate commitment to God. Though not a familiar story—hardly the parting of the Jordan River or the capture of Jericho—this obscure event provides some valuable lessons for us about faithfulness to God and confrontation and conflict with others. How do we challenge one another to be committed to Christ? How do we confront when it seems that commitment has been compromised? How do we respond when someone questions our commitment?

The Transjordanian tribes had done their job. For seven years they had stood beside the other nine and one-half tribes in conquering Canaan, and now it was time to go home. Joshua had nothing but commendation for them. But he reminded them that distance from the tabernacle might lead to distance from God: **Be very careful to keep the commandment and the law that Moses the servant of the LORD gave you: to love the LORD your God, to walk in all his ways, to obey his commands, to hold fast to him and to serve him with all your heart and all your soul.** The words **carried out the mission** could be translated "kept the charge." They refer back to Joshua's challenge and their response in chapter 1.

What a great tribute to these soldiers from the eastern tribes! For seven years they had sacrificed themselves to stand with their brothers and fight for land that they would not possess themselves. They had been away from their families and risked their own lives. They deserved to be commended for their work—and Joshua did just that.

22:6–9. Joshua blessed them and sent them home with their plunder from war. He followed a solid leadership pattern—commend, then command. He cheered their service and then challenged them to continued service. As followers of Christ we need commendation and we need challenge. We've all seen stories of employees who get their pictures in the paper. Those people are also motivated to continue to be good workers and perhaps even exceed their prior performance. And parenting is like that as well. Not just commanding and giving orders but motivating children through positive encouragement and affirmation.

Furthermore, they were told one of the basic lessons learned in kindergarten: share what you have with others. Joshua specifically says, **Divide with your brothers the plunder from your enemies**. But why did the people who stayed on the eastern side of the Jordan River deserve any of the plunder? Because there was work to do there in the guardianship of the land. Raising the crops, caring for the animals, and leading the families were just as important to those who stayed as to those who served as the primary military force for the conquest.

In another context Jesus said to his disciples, "Even now the reaper draws his wages, even now he harvests the crop for eternal life, so that the sower and the reaper may be glad together" (John 4:36).

Verse 9 emphasizes the geographic distinction between the nine and one-half tribes and the two and one-half tribes—**Shiloh in Canaan** and **Gilead, their own land**. What no one can ascertain in this great moment of future hope for all the tribes is the lurking danger of a possible civil war just days away. All around them stood half-vanquished Canaanites just waiting for any opportunity to pounce upon the invaders of their land. One would hope that the events of the rest of the chapter taught Israel a great lesson about unity. But we know from the later wars of the northern and southern kingdoms that the lesson, though poignant for the moment, was only temporary.

B Confrontation over Commitment (22:10–20)

> **SUPPORTING IDEA:** *Sometimes when we do things with the purest of motives, others misunderstand and quarrels can arise. That's what happens in these verses as the nine and one-half tribes are prepared to begin a civil war over an altar.*

22:10–14. We do not know exactly where Geliloth stood, but we can make a safe assumption that it was near Gilgal where they had first entered the land. That would have been southeast of Shiloh and familiar territory. With the purest of motives, the warriors of the two and one-half tribes **built an imposing altar there by the Jordan**. We learn later that they wanted some visible reminder of the union of the tribes and of their right and obligation to come back to Shiloh for worship. Presumably the altar could be seen across the river from the eastern bank as well as by the tribes living in Canaan.

So far in the text this behavior doesn't alarm us, but it certainly did the western tribes. They were concerned about the site that was in territory belonging to Manasseh or Benjamin, but they were much more concerned about the significance. What could have been so bad about this altar to cause them to think immediately about going **to war against them**?

The problem was that the western tribes thought the eastern tribes had built their own place of worship that would be more convenient than going all the way to Shiloh. That was unacceptable to them because it violated the direct command of God (Deut. 12:13–14). Although their reaction seems quick and harsh, at least the Israelites understood the danger of unfaithfulness. If this was an altar, the nation was in jeopardy.

Here we learn lessons both positive and negative. On the positive side, concern for faithfulness and strict adherence to God's law is commendable. Nevertheless, their knee-jerk response of considering war as the solution after they had fought shoulder to shoulder with these people for the last seven years seems outrageous.

At least they decided to send a delegation to get to the bottom of the problem. The phrase **whole assembly of Israel** seems striking since Joshua has repeatedly acknowledged that the two and one-half tribes living east of the Jordan River were part of Israel as well. "A survey of the rest of the chapter reveals that the narrator and the speakers consistently maintain such a distinction until the misunderstanding about the altar has been explained in a satisfactory manner" (Howard, 407). Furthermore, the delegation headed by Phinehas did not meet the two and one-half tribes at the altar but in **the land of Gilead**.

22:15–20. Suddenly "the whole assembly of Israel" (22:12) became **the whole assembly of the LORD**. Verbal excommunication had already taken place for these two and one-half tribes and the judgment had already been rendered: **How could you break faith with the God of Israel like this?** Phinehas remembered **the sin of Peor** back in Numbers 25 in which he played a significant role. In an emotional response, he has no intention of watching that kind of **plague** fall upon the nation again.

This business of crossing the Jordan River to worship was no small matter, for the Jordan is a river of some significance. Campbell tells us that

> . . . mountains on each side rise to heights above 2,000 feet and the Jordan Valley nestled in between is in effect a great trench 5 to 15 miles wide. During a part of the year the intense heat greatly discourages travelers. This then was a very pronounced river boundary and may have contributed to the fear of these tribesmen that they and their brethren would permanently drift apart. After all, "out of sight" is often "out of mind' (Campbell, *BKC*, 365).

So the Phinehas delegation used strong language to describe what they believed to be a major spiritual failure, comparing it not only with Peor but with the sin of Achan, who **acted unfaithfully regarding the devoted things**.

Howard sees in the delegates' critical remarks

> . . . the implication that Israel had never truly rid itself of this sin, that it always flirted with—if not participated in—idolatry and the allure of pagan religious systems. Achan's case was proof positive of this and the Cisjordan tribes feared that this altar represented another such case (Howard, 409).

But to their credit, the delegation offered a solution. If this altar had been built because the Transjordanian tribes were not happy with their land, then let them **come over to the LORD's land, where the LORD's tabernacle stands, and share the land with us**. Better to abandon physical material possessions including land and be close to worship than to allow distance from worship to corrupt one's life. This speech may indicate that the Canaan settlers never considered the land on the eastern side of the Jordan River to be a good choice. But Moses had given it to the two and one-half tribes, and Joshua had confirmed that allocation more than once.

Consider the three characteristics of this appeal by the Phinehas delegation:

1. It was *personal*. Instead of marching on the tribes, the Israelites chose a delegation headed by a priest. They delivered a sincere message before they picked a fight. That's a good approach.

2. It was *passionate*. The Israelites made the trip because they were concerned about faithfulness to God. They guarded God's reputation and holiness and his command about the central altar. By appealing to Peor and Achan, they recalled the time when Moabite worship brought a plague on the whole nation and twenty-four thousand Israelites died. They also remembered the time when the first battle for Ai was hopelessly lost. This delegation pled, begged, and tried to turn the eastern tribes from what they considered to be sin. Their motive was pure, even if their reasoning was faulty.

3. It was *purposeful*. The option of land grants west of the Jordan River shows a desire to restore these tribes and bring them back to a place where they could keep their commitment to God. Though wrong-headed, this whole process was right hearted.

Ⓒ Communication of Commitment (22:21–34)

SUPPORTING IDEA: *What a great example we find here from the behavior of the eastern tribes—a humble and gracious explanation rather than a hostile and defensive counterattack.*

22:21–29. Reuben, Gad, and East Manasseh wasted no time with their response. They began by invoking a combination of the three divine names *El, Elohim,* and *Jehovah.* In other words they pledged a solemn and majestic oath in their denial of the charge of rebellion and treachery (see "Deeper Discoveries"). They cut right to the question of motive and openly said in effect, "If our motive is wrong, **do not spare us this day.**" These eastern tribes were horrified to think that their altar was perceived as an act of rebellion. Yet they did not get defensive but offered a mature response by explaining their purpose.

It was not an alternative altar. It was a witness. A lasting remembrance that the tribes on both sides of the Jordan River shared a common commitment to the worship of God. A testimony to their unity rather than fragmentation. They tried to show that the wide Jordan River could not divide them from their commitment to God. Like Joshua's pile of stones in the Jordan, this altar served as a reminder that all twelve tribes belonged to God.

But would not a **replica of the LORD's altar** be an idol? No, not unless it were worshiped. The Transjordanian tribes had no intention of worshiping at this altar. Madvig notes:

> Its shape was an integral part of its witness, linking it to the true altar at the Tent of Meeting. Apparently the design of an altar indicated what deity was worshiped at that altar. Many years later in order to worship the god of the Assyrians, King Ahaz had to have an altar constructed in Jerusalem patterned after the altar in Damascus (2 Kings 16:10–16; 2 Chron. 28:22–25) (Madvig, 359).

Howard brings up a point that lies subtle in the text but looms large when we consider it:

> The altar's location should have been a clue from the beginning as to its purpose. Significantly the Transjordan tribes did not build it on their side of the Jordan, but across the river from where they would live. It served little useful purpose to them there; for it to have been used regularly to offer sacrifices, it would need to have been east of the river. Here, its imposing size comes into play. . . . There it would stand, west of the Jordan, out of practical reach for regular offerings, yet functioning as a silent reminder of the true altar at the Lord's sanctuary. It beckoned the Transjordan tribes to cross the Jordan to offer their sacrifices at the altar at which it was only a copy (Howard, 414).

22:30–34. To the credit of the tribes of Reuben, Gad, and Manasseh, the explanation was clear and their true motives were revealed. To the credit of the Phinehas committee, they recognized immediately that they had made a wrong judgment and admitted, **Now you have rescued the Israelites from the LORD's hand**. God received the glory because these tribes worked through this confrontation and reaffirmed their commitment. That alone was worth praising God about.

Thankfully, **they talked no more about going to war against them to devastate the country where the Reubenites and the Gadites lived.** Notice that the crisis went on for twenty verses, but the committee's response occupies only one. When God sends spiritual resolution and unity in the hearts of his people, it can be recognized immediately.

The chapter ends with the altar getting a name: **A Witness Between Us that the LORD is God.** We know the altar was a witness; now we know what the witness says. *The Nelson Study Bible* picks up on this to offer a reminder for Christians: "In a similar vein, Jesus told His disciples that people would know they were His disciples by seeing their love for each other; that is, their love would point people to Christ (John 13:35)" (392). *The Living Bible* puts an interesting twist on the altar's name: "It is a witness between us and them that Jehovah is our God, too."

Davis sums up the significance of this entire incident:

> The unifying factor in ancient Israel was not her culture, architecture, economy, or even military objectives. The long-range unifying factor was her worship of Jehovah. When the central sanctuary was abandoned as the true place of worship, the tribes then developed independent sanctuaries, thus alienating themselves from other tribes and weakening their military potential. The effects of this trend are fully seen in the period of Judges (Davis, 87).

MAIN IDEA REVIEW: *The nation of Israel, now divided by the Jordan River, had to learn there would be no variation in the singularity of their worship. They also had to learn not to criticize the worship of their brothers and sisters.*

III. CONCLUSION

Baptist Knees

According to Jane Shoemaker's report in *The Reader's Digest* (Nov. 1994), an orthopedist examined her painful knee and asked when she felt most uncomfortable. She told him it hurt most when she knelt to pray as Episcopalians do regularly in church every Sunday. After his technician took X rays, the doctor came back with them and said, "You may have to become a Baptist."

Without entering the many differences between Episcopalians and Baptists, or visiting the theological question of prayer positions, let's at least pick up on the divisions among denominations. In relation to this squabble in this chapter, Highland Dailege observes:

> For in as much as in all the promises and laws Canaan alone (the land of this side of Jordan, Num. 34:1–12) is always mentioned as the land Jehovah would give to His people for their inheritance. It was quite a possible thing that at some future time the false conclusion might be drawn from this, that only the tribes who dwelt in Canaan proper were the true people of Jehovah (Dailege, 221).

Denominations have some great benefits and provide helpful services to their local congregations. On the other hand, they do serve to divide us significantly and not just by theological position. Even two Baptist denominations, identical in faith statements, might come to verbal blows over something like rebaptism, support of certain missionaries, or fellowship with groups in different denominations. We are a people quick to criticize and complain and much too slow to affirm and acknowledge the validity of our differences while maintaining the strength of our unity.

Campbell says there are four major lessons we can learn from this chapter. All are relevant and applicable to today's church:

> (1) It is commendable for believers to be zealous for the purity of the faith; compromise of truth is always costly. (2) It is wrong to judge people's motives on the basis of circumstantial evidence. It is important to get all the facts, remembering that there are always two sides to every dispute. (3) Frank and open discussion will often clear the air and lead to reconciliation. But such a confrontation should be approached in a spirit of gentleness, not arrogance (Gal. 6:1). (4) A person who is wrongly accused does well to remember the wise counsel of Solomon, "A gentle answer turns away wrath, but a harsh word stirs up anger" (Prov. 15:1) (Campbell, 367).

PRINCIPLES

- We should acknowledge the faithful service of God's saints but never stop calling for that service to continue.
- When you confront someone about sin, your passion must be for the honor and glory of God.
- Rebellion against God and his commands should stir us up.

APPLICATIONS

- We should feel the same way about sin that God does—we must hate it.
- If you have a problem with someone, go to that person and talk it through.
- When we are forced to confront a person over sin, our goal is never to punish but always to restore.

IV. LIFE APPLICATION

Caution: Engage Brain Before Opening Mouth

Sports bloopers, commonly found in newspapers, magazines, and on circulating E-mail, indicate that if someone sticks a microphone in front of your face, you should probably think first and speak later—if at all. This collection of sports bloopers is only a minor sample of the kinds of things sports figures have said.

- "If I wasn't talking, I wouldn't know what to say" (Chico Resch, New York Islanders goaltender).
- "We have only one person to blame, and that's each other" (Barry Beck, New York Rangers).
- "A brush back pitch could permanently hurt a batter for a long time" (Pete Rose, Cincinnati Reds).
- "Fans, don't fail to miss tomorrow's game" (Dizzy Dean, sports announcer).
- "I've never had major knee surgery on any other part of my body" (Winston Bennett, University of Kentucky).

- "Winfield goes back to the wall. He hits his head on the wall and it rolls off! It's rolling all the way back to second base! This is a terrible thing for the Padres" (Jerry Coleman, Padres' announcer).
- "Even Napoleon had his Watergate" (Danny Ozark, Philadelphia Phillies).
- "I don't want to tell you any half-truths unless they are completely accurate" (Dennis Rappaport, boxing manager).
- "Today is Father's Day, so everyone out there: Happy Birthday!" (Ralph Kiner, New York Mets' announcer).

It seems clear in our chapter that the west bank Israelites spoke before they thought and arrived at a conclusion before they considered other possibilities. That was unwise behavior on their part. When we must confront someone, we should do so with the goal of restoration of relationship. Sometimes we need to confront in order to defend God's holiness. But we must do so personally, passionately, and purposefully.

V. PRAYER

Father, help us to think always before we speak and never to attribute motives to other people when we have no idea what they really intend. Amen.

VI. DEEPER DISCOVERIES

A. Names of God (22:22)

The Transjordanian tribes swore twice by God's three names—*El, Elohim, Yahweh*—translated "The Mighty One, God, the Lord!" Butler observes:

> *Elohim* is the generic name for God which is grammatically plural. . . . Most often, as here, it refers to the one God. Yahweh is the personal name of Israel's God revealed to Moses (Exod. 3:6). The defense case begins with a solemn vow that God knows the truth and the plea that Israel may soon learn. This is strengthened by an oath formula, directly to God, and asking that he not bring them victory if they are guilty. The assumption here is that the final word in

the dispute belongs neither to the excuser nor to the excused but to God. The term again gives military overtones to the scene (Butler, 248).

Elohim occurs about 2,570 times in the Old Testament. In 2,310 of these occurrences, it designates the true God. It first appears in the very first verse of the Bible but sometimes is applied to false deities (see Gen. 35:2,4; Exod. 12:12; 18:11; 23:24).

The plural form is unique to the Old Testament and appears in no other Semitic language. Many consider this to be a trinitarian plural, though this may be a form of reading the New Testament back into the Old Testament. Ryrie says, "It is a majestic plural. The fact that the noun is consistently used with singular verb forms and with adjectives and pronouns in the singular affirms this. This plural of majesty denotes God's unlimited greatness and supremacy" (Ryrie, 46).

Yahweh appears about 5,321 times in the Old Testament and comes from the root *Hawa,* which centers on existence. Again Ryrie says:

> Since *Yahweh* was God's personal name by which He was known to Israel, in post-exilic times it began to be so sacred that it was not pronounced. Instead the term *Adonai* was usually substituted, and by the sixth-seventh centuries A.D. the vowels of Adonai were combined with the consonants YHWH to remind the synagogue reader to pronounce the sacred name as Adonai. From this came the artificial word *Jehovah.* But all of this underscores the awe in which the name was held (Ryrie, 47).

Perhaps we should say that the rendering in the NIV is not the only possible translation of the Hebrew. One might read here, "The LORD, God of gods" or "Yahweh is God of gods." This wording is found again only in Psalm 50:1 where it is translated in exactly the same manner by the NIV: "The Mighty One, God, the LORD, speaks and summons the earth from the rising of the sun to the place where it sets."

Howard offers a significant paragraph:

> The piling up of the terms for God here, and their repetition, is unique in the Old Testament, and it indicates the agitated state of

mind of the Transjordan tribes and their eagerness to have their position vindicated. They affirmed as forcefully as possible their loyalty to this God. After the string of terms for God is ended, we find an interesting sequence in which the idea of knowing is important: the tribes affirmed that, as for God, "he knows!" Then they stated that, as for Israel, "it *will* know!" . . . In affirming God as they did, these tribes were also appealing to him as their witness to vindicate them. Then their Israelite brethren would know the truth (Howard, 412).

B. The Transjordanian Choice

We referred to this several times throughout the commentary, and still it looms as an issue. There is no question that the tribes of Reuben, Gad, and East Manasseh had every right to choose to stay on the eastern side of the river. The choice cannot be wrong, but was it wise? This chapter reopens the nagging question of whether these tribes were really in God's will in settling east of Jordan.

Many scholars blame Reuben, Gad, and East Manasseh for choosing their inheritance in Transjordania. But in my opinion that view is historically incorrect. God had delivered the land of Sihon and Og to Israel, and someone had to inherit it. Certainly the original promise to Moses extended all the way to the Euphrates River and encompassed the land of the east Jordanian tribes.

Today we think the Jordan River is the eastern boundary of Israel/Palestine, but this has no basis in the biblical text. Even if we shrink the boundaries considerably east of the Euphrates River, we still must acknowledge that the mountain range of Gilead that separates it from the desert to the east forms a natural boundary. The two and one-half tribes were as much in Palestine as the other nine and one-half tribes, though they may not have been actually in Canaan.

In verse 19, the Phinehas delegation says, "If the land you possess is defiled, come over to the LORD's land," an insinuation

> . . . that Transjordan lay outside the sphere of the Lord's blessing and that the two and one-half tribes were building the altar to offer sacrifices and to sanctify it. When the nine and one-half tribes called

the land of Canaan "the Lord's land," it is clear that they did not regard Transjordan as a part of the promised land (see also Num. 32:6–9). The presence of "the Lord's tabernacle" was further evidence to them that the land west of the Jordan was especially blessed. Their willingness "to share the land" reveals a beautifully generous spirit and is proof of the sincerity of their concern for orthodox worship (Madvig, 358).

All true. But the opinions of the Phinehas delegation do not necessarily reflect the opinion of Joshua, who earlier in the chapter blessed the eastern tribes and sent them on their way. He called their homestead "the land that Moses the servant of the LORD gave you on the other side of the Jordan" (v. 4).

To repeat, the choice of land east of the Jordan River was legitimate and legal and very much a part of the land God intended to give Israel. Whether it was a smart choice to live so close to pagan peoples and to be the first to take the crushing blows of Assyria and Babylonia is an entirely different question.

VII. TEACHING OUTINE

A. INTRODUCTION

1. Lead Story: No Laughing Matter
2. Context: This chapter is important in the flow of the Joshua narrative. We have watched the two and one-half tribes struggle beside their brothers for seven years with the written report going all the way back to chapter 1. We have wondered and worried about their people back on the other side of the river, how soon they might return, and what the consequences might be. Our historian picks up all of that in this chapter and leaves us with a strong affirmation: "A Witness Between Us that the LORD is God" (22:34).
3. Transition: The last three chapters of Joshua are all farewell chapters. In this chapter the two and one-half eastern tribes say farewell to their mainland brothers. In the next chapter Joshua says farewell to the leaders of Israel.

B. COMMENTARY

1. Call to Commitment (22:1–9)
2. Confrontation over Commitment (22:10–20)
3. Communication of Commitment (22:21–34)

C. CONCLUSION: CAUTION: ENGAGE BRAIN BEFORE OPENING MOUTH

VIII. ISSUES FOR DISCUSSION

1. What procedures does your church teach when Christians disagree with one another over spiritual things?
2. Memorize and utilize Proverbs 15:1.
3. Think about a time when you have impugned others' motives. How might you have acted differently on the basis of lessons learned in this chapter?

Joshua 23

Passing the Torch

I. INTRODUCTION
The Squatters of Barton's End

II. COMMENTARY
A verse-by-verse explanation of the chapter.

III. CONCLUSION
Finishing Well

An overview of the principles and applications from the chapter.

IV. LIFE APPLICATION
Surgeon General's Warning

Melding the chapter to life.

V. PRAYER
Tying the chapter to life with God.

VI. DEEPER DISCOVERIES
Historical, geographical, and grammatical enrichment of the commentary.

VII. TEACHING OUTLINE
Suggested step-by-step group study of the chapter.

VIII. ISSUES FOR DISCUSSION
Zeroing the chapter in on daily life.

"*I* think if I had to preach week in and week out, especially in a culture saturated with entertainment, I would tack a reminder to myself in the pulpit: 'It's about God, stupid!'"

William D. Hendricks

Joshua 23

IN A NUTSHELL

*J*oshua had led the Israelites for some thirty years, and he had been faithful to the Lord and faithful to the people. As he neared the time of his death, he was ready to pass the torch to other leaders of Israel.

Passing the Torch

I. INTRODUCTION

The Squatters of Barton's End

In 1555 John Barton of Kent, England, built a secluded farmhouse for his son. The young man moved in with his family and servants that year. Already, however, pinhole borers and wood beetles had taken over. Soon after the family moved in, birds, bats, worms, and insects joined them. Three years after the house was finished, it had 1,092 tenants—only seven human. After the first wave of invaders, Noctule bats and the smaller Pipistrelle bats arrived in the loft, bringing their own insect parasites to increase the numbers. Mice moved in from the fields, and rats visited for meals. By 1660 earthworms, wood lice, snails, centipedes, millipedes, slugs, and aphids all thrived in the Barton house.

By 1860 the population at Barton's End had reached its peak—119 species—plus the family. The house has been studied through history. It reached a high of 3,300 countable creatures and insects—and one can only guess at those that could not be seen. At the last census of Barton's End, only some 450 inhabitants were estimated, an average number for a well-scrubbed modern home.

When I read that story, it reminded me of one of Aesop's fables. The beasts and the birds were engaged in a war, and the bat tried to belong to both sides. When the birds were winning, he would fly around announcing he was a bird. When the beasts were victorious, he would assure everyone he was a beast. Soon his hypocrisy was discovered, and he was disowned by both sides. Which is why, according to Aesop, the bat can now only come out at night.

Jesus reiterated this principle in the New Testament: "No one can serve two masters" (Matt. 6:24). In this chapter Joshua said to the Israelites, "Hold fast to God and keep your hands off the Canaanite gods." For us it means basically the same thing: "Hold fast to God; don't dabble in the things of the world." The word for *hold fast* is the same word used in Genesis 2:24 for "cleave." As a man is to hold on tight to a relationship with his wife, so are Christians to grab and steadfastly maintain their relationship with God.

II. COMMENTARY

Passing the Torch

> **MAIN IDEA:** *One of the most important concepts in this book is reiterated by Joshua in this speech: godly living is not accomplished by winning a single skirmish but by enlisting for lifelong service. For Joshua and Israel, the clashing of swords had stopped, but the need for a faithful, diligent commitment was greater than ever.*

A Look Back on God's Works (23:1–5)

> **SUPPORTING IDEA:** *Joshua realized when he came to the end of his years that all the victories he had won belonged to the God who had fought those battles for him.*

23:1–2. Everything was not well in Canaan land. After the struggle to get the tribes settled, there were still many enemies to be conquered. Joshua seems to have observed a growing fascination on the part of Israel with the Canaanite gods around them. Complacency and temptation marked the people who just a few years ago had marched victoriously against Jericho and watched the walls come tumbling down. There is some thought among scholars about the relationship of Joshua 23 and 24 and "some have suggested that these final chapters contain two reports of the same event. It seems better to view chapter 23 as Joshua's challenge to Israel's leaders, and chapter 24 as his charge to the people" (Campbell, *BKC*, 367).

Basking in thirty-four medals at the 2002 Winter Olympics, Americans reported it the greatest Olympics in modern memory. One of the exciting moments carried out weeks before the actual games began was the passing of the torch from runner to runner, from city to city, until it was lit by the captain of the famous gold-medal-winning hockey team of some twenty years earlier. Before he could take the torch and light the flame on site, however, he had to await the passing of the torch from hand to hand over all those miles. There must be a handing off, and there must be a taking hold of that which is handed. And that's where we find Joshua at this point.

The final words of a great leader nearing death should perk up our ears. Especially someone who walked so closely with God, who lost only one battle during the entire seven-year military campaign. Especially someone who had taken a vast group of wilderness nomads and brought them into their own promised land to become an established and respected nation. If Joshua had something to say, the leaders of Israel knew they needed to listen. We should listen too.

Throughout this study we have noted how the promised land conquest mirrors the Christian life. If we have battles to fight, enemies to evict, and ground to be taken, we need both the courage to fight and the faith to trust God for the victory.

There is debate over the words **long time** in verse 1. Howard is correct in assessing

> . . . that the "long time" should be calculated from the *completion* of the process (i.e., that the speeches in chaps. 23 and 24) came "a long time" after the land distribution was completed, when God had finally given true rest to the land. . . . . [Joshua] was 110 years old when he died (24:29), and, if he was anywhere near Caleb's age of eighty-five when the land was distributed (see 14:10), then his farewell speeches would have come about twenty-five years after the main events in the book (Howard, 419–20).

23:3–5. Joshua reminded the leaders that they had been eyewitnesses to the way God had fought for them and given them victory after victory. They had been given their inheritance in the land. They had taken possession and set up their homes and cities. God had been faithful. And that proven faithfulness led Joshua to speak for the future. God had promised and God would help them to continue driving out their enemies. God would continue to help them take possession of the land. God had the power and desire to do so.

Within the last two years my wife has traveled to Ohio to join her family in celebrating both of her sisters' fiftieth wedding anniversaries. She enjoyed the food and cake, the old wedding and family pictures, and the friends. But she also took note of the focus on God's faithfulness in their marriages. They celebrated fifty years of God's goodness in their lives, a collective century of Christian family living.

We need to celebrate God's goodness on a regular basis. Sometimes we get so caught up in our troubles, needs, and hurts that we forget to proclaim God's goodness. He cares about our troubles, meets our needs, and heals our hurts. But for that very reason, we must make the effort to declare those blessings.

One of the key words in these verses appears in verse 4: **allotted**. It's difficult for us to understand how slowly the Israelites drove out their Canaanite enemies and how long this process would continue. Nevertheless, we remember Exodus 23:30 and its emphasis on "little by little." Like Joshua, we patiently wait for this drama to unfold until finally in David's time we see the complete fulfillment.

B Hold Fast to God's Word (23:6–11)

SUPPORTING IDEA: *Israel faced a great threat in Canaan. All the forces of pagan culture around them tried to force their attention away from God, who had delivered them from Egypt and given them this land.*

23:6–11. Joshua moves from celebrating God's faithfulness to challenging the leaders to be faithful people. The words of verse 6 sound familiar. They reflect almost exactly what God had said to Joshua years before when he gave him this leadership position (1:7–8). Joshua had found this to be the secret of his success. He led the people for thirty years with this priority of steadfast obedience to God's commands. Now he calls on these leaders to lead with the same priority. He does not ask them to take off in new directions, discover creative paradigms, and live on the cutting edge of change so they can prove their creative leadership ability. They are to stay centered on their obedience to God.

So the standard of godly living in the land was God's Word, and the form was separation from sin and sinners. These verses do not indicate racial prejudice on God's part. There is no attempt here to keep the purity of the race for other than spiritual reasons. In fact, God allowed for intermarriage when aliens chose to worship him. Again, Rahab is our best example. Spiritual intermingling was the problem and the danger. The people dared not mix their worship of Jehovah with the worship of other gods. They could not serve both. So Joshua warned the leaders of this danger.

Madvig comments:

> For the first time in Joshua, we find an explicit warning against intermingling with the native population whose immorality and degradation were closely tied to their religious practices. Because Israel replaced a people whose culture was far more advanced than

their own, the temptation to worship the gods of the Canaanites must have been overwhelming. Yet if the Israelites were to adopt their wicked practices they too would be subject to punishment (Deut. 8:19–20). God does not show any partiality. Israel was to remain separate from the nations living in the land of Canaan. . . . "Invoke the names," "swear," "serve" and "bow down" are four expressions of worship that are specified here to show that no form of worship whatsoever must be accorded to these pagan deities (Madvig, 362).

So there is a standard, a form, and also a motive. Joshua did not offer this challenge to obedience without another reminder of how miraculous God's work had been. The nations they drove out were not puny little punks with sticks and stones for weapons. And besides that, in nearly every battle the Israelites had been outnumbered. No heat-seeking missiles. No bombs that explode in a cave and suck out all the air, killing everyone inside. No night scopes and radar. It is as if one Israelite could rout a thousand Canaanites because **the LORD has driven out before you great and powerful nations**.

We must see here Joshua's connection between love and obedience. They go together. Joshua didn't tell them to obey out of hard, cold duty, nor did he tell them just to love God and not worry about the rest. Perhaps Jesus said it best: "If you love me, you will obey what I command" (John 14:15).

Ⓒ Watch Out for God's Warning (23:12–16)

SUPPORTING IDEA: *Everything that happened to Israel and Canaan demonstrated that God's blessing falls on people who are willing to devote themselves to his cause. God's judgment awaits people who participate in the pagan behavior around them.*

23:12–13. Joshua used positive reenforcement first, seeking to motivate the Israelites to obey out of appreciation for God's faithfulness to them. But if that didn't work, there was always the fear of consequences. Those consequences were not an empty threat. The text says, **Then you may be sure that the LORD your God will no longer drive out these nations before you**. What's the potential problem here? Alliance and casual intermarriage—not military decline, a political coup, an economic recession, a natural disaster, or a national plague. The greatest danger facing Israel as the generations would unfold was to turn away from God and connect with the pagan culture around them.

Joshua wasn't just a general; he was also a prophet! Let's look at another prophet who, sitting in the hollow shell of a prison in what used to be Jerusalem, prayed to God and said,

> You gave them this land you had sworn to give their forefathers, a land flowing with milk and honey. They came in and took possession of it, but they did not obey you or follow your law; they did not do what you commanded them to do. So you brought all of this disaster upon them (Jer. 32:22–23).

Richard Halverson, former chaplain to the U.S. Congress, once applied this to our nation, saying, "We have become technological giants . . . and moral adolescents. Our progress in ethics and morals and humanness has declined in inverse ratio to our technical and scientific expertise." Joshua knew that Israel's problems would be moral not military.

Joshua used picturesque language to emphasize that the problems would come from the Canaanites themselves: **They will become snares and traps for you, whips on your backs and thorns in your eyes, until you perish from this good land, which the LORD your God has given you**. First they would get caught (tempted to sin), then whipped (enslaved by sin), then hurt (thorns in the eyes), and eventually killed. The same God who blessed them so profusely would just as certainly bring destruction and punishment on them if they broke the covenant. The potential problem could very easily yield a risky result.

Madvig observes that "the message of this entire book is a warning against apostasy. . . . The devotion that belongs exclusively to the Lord must not be directed to any other" (Madvig, 363).

23:14–16. Joshua ended his speech to the leaders on a negative note because he wanted them to grasp the consequences of turning against the Lord. We tend to downplay the wrath and destructive power of God in our modern world, but God is just as serious about our worship and reverence as he was then. The writer of Hebrews says, "Therefore, since we are receiving a kingdom that cannot be shaken, let us be thankful, and so worship God acceptably with reverence and awe, for our 'God is a consuming fire'" (Heb. 12:28–29).

Of these verses Tom Lee writes:

> These words pick up on the description of God in Deuteronomy 4:24. This awesome view of God was derived from the descriptions of God at Sinai (Exod. 19:16–25). The term shows that God is righteous and that he demands righteousness in his children. He will not change his demands for sinful human beings. Our reading and reflecting on these words should develop in us a sense of awe and reverence for God and a commitment to obey him. These words bring out a feature of the divine character which we must accept along with the emphasis on God's grace and mercy. They remind us of the need to be prepared for God's all-searching judgment at the time of Christ's return (2 Cor. 5:10; 2 Thess. 1:6–10) (Lee, 230).

Have you ever seen Niagara Falls? They look beautiful and peaceful from far away. Even from the top of the falls, the water seems quiet and peaceful. But when you stand at the bottom on the "Hurricane Deck," you can feel and hear the awesome power and fury of the falls. So it is with our God. When he accepts our love and obedience, he flows like a peaceful, calm river through our lives, but disobedience and apostasy can put us at the base of the falls.

So Joshua passed the torch of responsibility to the leaders of Israel. As Moses had passed it to him and as Paul would later pass the torch to the elders at Ephesus (Acts 20). These leaders would then pass the torch to the people—and on down through the history of the Old Testament. This chapter reminds us to *look back on God's works, hold fast to God's Word, and watch out for God's warning.*

MAIN IDEA REVIEW: *One of the most important concepts in this book is reiterated by Joshua in this speech: godly living is not accomplished by winning a single skirmish but by enlisting for life-long service. For Joshua and Israel, the clashing of swords had stopped, but the need for a faithful, diligent commitment was greater than ever.*

III. CONCLUSION

Finishing Well

Since I am "old and well advanced in years," I receive little reminders from my friends in cards and E-mails lest with these rapidly encroaching years I forget my own age. One of those little pieces drags on for multiple verses, but I reproduce just a few here for other souls who might wander the bypaths of this commentary after I have left it.

> Just a line to say I'm living
> That I'm not among the dead
> Though I'm getting more forgetful
> And all mixed up in my head
>
> I got used to my Arthritis
> To my dentures I'm resigned
> I can manage my Bifocals
> But dear God I miss my mind.
>
> For sometimes I can't remember
> When I stand at the foot of the stairs
> If I must go up for something
> Or have I just come down from there?
>
> And before the fridge so often
> My poor mind is filled with doubt
> Have I just put some food away?
> Or have I come to take something out?
>
> And there's a time, when it is dark
> I stop and hold my head
> I don't know if I'm retiring
> Or am I getting out of bed?
> (Wes Bush, "Just a Line to Say I'm Living")

Hardly words spoken by Joshua, I'm sure, though he may have exhibited at least some of the symptoms. Remember our title—"Passing the Torch." Those of us who are aging, even approaching middle age and passing the torch of faith to an emerging new generation of young adults, can take heed from this chapter. Like Joshua's call to Israel, we do not want our children intermarrying with those of the faithless generation around us or developing their value systems from television, the Internet, and worldly friends. Separation is a genuine issue in godly living and hardly only related to the modern day, as this chapter shows.

There is an old story about a businessman interviewing drivers for a dangerous mountain road. The first candidate said, "I'm the fastest driver you can find. Even on curvy mountain roads, I'll get you the deliveries fast." The second claimed, "I know how to take the curves. I can drive right to the edge, even on the shoulder, and still keep control of the vehicle." The third, however, affirmed, "I am committed to driving at a safe speed in the center of the road and keeping the cargo I'm delivering safe at all costs."

God is looking for "center of the lane" Christians who don't push the wheels of their lives as close to the edge as possible just for the thrill or to see if they might go off the edge and fall down the rocky precipice of sin.

PRINCIPLES

- The greatest danger in your life is not that you will lose your job or your health, or even your friends and family, but that you might lose your faith.

- The result of abandoning God is nothing short of a divine disaster.

- God is gentle, loving, and kind, but he also deals directly, seriously, and swiftly with sin.

APPLICATIONS

- We must heed Joshua's warning and make certain that we do not turn our backs on God's faithful blessings.

- If God has blessed you and been faithful to you, tell someone about it.

- Challenge someone, particularly your children and friends, to a life of obedience and love—pass the torch.

IV. LIFE APPLICATION

Surgeon General's Warning

Since few people know about the role of the office of the surgeon general of the United States, people hardly noticed when Dr. David Satcher slipped out the door early in 2002. But as he left, he offered a final warning on a subject that he had spoken about many times—obesity. Americans spend more than thirty billion dollars a year on weight-loss products and programs. Nevertheless, obesity is epidemic in this country. In the early twenty-first century, thirty-seven states have obesity rates of 15 percent or higher. Thirty-three more than ten years ago.

Sixty-one percent of Americans are overweight or obese primarily because they eat imprudently and exercise little. Smoking-related illnesses kill four hundred thousand people a year, but illness related to obesity (heart attacks, strokes, diabetes, and some cancers) now kill three hundred thousand a year and will soon surpass smoking as the leading cause of death.

One expert claims that what we eat has changed more in the last forty years than in the previous forty thousand and that Americans now spend more on food than on higher education or new cars and mostly at fast-food restaurants. Every month 90 percent of children ages three to nine visit a McDonald's whose serving of french fries is three times larger than it was a generation ago. Doctor Satcher's warning is based on sound statistics and makes a prophecy that cannot be dismissed or forgotten by gulping down a large piece of chocolate cream pie.

Such is the message we have in this chapter and throughout this book. Those who are on the edge, on the danger zone of flirting with worldliness, had better give careful attention to obedience and love of God and a rejection of their sinful surroundings. The same trends of being overweight are spiritually visible in this country with respect to becoming overworldly. Even if we are not "old and well advanced in years," we have responsibility to guard ourselves against worldliness and grasp opportunities to share our experience with God with other people. We have a torch to pass on and warnings to issue.

Every adult is a mini-Joshua standing somewhere along the path of life and leading others (especially his or her own children) into spiritual warfare, warning them what disobedience to God might bring. We are torch-passers. Maybe you can do that by teaching kids in a Sunday school, by coming alongside a friend, by conducting regular family devotions, or by preaching and teaching in a formal setting. God is looking for leaders who will model godliness and separation as a Christian lifestyle.

V. PRAYER

Father, help us to take seriously the warnings of Joshua to Israel and apply them to the worldliness and apostasy of our own day. Amen.

VI. DEEPER DISCOVERIES

A. "Way of All the Earth" (23:14)

This phrase is a common idiom for death that also appears in 1 Kings 2:2 where David said to Solomon, "I am about to go the way of all the earth." In Romans 5:12 we read the familiar words that because of sin "death came to all men, because all sinned." We talk about people "passing," "going to sleep," "departing," and "no longer with us"—all euphemisms for death exactly like the one Joshua used here. Butler points out how Joshua used his death as an emotional motivational tool to get Israel to think seriously about their spiritual state:

> Will not they listen to the voice of an old, dying man? Can they not accept his personal testimony? If not, can they not look deep within themselves and accept the reality of what they know? God has failed in nothing. Everything he said, he has done. God has been, is, and will be faithful. What is Israel's response? (Butler, 256).

Redpath says of this chapter:

> If I could choose the subject for the last sermon I ever preached, this would be my text. I'm quite sure that if the saints of God of past generations could speak in the light of what they have seen of eternity, in light of what they know of heaven and hell, they would say only these words to us all—"take heed to love." For the greatest

safeguard against carelessness of walk, prayerlessness of spirit, cold-
ness of heart, is love. That which lifts the life of the Christian and of
the church on to a new level of fullness of experience, the greatest
factor for revival in the church today, is not our advocacy of truth,
but the love of our hearts filled with the Holy Spirit (Redpath, 238).

B. Conditional Blessing (23:15–16)

Joshua 23 and 24 emphasize more strongly than any other part of the book
the conditionality of the promise of the land. In one sense the covenant with
Abraham is nonconditional. Ultimately, Israel will possess all the land that was
promised to that great patriarch. But contentment, peace, and rest in the land
depend upon the behavior of the nation. Divine sovereignty and human
responsibility are complementary truths rather than contradictory positions.
Furthermore, if the conquest of the land and the settling of the allotment of the
tribes is the promised rest, what do we do with 2 Samuel 7:1,11? How could we
find passages like 1 Chronicles 22:9 and 1 Kings 8:56 suggesting Solomon
brought rest to the land? What is the relationship in this conditional covenant
between the spiritual and the material aspects of rest and ownership?

Kaiser helps us out:

The resolution of these matters can be found in the Old Testament view of fulfillment. Specifically named generations received
their share of the completion of the single plan of God. This had
once served as a partial confirmation of God's long-standing word
and a contemporaneous installment on the fulfillment. This, in turn,
simultaneously functioned as a means of connecting that word to its
ultimate or climactic fulfillment since these periodic installment
type of fulfillments were general part and parcel with that ultimate
event. Thus there was a single meaning in the mind of the author
even though he might know of or experience multiple fulfillments of
that single meaning! The promise was not to be thought of as having
been given its final effect even in the aspect of the land. Hence rest
was more than entry and division of the land to all the tribes; it also
was to be a final condition which pervaded the land. Thus after
Israel entered the land, she was warned that she would only enjoy
the quality of life God had intended for her if she continually obeyed

his commandments (Deut. 4:10; 12:1; 31:13). The extent of Israel's possession of the land was likewise important before the promise could be said to have been completely fulfilled (Kaiser, 129).

VII. TEACHING OUTLINE

A. INTRODUCTION

1. Lead Story: The Squatters of Barton's End
2. Context: As we have noted, Joshua 23 and 24 seem to be a seamless garment with the exception that Joshua speaks first to the leaders and then assembles all the tribes. As the book winds down, chapter 23 serves as a subclimax to which chapter 24 will be the climax.
3. Transition: Our author gives us a long lead time between the end of chapter 22 and the beginning of chapter 23 when he says in verse 1: "After a long time had passed and the LORD had given Israel rest from all their enemies around them." But there seems to be no such time between chapters 23 and 24 since Joshua, now at the end of his life, must emphasize this final message against disobedience and apostasy. First to the elders, leaders, judges, and officials and then to all the tribes.

B. COMMENTARY

1. Look Back on God's Works (23:1–5)
2. Hold Fast to God's Word (23:6–11)
3. Watch Out for God's Warning (23:12–16)

C. CONCLUSION: SURGEON GENERAL'S WARNING

VIII. ISSUES FOR DISCUSSION

1. How might attitudes in your family change if you spoke like Joshua? If you announced God's faithful blessings to all family members on a regular basis?

2. To whom specifically should you be passing the torch? Your own children? A Sunday school class? A congregation? Grandchildren? Students in your classes?

3. Review what Joshua meant in 23:6 when he urged the leaders to "obey all that is written in the Book of the Law of Moses."

Joshua 24

It's Your Call!

I. INTRODUCTION
"It Is Well with My Soul"

II. COMMENTARY
A verse-by-verse explanation of the chapter.

III. CONCLUSION
Joshua's Song

An overview of the principles and applications from the chapter.

IV. LIFE APPLICATION
Read Me My Rights!

Melding the chapter to life.

V. PRAYER
Tying the chapter to life with God.

VI. DEEPER DISCOVERIES
Historical, geographical, and grammatical enrichment of the commentary.

VII. TEACHING OUTLINE
Suggested step-by-step group study of the chapter.

VIII. ISSUES FOR DISCUSSION
Zeroing the chapter in on daily life.

Joshua 24

> ### Quote

"Whether Christian or non-Christian, we're called upon to make choices which will have significant results."

Francis Schaeffer

GEOGRAPHICAL PROFILE: GIBEAH

- Burial place of Eleazar, son of Aaron
- Site of the palace of Israel's first king, Saul
- Located just northeast of Jerusalem in the territory of Benjamin

PERSONAL PROFILE: BALAK

- King of Moab who fought against Israel in the wilderness (Num. 22)
- Called for a false prophet by the name of Balaam to curse Israel
- After a conversation with his donkey, Balaam uttered an oracle of blessing rather than a curse

IN A NUTSHELL

We've marched with Joshua from the eastern side of the Jordan River, through it, over Jericho and Ai, and throughout all of Canaan. Seven years of war and twenty-three years of settling into the land have taken place. Walls have fallen; altars have been built; the sun stood still; cities were constructed; and civil war was narrowly averted. Now at approximately 110 years of age and about to pass on to his heavenly reward, Joshua gathers all Israel and their leaders at Shechem for his final words to them.

It's Your Call!

I. INTRODUCTION

"It Is Well with My Soul"

The Spafford family—Horatio, his wife, and four daughters—were scheduled to travel to Europe in November 1873. Delayed by business, Mr. Spafford stayed in Chicago while the rest of the family sailed aboard the *Ville du Havre*. The ship collided with an English sailing vessel and sank in the Atlantic Ocean. All four daughters drowned. Mrs. Spafford cabled her husband two words—"Saved alone." Mr. Spafford sailed immediately, asking the captain of the ship to show him the area where his daughters had drowned. There, at the scene of the tragedy, he wrote the hymn we know and love so well.

We can't imagine these words being sung to any other tune, but three years passed between the writing of the text and the composition of the tune by Philip P. Bliss. Spafford's wonderful lyrics call us to display the reality of Christ's peace in our lives, in spite of the struggles and tragedies we face.

> When peace, like a river, attendeth my way,
> When sorrows like sea billows roll,
> Whatever my lot, Thou hast taught me to say,
> It is well, it is well with my soul.

When circumstances and surroundings offer us no peace, in those dark moments we can allow the peace of Christ to rule in our hearts.

Two New Testament passages come to mind as we think of the hymn text and also remember Joshua's serene and peaceful departure at the end of the book: "Let the peace of Christ rule in your hearts, since as members of one body you were called to peace. And be thankful" (Col. 3:15). "Peace I leave with you; my peace I give you" (John 14:27).

Joshua challenged the tribes once again to serve the Lord God alone. Joshua 1 and 24 serve as great bookends to a wonderful story. There is no doubt that our narrator intends a great highlight to Joshua's leadership career as he brings his story to a close.

II. COMMENTARY

It's Your Call!

> **MAIN IDEA:** *Joshua reviews Israel's covenant history, their covenant commitment, and their covenant action. The chapter presents a vivid and dramatic picture of what it means to be in a covenant relationship with God.*

🅐 Review of Covenant History (24:1–13)

> **SUPPORTING IDEA:** *The nation of Israel had a history with God—a record of how God had provided and remained faithful to them through the years. In the years ahead they would find it necessary to review that history periodically.*

24:1–4. God took Abraham out of a culture of idolatry. It all started beyond the Euphrates River with God's unexpected and unexplained grace taking Abram out of paganism and into the land of promise. As he speaks to the gathered tribes of Israel at Shechem with **the elders, leaders, judges and officials** standing on full display, Joshua goes all the way back to Terah and Abraham to remind them that just as God provided for the patriarchs he provides for Israel out of their sin and into his grace. God promised Abraham many descendents. But he had only one son of promise, Isaac, who had only two sons, Jacob and Esau. Esau was no more in the promised land than was Ishmael, and Jacob's family had ended up in Egypt as slaves. One could assume that God was in no hurry to fulfill his promise to Abraham.

Joshua had selected the perfect place for this gathering—Shechem—just a few miles northwest of Shiloh where Abraham first received the promise that God would give his seed the land of Canaan. Perhaps he even stood by Abraham's altar (Gen. 12:6–7). Jacob also stopped at Shechem, and Joshua had built an altar there (Josh. 8:30–35). This was an excellent place for this speech, since the stones on which the law had been written were probably still standing—a vivid visual aid of that significant event.

From the time of Abraham through the time of Joshua on to the time when Jesus would speak to the woman at the well in John 4, Shechem was a special place. Campbell observes:

The literary form of this discourse has occasioned much interest and comment. It is now rather well known that the rulers of the Hittite Empire in this period (ca. 1450–1200 B.C.) established international agreements with their vassal states obligating them to serve the Hittite kings in faithfulness and obedience. These suzerainty (overlordship) treaties followed a pattern and required periodic renewal. Joshua 24 contains, in the standard suzerainty treaty form of that time, a covenant-renewal document in which the people of Israel were called on to confirm their covenant relationship with God (Campbell, *BKC*, 369).

24:5–7. The exodus had been Israel's first experience with God's awesome power. The plagues, the fire, the darkness, and the Red Sea. Their forefathers experienced God's miraculous deliverance as he defeated the Egyptian army. After that they **lived in the desert for a long time**.

This covenant, this suzerainty treaty, obligated only the vassal to take an oath of obedience. While the vassal was obliged to trust in the benevolence and protective support of the monarch, the monarch maintained his sole right of self-determination and sovereignty by not binding himself to specific obligations. In the case of the Mosaic covenant, the Israelites and the mixed multitude adopted the position of the vassal peoples while Jehovah was their divine sovereign.

We do well to remember that the Mosaic covenant was different from the Abrahamic covenant. The Mosaic covenant is nowhere proclaimed as an everlasting covenant since it had to be renewed periodically—at least in every generation. Like the Hittite treaties, it was not regarded as binding in perpetuity from the first. Review and renewal were always essential. That review, as here, took into account the history of the vassals with their overlord. Since this ceremony in chapter 24 is obviously a renewal of the covenant, mention of the original covenant made at Sinai is not necessary because Joshua has just emphasized that in 23:16. Israel needed to remember that every time they were helpless, God was at work.

24:8–10. In line with the plagues and the Red Sea, Joshua chose to mention Balaam (though the real hero, the donkey, is omitted). God had used a speaking donkey to correct a prophet who had been hired by the enemies of Israel to curse them. Instead of cursing Israel, Balaam was forced by God to bless them. Once again God took what someone intended as evil and turned it into something good for his people.

Balaam makes it into the pages of the New Testament as the complete demonstration of an evil person. In speaking of the apostates of the first century, Peter wrote, "They have left the straight way and wandered off to follow the way of Balaam son of Beor, who loved the wages of wickedness. But he was rebuked for his wrongdoing by a donkey—a beast without speech—who spoke with a man's voice and restrained the prophet's madness" (2 Pet. 2:15–16). In the letter to the church at Pergamum, John wrote, "Nevertheless, I have a few things against you: You have people there who hold to the teaching of Balaam, who taught Balak to entice the Israelites to sin by eating food sacrificed to idols and by committing sexual immorality" (Rev. 2:14).

Once again, the battle belonged to the Lord as Balaam issued blessing instead of cursing and God delivered Israel **out of his hand**.

24:11–13. The words in these verses summarize the Book of Joshua—the whole conquest. God not only gave them victory over every enemy; he also handed them ready-made land to live in. Houses, cities, roads, fields, and trees. They just walked in and set up shop. God provided for their every need. We will deal with the **hornet** in "Deeper Discoveries." Let's emphasize here that God not only marched with the armies of Israel; he was also before them every place they went. The seven nations here are the same as those listed in 3:10, simply arranged in a different order. Regardless of how we interpret the **hornet**, the general point of the paragraph is that God fought for Israel wherever they went.

Ⓑ Renewal of Covenant Commitment (24:14–24)

SUPPORTING IDEA: *Having reviewed the history of Israel in brief form, Joshua calls upon the nation to "fear the LORD and serve him with all faithfulness" and offers himself and his household as the model.*

24:14–15. Following the history of God's grace and a long record of promises kept, the only response is the one Joshua himself claims. As Joshua put it, anyone who chose not to serve the Lord could have his choice of any non-gods. The gods that Abraham's family worshiped beyond the Euphrates River, the gods of Egypt, the gods of Canaan—they are all cut of the same cloth, made of the same wood and stone. The idea that any Israelite listening to Joshua that day would decide against the God who blessed the nation was so obviously absurd. Any other choice was meaningless.

Furthermore, they saw where Joshua stood. No matter what anyone else said or did or decided, Joshua held firm in his commitment to serve the Lord only. That's the way it must be.

> With his famous words, Joshua clearly and unambiguously took his stand on the side of the living God. Joshua modeled a perfect leader's actions. A leader must be willing to move ahead and commit himself to the truth regardless of the people's inclinations. Joshua's bold example undoubtedly encouraged many to follow with the affirmations of vv. 16–18 (*Nelson Study Bible*, 394).

We must not read into Joshua's challenge an open invitation to choose Canaanite gods. The contrast makes such a selection ludicrous in view of what he had already pointed out about God's faithfulness and power. Of particular concern were the gods around them, the proliferation of idols in the land of the Canaanites (Amorites). Madvig notes:

> The fertility cult of the Amorites with its many corrupt and immoral practices held a special appeal to the Israelites, who were settling down to agricultural life after so many years of wandering. This cult continued to be a strong temptation for many years. Our individualistic approach to salvation must be modified by the fact that here (and in Acts 16:31) individuals are challenged to involve their entire households (Madvig, 368).

24:16–24. Immediately **the people answered** that they stood in unanimous agreement with Joshua and would never **serve other gods**. They reviewed God's leadership in their nation and blessing upon their lives and loudly proclaimed, **We too will serve the LORD, because he is our God.**

But the verses which follow seem to suggest that they were unable to convince Joshua by this great acclamation. What they said should have pleased him. But it seems as if Joshua were stopping them as they rushed to the altar to make their commitment and sending them back to rethink it. He appears to say, "You don't know what you're committing to. You're not serious enough about this. You don't realize how holy God is and that he won't just ignore your sin and idolatry. You haven't yet counted the cost of serving God." He actually told them that this **jealous God . . . will not forgive your rebellion and your sins**, a point we will return to in "Deeper Discoveries." But they persisted and repeatedly said, **We will serve the LORD.** They were willing to be witnesses against themselves to this covenant commitment.

Christians today need to count the cost of following Jesus. We need to be humble enough to recognize the pitfalls and the potential of our own failures. All pride is sin, but spiritual pride is particularly heinous. We need to be willing to make right, godly, and moral choices for life even if people around us do not. We need to stay faithful in our personal devotional walk with God, even when there are so many distractions and demands upon our time.

Recording of Covenant Action (24:25–33)

> **SUPPORTING IDEA:** *Israel needs more stones with ears to record their private prayers and public promises to God about their national affirmation of faithfulness and purity.*

24:25–27. Literally, Joshua "cut a covenant" which probably involved a sacrifice. Everything was written and recorded to be passed on. And in appropriate Joshua form, he erected one more stone memorial, possibly a pillar or a slab as a reminder and witness of the day's events. A rock with ears that heard God's promises from Israel as well as God's promises to them.

The words **decrees and laws** are actually in the singular and could be translated "a statute and an ordinance." Howard recalls:

> They are used forty-one times together, five times in the singular. . . . What is in view is a specific ordinance for the specific context. In Ezra 7:10 the large context of the law is in view as it is many times when two terms are plural. . . . Here in Joshua 24 the "decree and law" that Joshua established centered around a specific ordinance, which was the primary concern and focus of the chapter, namely, that Israel would be committed to Yahweh alone. By extension, of course, such a commitment would entail Israel's keeping the entirety of the law, but the immediate focus is more intensely concentrated on this single-minded and whole-hearted commitment to God (Howard, 440).

The words *serve, served,* or *serving* occur thirteen times in verses 13–24. What do you think happened every time Israel passed this stone in a very obvious and sacred place? Conviction? Remembrance? Accountability?

We need stones with ears in our lives. We need reminders of who we are and whose we are. When I see my wife's picture, I am reminded of my commitment to her. When I see my ordination certificate, I am reminded of my commitment to ministry. When I see the American flag, I remember my commitment to my country. And when I sign my income tax forms, I remember my commitment to the laws and financial statutes of our nation.

Stones with ears. Visual reminders of our commitments to God, his word, his work, his people. Perhaps in a picture or even a bookmark. Maybe a poster or plaque on the wall. Maybe a special letter in a purse or wallet. We need stones with ears to remind us of our commitments to God as well as his commitments to us.

24:28–33. Joshua's life and ministry had finished. He died **at the age of a hundred and ten,** and they buried him in his city. What a tribute to a pastor or Christian leader—**Israel served the LORD throughout the lifetime of Joshua and of the elders who outlived him and who had experienced everything the LORD had done for Israel.** Some commentators criticize Joshua for not training a single successor the way Moses did. But that was obviously not God's plan. Joshua represents the classic transition into team leadership. The team that he pulled together and charged did not fail, as verse 31 tells us.

All three funerals at the end of our chapter took place in the territory of Ephraim. Joshua was buried at Timnath Serah, Joseph at Shechem, and Eleazar at Gibeah. As we think back on Joshua's leadership, we are continuously reminded that he never exalted himself. Up to his final speech he exalted God. What a stark contrast to many political and religious leaders of our day. We watch conventions of "candidate glorification" with balloons, banners, lights, cameras, speeches, chants, flags, funny hats, and clichés. Instead, we need to focus on the history of what God has done for us and let that motivate us to stand firm in our commitment to serve him. Joshua 24:15 raises the flag high over this entire book: "But as for me and my household, we will serve the LORD."

MAIN IDEA REVIEW: *Joshua reviews Israel's covenant history, their covenant commitment, and their covenant action. The chapter presents a vivid and dramatic picture of what it means to be in a covenant relationship with God.*

III. CONCLUSION

Joshua's Song

James Stewart, a budding musician now in his mid-twenties, has written "Joshua's Song," a loosely rhymed poem set to music and based on Joshua 23 and various verses in 1 Corinthians 1.

> You who wandered in the desert
> You who crossed a mighty sea
> You who fought the nightless battle
> Living in the land of victory.
> Do you now see that it was he
> Who led and guided you?
> And do you see your victory
> Was given by his hand?
> From Egypt on to Jericho,
> From desert to the sea,
> From slavery to rulership
> Of all the land you see,
> All that he has promised
> Has finally come true.
> All the covenant he spoke
> Has now been given to you.
> You who wandered in the darkness
> In the bondage of your sin,
> You who fought the endless battle,
> The battle you could never win,
> Do you now see it was he
> Who always came to save you?
> And do you see how freely

Grace was given by his hand?
From slavery to freedom,
From prisoner to heir,
From scarlet sin to white as snow
Washed 'neath the crimson tear,
All his promise is made real in you,
The blood of Christ shed just for you.

We've seen choices throughout the Book of Joshua. From Joshua's choice to follow God and accept his leadership role in chapter 1 to the choice of the two and one-half tribes to surrender their freedom temporarily and fight for seven years in Canaan. We see also the choice of Achan to keep the treasures of Ai and the choice of God to give defeat followed by victory after forgiveness. We see the two and one-half tribes returning to the eastern side of the Jordan River and the erection of the cities of refuge.

Schaeffer says it well:

So we find throughout the entire Book of Joshua an emphasis on choice—choice that makes a tremendous difference in history for individuals, for groups, for future generations. The Bible insists, "Don't forget who you are. You are not a puppet or a machine. You don't obey universal laws of cause and effect in a closed system. Rather you are made in the image of God, and, as such, you must choose, and choose rightly, at every point." Adam chose wrongly, and we all bear the marks of his error. Abraham believed God, and his choice was counted to him for righteousness. Joshua chose rightly too. For those of us today, the situation is the same. For the Christian or non-Christian, we are called upon to make choices which will have significant results (Schaeffer, 213).

PRINCIPLES

- Joshua didn't focus on what he did but on what God did.
- It is wise to remember our collective and individual histories with God.
- You can't choose God and someone else; serving the Lord is all-out, sold-out, wholehearted commitment.

APPLICATIONS

- Take some time to write down what God has done in your life.
- Honor your commitments and leave the problems in the Lord's hands.
- Take time to pass on to others what God has done for you.

IV. LIFE APPLICATION

Read Me My Rights!

One short but complicated paragraph will be repeated dozens of times today throughout the United States. Those who use it don't want to say it. Those who hear it don't want to receive it. For some it's routine; for others it's frightening. These are not words you want to hear. But be careful, because sometime, somewhere, somebody might walk up to you and say:

> You have the right to remain silent. Any statement you make may and probably will be used in evidence against you at your trial. You have the right to have a lawyer present to advise you either prior to any questioning or during any questioning. If you are unable to employ a lawyer, you have the right to have a lawyer appointed to counsel with you prior to or during any questioning. You have the right to terminate the interview at any time.

This is just one version of the famous "Miranda" warning which stems from the trial of Ernesto Miranda some forty years ago. On March 3, 1963, an eighteen-year-old woman employed by a Phoenix theater was kidnapped, driven into the desert, and raped. Ten days later police arrested Ernesto Miranda, and interrogators persuaded him to confess.

But that twenty-three-year-old indigent and the officers who arrested him were caught in the vortex of history. On June 13, 1966, the Supreme Court upset the conviction. The decision, labeled *Miranda vs. Arizona*, became practice for every law enforcement officer in America. You might remember the wording differently from television police shows, but Miranda warnings in some form are now the law of the land based on an interpretation of the Fifth Amendment of the U.S. Constitution.

The court decision didn't necessarily aid Ernesto Miranda himself. On February 24, 1967, a jury again found him guilty of rape and kidnapping (without the confession). He was sentenced to prison for a term of twenty to thirty years, and on December 12, 1972, paroled.

Perhaps more than any other words in America, the Miranda warning illustrates a society obsessed with rights. We have observed in the last thirty years a focus on civil rights, women's rights, children's rights, rights of the aging, rights of incarcerated prisoners, rights of animals, and probably a dozen or so more. American children learn at a very young age to say to a playmate in a sandbox, "Hey, move over! You're violating my rights."

All that may be fine and very North American. But it hardly reflects the attitude that the Bible requires from the servants of Jesus Christ. Like Joshua 24, the focus of Scripture centers on *responsibility* rather than *rights*. We're slaves, a metaphor regularly used to describe Christians in the New Testament. Just like the vassals and the overlord in the covenant described in Joshua 23 and 24. Slaves have virtually no rights in relationship to their masters.

In Luke 12, Jesus teaches the crowds and his disciples about *witnessing, greed, anxiety,* and *readiness* for his return. Of great relationship to Joshua's commitment in 24:15 is Luke 12:48: "But the one who does not know and does things deserving punishment will be beaten with few blows. From everyone who has been given much, much will be demanded; and from the one who has been entrusted with much, much more will be asked."

The first part of the verse is one of the clearest indicators in the Bible that there will be levels or degrees of punishment in hell. A specific application requires us to see the fate of false servants in a passage like this. More generally, we see that those who postpone their duties because they lose track of the Lord's imminent return may awaken to that reality too late. How did Peter understand all this? Just a guess, of course, but I suspect the last half of verse 48 rang in his ears much as it has in mine day after day for decades of ministry. The central idea of the parable demands that serving the Lord is a matter of responsibility, not rights—precisely the central principle of Joshua 24.

All this reminds us that God will hold you and me—people who have had unparalleled and in some way unprecedented privileges—responsible for greater performance in ministry. Perhaps a fitting close to the parable and this life application would be a paraphrase of the famous Miranda warning:

> You have the right to unquestioned obedience. Any statement you make may and probably will be used in evidence either for or against the cause of Jesus Christ. You have the right to have the Holy Spirit present to advise your leadership decisions. And if you choose not to carry out ministry on the Master's terms, you have the right to bail out at any time.

V. PRAYER

Father, make us like Joshua—resolute, courageous, and faithful to the end—and may our households follow us in our determination to serve God whole-heartedly. Amen.

VI. DEEPER DISCOVERIES

A. The Hornet (24:12)

Joshua obviously refers here to Exodus 23:28 where God promised to "send the hornet ahead of you to drive the Hivites, Canaanites and Hittites out of your way." Some interpreters have tried to identify the hornet as a specific pagan leader such as the Pharaoh of Egypt, whose leadership was symbolized in this way. Garstang takes this view and says:

> The sovereignty of the Pharaoh over united Egypt was expressed by a hieroglyphic formula, *ny-swt-byt* in which the second member, a reed, symbolizes Upper Egypt, and the third member, which denotes in particular the kingship of Lower Egypt, is probably a hornet though commonly taken for a bee. In current hieroglyphs the bee and hornet were not distinguished, though the honey-bee was called the "fly of honey." When drawn out pictorially, however, as in some of the Theban Tombs, the insect is seen to possess features which in the opinion of zoologists are particular to wasps (Garstang, 259–60).

Others find specific incidents in the history of warfare where insects such as hornets were used. However, nothing in the text of Joshua, or for that matter the Pentateuch, leads us to conclude anything other than a metaphor here—not Egypt, not other battles, and certainly not literal hornets. Howard puts it well: "Thus, the first possibility appears to be the most likely (i.e., that we are dealing with a metaphor here). We should remember, however, that the larger point is that God fought for Israel, regardless of how we interpret the reference to 'the hornet'" (Howard, 433).

B. "He Will Not Forgive" (24:19)

What could Joshua possibly have meant here? We struggle with the words "you are not able to serve the LORD," taking them to mean that the people should reconsider the swiftness with which they made their response to Joshua's challenge. But in emphasizing that God "is a holy God; he is a jealous God" Joshua goes so far as to state firmly, "He will not forgive your rebellion and your sins." The point we must make here is that the Mosaic covenant of the land was conditional unlike the Abrahamic covenant. We have already seen how the prophet Jeremiah lamented the fact that disobedience caused the Babylonian captivity.

Long before that, we see during the time of the judges constant struggles to maintain the land of Canaan, hitting rock bottom at the end of that book and seeing deliverance only with the rise of Saul, David, and the monarchy. Campbell reminds us:

> Of course Joshua did not mean that God was not a God of forgiveness. He meant God was not to be worshiped or served lightly, and that to forsake Him deliberately to serve idols would be a presumptuous, willful, high-handed sin for which there was no forgiveness under the Law (Num. 15:30). Such sin would result in disaster (Campbell, *BKC*, 370).

Madvig adds the following note: "The statement 'he will not forgive' is hyperbole and is contrary to the nature of God, who is presented throughout the Old Testament as a God of forgiveness and grace" (Madvig, 369). True, and well based on Exodus 34:6–7a. Nevertheless, the warning of judgment for failure to drive out the Canaanites and the warning against yielding to the temptation to turn to Canaanite gods carried with it the idea that if Israel followed that pattern, God would bring punishment upon them.

VII. TEACHING OUTLINE

A. INTRODUCTION

1. Lead Story: "It Is Well with My Soul"
2. Context: The text of Joshua ends as it began with a focus on the man whom God used to lead the people through the conquest and distribution of the promised land. He began faithful and he finished faithful; he began courageous and he finished courageous.
3. Transition: As chapter 23 blends into chapter 24, they serve together to offer an ending—a happy ending—to this important Old Testament book.

B. COMMENTARY

1. Review of Covenant History (24:1–13)
2. Renewal of Covenant Commitment (24:14–24)
3. Recording of Covenant Action (24:25–33)

C. CONCLUSION: READ ME MY RIGHTS!

VIII. ISSUES FOR DISCUSSION

1. What needs to change in your family to make it more like Joshua's household?
2. What temptations do we face today that parallel the godless idolatry of the Canaanites?
3. What spiritual pillars must be in place for Christians to end well as did Joshua and Eleazar?

Glossary

consecration—Setting apart for God's use

covenant—A contract or agreement expressing God's gracious promises to his people and their consequent relationship to him

exodus, the—The most important act of national deliverance in the Old Testament when God enabled the Israelites to escape Egypt

high priest—The chief religious official for Israel and Judaism appointed as the only person allowed to enter the holy of holies and offer sacrifice on the Day of Atonement

holy—God's distinguishing characteristic that separates him from all creation; the moral ideal for Christians as they seek to reflect the character of God as known in Christ Jesus

idolatry—The worship of that which is not God

inheritance—Humanly, a legal transmission of property after death; theologically, the rewards God gives his children who are saved through Jesus Christ

law—God's instruction to his people about how to love him and others; when used with the definite article "the," *law* may refer to the Old Testament as a whole but usually to the Pentateuch (Genesis through Deuteronomy)

miracle—An act of God beyond human understanding that inspires wonder, displays God's greatness, and leads people to recognize God at work in the world

obedience—Hearing and following instructions and directions from God; expected of believers

pagans—Those who worship a god or gods other than the living God to whom the Bible witnesses

Pentateuch—First five books of the Hebrew Bible: Genesis, Exodus, Leviticus, Numbers, Deuteronomy; only Scriptures recognized by Samaritans and by Sadducees

polytheism—Belief in more than one god; heresy prevalent in biblical times

priesthood—The body of those who represent God and give his instructions to people as well as interceding with God and offering sacrifices to him; all believers for whom Christ has opened the way for personal intercession with God and responsibility to represent God to the world

sacrifice—According to Mosaic Law, an offering to God in repentance for sin or as an expression of thanksgiving

sin—Actions by which humans rebel against God, miss his purpose for their life, and surrender to the power of evil rather than to God

Bibliography

Beers, V. Gilbert. *The Victor Handbook of Bible Knowledge.* Wheaton, Ill.: Victor Books, 1981.

Bornstein, Steven M., and Anthony F. Smith. "The Leader Who Serves," in *The Leader of the Future.* F. Hesselbein, M. Goldsmith, R. Beckard, and R. Schubert, editors. San Francisco, Calif.: Jossey-Bass, 1998.

Butler, Trent C. *Joshua,* in The Word Biblical Commentary. Waco, Tex.: Word Books, 1983.

Calvin, John. *Commentaries on the Book of Joshua.* Grand Rapids, Mich.: Eerdmans, 1949.

Campbell, Donald K. *Joshua: Leader Under Fire.* Wheaton, Ill.: Victor Books, 1981.

Campbell, Donald K. *Joshua,* in The Bible Knowledge Commentary. John Walvoord and Roy Zuck, editors. Wheaton, Ill.: Victor Books, 1985.

Davis, John J. *Conquest and Crisis: Studies in Joshua, Judges, and Ruth.* Grand Rapids, Mich.: Baker, 1969.

Day, George E. *Oehler's Old Testament Theology.* New York: Funk & Wagnall's, 1883.

Durant, Will. *Our Oriental Heritage.* New York: Simon & Schuster, 1954.

Garstang, John. *Joshua and Judges.* Grand Rapids, Mich.: Kregel, 1978.

Getz, Gene A. *Joshua: Defeat to Victory.* Glendale, Calif.: Regal Books, 1979.

Gilmore, Thomas. *Making a Leadership Change.* San Francisco, Calif.: Jossey-Bass, 1988.

Gridlestone, Robert B. *Synonyms of the Old Testament.* Grand Rapids, Mich.: Eerdmans, 1956.

Hamlin, E. John. *Inheriting the Land.* Grand Rapids, Mich.: Eerdmans, 1983.

Howard, David M., Jr. *Joshua,* in The New American Commentary. Nashville, Tenn.: Broadman & Holman, 1998.

Kaiser, Walter C., Jr. *Toward an Old Testament Theology.* Grand Rapids, Mich.: Zondervan, 1978.

Keil, C. F. *The Book of Joshua.* Reprint. Grand Rapids, Mich.: Eerdmans, 1975.

Keil, C. F., and F. Delitzsch. *Joshua, Judges, Ruth.* Grand Rapids, Mich.: Eerdmans, 1950.

Lea, Thomas D. *Hebrews and James,* in The Holman New Testament Commentary. Nashville, Tenn.: Broadman & Holman, 1999.

Madvig, Donald H. *Joshua,* in The Expositor's Bible Commentary. Frank E. Gaebelein, editor. Grand Rapids, Mich.: Zondervan, 1992.

Bibliography

Radmacher, Earl D., general editor. *The Nelson Study Bible*. Nashville, Tenn.: Thomas Nelson, 1997.

Redpath, Alan. *Victorious Christian Living*. Grand Rapids, Mich.: Revell, 1960.

Ryrie, Charles C. *Basic Theology*. Wheaton, Ill.: Victor Books, 1982.

Schaeffer, Francis A. *Joshua and the Flow of Biblical History*. Downers Grove, Ill.: InterVarsity Press, 1975.

Thompson Chain-Reference Bible. Frank Charles Thompson, compiler and editor. Indianapolis, Ind.: B. B. Kirkbride Bible Company, Inc. and Grand Rapids, Mich: Zondervan, 1983.

Wilmington, Harold L. *Wilmington's Survey of the Old Testament*. Wheaton, Ill.: Victor Books, 1987.

Woudstra, M. H. *Book of Joshua*, in The New International Commentary on the Old Testament. Grand Rapids, Mich.: Eerdmans, 1981.

The Ultimate "Ever
for Study or Se

No other reference series gets to the heart of the Bible as efficiently as do Holman's Old Testament and New Testament Commentaries.

Designed to offer a detailed interpretation when time allows, or an essential understanding of the text when time is short, the Holman Old Testament Commentary series and the Holman New Testament Commentary series provide unsurpassed clarity and convenience.

OLD TESTAMENT

Genesis (Vol. 1) 978-0-8054-9461-7
Exodus, Leviticus, Numbers (Vol. 2) 978-0-8054-9462-4
Deuteronomy (Vol. 3) 978-0-8054-9463-1
Joshua (Vol. 4) 978-0-8054-9464-8
Judges, Ruth (Vol. 5) 978-0-8054-9465-5
1 & 2 Samuel (Vol. 6) 978-0-8054-9466-2
1 & 2 Kings (Vol. 7) 978-0-8054-9467-9
1 & 2 Chronicles (Vol. 8) 978-0-8054-9468-6
Ezra, Nehemiah, Esther (Vol. 9) 978-0-8054-9469-3
Job (Vol. 10) 978-0-8054-9470-9
Psalms 1-75 (Vol. 11) 978-0-8054-9471-6
Psalms 76-150 (Vol. 12) 978-0-8054-9481-5
Proverbs (Vol. 13) 978-0-8054-9472-3

Ecclesiastes, Song of Songs (Vol. 14) 978-0-8054-9482-2
Isaiah (Vol. 15) 978-0-8054-9473-0
Jeremiah, Lamentations (Vol. 16) 978-0-8054-9474-7
Ezekiel (Vol. 17) 978-08054-9475-4
Daniel (Vol. 18) 978-0-8054-9476-1
Hosea, Joel, Amos, Obadiah, Jonah, Micah (Vol. 19) 978-0-8054-4977-8
Nahum-Malachi (Vol. 20) 978-08054-9478-5

Complete Holman Old Testament Commentary - $299.97
978-0-8054-9523-2
Individually $19.99

nan's" Commentary
non Preparation!

The Holman Old Testament Commentary series is available in individual volumes or as a collected, cost-saving, 20 volume set.

The Holman New Testament Commentary series is available in individual volumes or as a collected, cost-saving 12 volume set.

HCSB